UPSTART

Owen Swift

ISBN: 1545457476
ISBN 13: 9781545457474
Library of Congress Control Number: 2017907485
CreateSpace Independent Publishing Platform
North Charleston, South Carolina

THANKS

to Roger & Kippy,   for their help and encouragement

to my friends,   who took the time to read and critique
                     my effort at storytelling

to EW,   for her attention to the details that I missed

Editor: Kippy Requardt
Cover: Phil Cone

1

8-15-94

Into the summer twilight on Emigration Canyon Rd, an entertaining two lane blacktop that twists and drops from the mountain heights east of Salt Lake City, roared an older black Porsche 911 at speed, the tuned exhaust note crackling, rising and falling with the shifting gears, echoing off the canyon's walls and competing for Owen's attention with Emmylou, cranked up loud as the Blaupunkt would go, blasting out Willy Nelson's ode to Poncho & Lefty through the open windows as the car accelerated toward the next bend. Owen singing along, something he would never even consider if there was anyone within earshot:

"Poncho was a bandit boy, his horse was fast as polished steel, he wore his gun outside his pants for all the honest world to feel..."

I get stopped by the cops I'll plead DWE, driving while exuberant, Owen thought, as he slowed for the city streets, amazed as always at how Pavlovian a response he still had to loud music, thinking how much he loved hustling this car. Love everlasting, that Hallmark invention he had so much difficulty proclaiming to the opposite sex but one which seemed to perfectly describe his feelings about the Porsche. The relationship had lasted twice as long as any he'd had with a woman.

The 911 was an extravagance in his present financial circumstances, no question about that. An appropriate gift to himself when he had checked out as an Eastern Airline DC9 Captain in Miami decades ago but a completely inappropriate vehicle for the mountain winters, Owen stored the old girl in a Salt Lake garage and drove his ten-year-old Subaru wagon till the snow melted and the road salt washed away. Ten minutes at the car's limits was all the mental therapy he needed to put a smile on his face, an entertainment he was loath to give up despite the increased financial strain created when the car needed repair.

Owen was going to work, heading to the east side of the Salt Lake airport, the "other" side, the side the traveling public rarely saw; National Guard buildings, corporate offices and hangers, private airplanes overnighting at the fixed base operator's facility, the air freight area.

He pulled into employee parking and found a spot alongside a sad looking, corrugated metal sided hanger. A faded sign above the door proclaimed it the headquarters of Majestic Airlines. With its fleet of eleven leased aircraft; ten piston engined Beech 18s circa the 1950s and one Beech-99; an aging but not as ancient turboprop airplane that had, to borrow the cowboy expression, been rode hard and put away wet, there was a greater impression of fly-by-night than majesty in evidence. Owen thought the only thing "Majestic" about the company was the radio call sign used to communicate with ATC (air traffic control). The major carriers used their corporate names, United, American, SouthWest followed by the flight number. Boring. America West used "Cactus" which had a nice ring to it but Majestic used "Magic" which to Owen's ear sounded even sexier, especially in his pack-a-day husky pilot's voice. Magic 101 would be the call sign of his flight this evening to Denver.

Unfortunately, the call sign only partially made up for the company's many shortcomings but this was the only flying job he had been able to find. 1994 had not been a good year to be seeking pilot employment.

Owen unfolded from the Porsche, pulling his battered canvas overnight duffel with him. It was packed with aviation charts, approach plates, two spare flashlights, a multi-function screwdriver and pliers with a wire cutter in one compartment; extra pair of jeans, shirt, socks, underwear and a dopp kit in the other. He walked across the concrete ramp toward the Beech B-99 parked in a line with four of the 18s. With a quick flick of the wrist and an upward tug he opened the cockpit entry door, leaning back as it rose with a hydraulic hiss to avoid the blast of heat that surged from the airplane's interior. It was like opening a wall-mounted oversized oven set on broil.

More of an escape hatch than an actual door, installed on the freighter conversions to allow the pilot a path that didn't require climbing over a load of smashed or burning cargo, it also allowed the pilot to wait until the airplane was ready for departure, the cargo door about to be closed and locked, before he wiggled through the narrow opening into the heat-soaked cockpit. The outside air temperature in the valley had been in triple digits most of the afternoon and even with the sun about to set it remained in the high 90s. The inside of the aircraft was hot enough to roast a turkey.

Owen dropped the overnight bag behind the two pilot seats, reached behind the captain's seat and grabbed the two step boarding ladder, clicked it into its brackets at the bottom of the door frame, stepped up one rung, high enough to get his eyes level with the instrument panel and leaning into the cockpit flipped the battery switch on then checked the fuel gauges.

Enough Jet A had already been added to bring the total onboard to 1,200 pounds, 180 gallons, the minimum for the 1:50, 345 mile flight to Denver plus the 45 minute reserve to cover the FAA requirement for any surprises that might delay the landing. In Owen's mind it was not enough. The scene replayed itself practically every flight. The Chief Pilot wanted everyone to operate with minimum fuel. "Less weight, less cost," he claimed, which was unmeasurable nonsense in a plane this small. It was an airline mantra that Owen had challenged when he was a Captain at Eastern. He had come close to running out of fuel a few times during his career and those memories spoke more loudly than the young Majestic Chief Pilot. Owen glanced at the front of the hanger. There was the fuel truck, driver in the cab waiting for the signal he knew would be coming. Owen waved him over, requested another 75 gallons, an extra hour's worth of flight, then poked his head back in the cockpit and quickly scanned the flight instruments while the battery switch was on. There were no red warning flags visible, everything seemed to be working. The Hobbs hour meter read 18,242 hours, same as it had two days ago when he had parked the airplane in this exact spot. It hadn't turned a wheel since Saturday morning.

"Owen"? He turned off the battery switch backing his head and shoulders out of the cockpit, his forehead already breaking into a slight sweat, turned and saw a man and young girl walking toward him.

"George, surprised to see you this time of night."

George worked the day shift as a mechanic for Majestic. He was the one Owen went to with complaints about the 99, though both knew there was never enough time or money allocated to actually fix anything.

"This is kind of a last minute deal," George apologized, "I know I was supposed to call earlier to make sure the seat was available but the decision was only made an hour ago. My daughter Susie," George half turned and motioned her forward, "wants to go to Denver. We have family there and they're going camping. My wife has heard me complain endlessly about the sorry state of repair Majestic's fleet is in and she's somewhat concerned."

Owen shrugged, "The airplanes are not state of the art, no question, but I don't think any of it is life threatening or I wouldn't work here." Owen looked at the girl who was listening intently.

"You worried about this Susie?" Owen asked.

She shook her head, "No, my mom's the worrier. Dad claims you're a really good pilot and have tons of experience so if you're not worried I don't see why I should be."

"OK then," Owen said with a smile. "I do have tons of experience. Seat's yours if you want it."

"Oh yeah I want it. I've been in the back of big airplanes a bunch of times, never in the cockpit. This should be a lot more exciting." Susie smiling at him now, "What do I do?"

Owen took her backpack from George and set it behind the right seat. "I was just starting the preflight. You can walk around with me if you like,"

Twenty-three years old, and smart, Susie had recently graduated from the University of Utah with honors in applied mathematics. Looking at an advanced degree in computer programming, her proud father had bragged on more than one occasion, work on Wall Street, make a lot of money.

Susie dismissed her father with a quick peck on the cheek: "Thanks, Dad, I'll see you in a week or so," George hesitated, "Her aunt called our house an hour ago with the local weather forecast. Weatherman said there was going to be thunderstorms, maybe some big ones. Susie's mother's pretty worried and wanted to cancel but Susie doesn't like being told what to do, at least not by her parents. I told the wife there was no pilot I trusted more than you, that you're not some thrill-seeking kid, but do me a favor and have her call us as soon as you get on the ground." George looked a little worried himself but he called goodby to his daughter, turned and walked into the parking lot, behind the hanger and out of sight.

Owen nodded at Susie who followed him around the left wing to the cargo door, watched as he pulled it open, listened as he explained that the slight breeze generated wouldn't do much to lower the interior temperature. They wouldn't cool off until they had climbed above 10,000 feet or so during the departure when the outside air flowing through the cockpit vents would begin to feel like air conditioning. The onboard air conditioner had been removed to save weight and maintenance expense when the aircraft had first been put into service at Majestic. Management wasn't particularly concerned with their pilots' comfort.

Converting the aircraft for freighter duty included removing the fifteen passenger seats. That left only the front two, Captain on the left, Copilot (First Officer) on the right, though a Copilot was not required by the FAA if there were no paying passengers. The right seat was given out on a first come basis to pretty much anyone who wanted to go for a ride to Denver, one of the younger Majestic pilots trying to log some "turboprop" time, sometimes a Park City friend of Owen's, even the occasional lady friend.

Company in the cockpit? Owen enjoyed the young pilots enthusiasm despite his admonishments that they should switch to a career in dentistry if they wanted to own a Porsche. They were on the way up. Most had been flight instructors, an even lower rung on the pilot ladder than the multi-engine freight experience they were now accumulating. There was a company rumor that the Beech 18s were about to be traded in for more 99s, more turbine time available and another step closer to their dream of getting an airline job.

Friends or acquaintances just along for the ride? Every professional pilot knew that flying could be stupefyingly boring for hours then surprise with astonishing beauty or fear. This evening's flight to Denver would be an eye opener for someone like Susie whose only exposure to the wonder of flight had been in the back of a crowded airliner. Owen liked sharing that. It reminded him of all he had gotten from his chosen career. Memories that lately had started to fade.

Directly behind the pilot seats was a flat aluminum floor with straps and netting to keep the cargo from shifting during flight and, it was hoped, from crushing the pilot in the event of a sudden and violent stop.

Continuing his preflight, Owen circled the exterior looking for problems and explaining as they went: the tires still appeared properly inflated, as did the gear struts. The wings weren't leaking any fuel. Owen had checked the engine oil levels on Saturday while the oil was still warm. Now, there was no oil visible at the bottom of the engine nacelles or dripping on the ground beneath them. The hydraulic brake reservoir was still full and nothing looked like it was about to fall off.

Owen removed the aileron control locks he had installed before he left the airplane Saturday. They were meant to prevent damage to the flight controls if a storm rolled through and the wind kicked up while the aircraft was unattended, but would render the airplane uncontrollable if left in place during takeoff. Dumb as that kind of mistake might seem, people had died on more than one occasion by missing that critical step of the pre-flight.

Finished, Owen walked the hundred feet to the wood slated bench facing the aircraft ramp at the side of the hanger, explaining to Susie that he was going to smoke. She said she was going to visit the ladies room in the hanger.

"Just be back when you hear the 727 pull up," Owen cautioned.

He sat and lit a Chesterfield. Owen knew he could have done the preflight without leaving the bench, at least to his satisfaction; a leak big enough to worry about would leave a stain on the concrete visible from where he sat. All the important gauges, lights and warnings in the cockpit had been working when he had parked the airplane Saturday morning. Testing them now would mean that system had just worked, not that it would next time you pressed the switch or when you really needed it. Minor mechanical failure was not something Owen worried much about anymore. A wing about to fall off or an engine that was going to catch fire? Those were not detectible faults no matter how thorough the pilot's preflight, but the preflight procedure was spelled out in detail in the FOPM (flight operations procedure manual).

Despite Owen's general disdain for any list of rules, but especially aviation rules that seemed to have been hatched by a bunch of lawyers, in this case getting caught was a violation of Federal law and had career-ending potential. FAA inspectors were easy enough to spot and avoid since they were usually the only ones on the freight ramp wearing a sport coat and tie. It was just easier to play their game and feign interest and obedience.

Owen checked his watch. The inbound Fedex 727 bringing whatever freight and mail he would take to Denver was late. He pulled the clipping from the help wanted section of Sunday's Salt Lake Tribune out of his shirt pocket and read it again: "Airline Captains wanted." In his previous four years of looking, there had never been mention of any sort of pilot job in the paper, let alone Captain positions. No existing US carrier would hire Captains off the street so it had to be a new entrant or foreign. At the bottom of the ad was a St. Louis address and phone number for Flight Safety, an aviation training company he had heard of, though Owen thought they trained for corporate aircraft; the major carriers did their own pilot training. Owen had called yesterday to check and the number did indeed belong to Flight Safety in St. Louis. A recording informed him that the office was closed until Monday at 8:00am. Not wanting to miss out, he had called this morning at 7:50, then waited patiently until the call was answered.

Deregulation had begun in 1978 and many of the legacy carriers had failed: Eastern, Pan Am, Braniff, as well as more than one-hundred new entrants. There had been a lot of ex airline Captains wandering around since then, looking for work.

His call had been transferred to a woman in HR who explained the reason for the ad; there was a start-up airline in the final stage of the FAA regulatory process for certification as a US part 121 passenger airline.

Captain applicants must possess at a minimum: a current Class One medical, an airline transport pilot license with one or more type ratings and a minimum of 1,000 hours of turbine PIC (pilot in command) time. Preference would be given to applicants with prior airline experience and a type rating in the Boeing 737.

737? Shit, Owen thought. He had type ratings and had flown as Captain on the DC9/MD80, the 727 and the 757/767. He had never even been in the cockpit of a 737.

When Owen asked what other details she could share he was told it would be a passenger carrier, they had lease arrangements for 737s but no bases or routes had yet been announced. He gave his address and the woman promised that a pilot application would be overnighted. "You do sound like what they are looking for but the ad ran in fifteen papers over the weekend and we've been swamped with calls. Interviews are set to begin in two weeks in St. Louis." He would need a little luck to get in this door ahead of the mob. About time his luck changed.

Owen would readily admit to the necessity of an occasional stroke of good fortune. His first airline job had come about because a number of unlikely events had occurred in a sequence that he had little to do with, then concluded when he knocked on the right door on the right day and got hired by The Flying Tigers Airline. Tigers was an airfreight carrier operating four-piston-engined, 70 ton Lockheed Constellations. Why he got the job, only nine months after his first flight lesson and never having flown anything larger than a single engine Piper, was an enduring mystery.

Owen's love life had been similarly lucky, stumbling onto terrific women with little effort or intent on his part. That he'd come to know a number of beautiful women was, for him, another enduring mystery.

In clement weather Owen walked for exercise. On most days the return flight to Salt Lake had him on the ground and in his car heading up the mountain by 8:30am, and in his green shag carpeted rented condo behind the Albertson's shopping center by 9:15.

After a few minutes of stretching, wearing hiking shorts and a tee shirt, he'd set off past the city park and up the mountain toward Stein's lodge on a 10 mile loop with a 2,000 foot vertical ascent up Royal Street, then over the back side of Deer Valley and down Ontario Canyon Road to the top of Main Street and a seat at the Wasatch Brew Pub for a couple of beers and a cheeseburger before returning to his apartment, a nap, hit a bucket of balls or squeeze in 9 holes, then back to the airport; start the whole process again.

When Andrea, a willowy thirty-something new age mountain girl, who taught at the Park City elementary school in the winter and augmented that meager salary as a waitress at the pub, discovered that not only was he a pilot, but he could offer her a ride over the mountains in the front of a "little" airplane, she jumped at the chance. She liked new and different.

Andrea possessed a charming smile, Owen's favorite long limbed and athletic female body shape, and a fondness for a toke, now and then, off the joint she kept in her sequined purse. Sex was also high on her list of favorite sins.

Owen had no problem with either of her admitted vices, he admitted to a few of his own, though his preference was for vodka not wine and more vodka instead of a puff of the dope. The sex? They shared a consideration for the other's pleasure, which in Owen's experience was the key ingredient in a satisfying sex life. Andrea wasn't looking for long term, she said repeatedly. Owen readily admitted that he wasn't either.

Yesterday had been Owen's birthday. Fifty years old. Just beginning his second half-century. Hadn't thought twice about turning forty but then he was employed as an airline Captain with his future seemingly secure. Now? Still in good shape physically and mentally, but financially...? He wouldn't normally dwell on a negative but this one was getting harder to ignore.

They had agreed on a private night, no party, couple of vodkas for the birthday boy, great sex, both in the shower, then in the Porsche, headed to the Spring Chicken Inn with a good bottle of Shiraz. Not the easy way; east on I-80, but the fun way through Brown's canyon. Best fried chicken ever, wandering back on the interstate, listening to Brubeck's quartet, stuffed and content, then Andrea had surprised him, turned off the tape deck, shifted in her seat to face him and asked:

"Have you given any thought to the long term, you know? You and me? I need you to at least think about it, then we should talk about it. We have been going together for three months and it's been... great fun...great sex and everything...but I'll need more, eventually, you know?" She shrugged apologetically, "I know it's not what you signed up for, it's just that I met someone, we've gone out a few times, and he is interested...in the long term."

Going together? Owen wasn't quite sure when they had stopped dating and started going together but he had agreed to think about it.

It was not something you thought about coming down a mountain road at ninety miles an hour. Sitting on this bench there was little else for him to do until the FedEx 727 showed up with tonight's load of overnight mail.

Owen sat smoking as he watched the airliners departing to the south in the fading sunlight. One after another they lifted off, part of the evening's departure crush, a reminder of his past life. He watched as a United 737 began its takeoff roll. It accelerated more slowly and lifted off the runway later than the airplanes that had preceded it. An early series 200, Owen thought, with the little engines, and it jogged a memory: Colorado Springs, three years ago, a United 737 crash that pulverized the aircraft, killing all on board. The NTSB had given up after an eighteen month investigation, admitting that they had been unable to discover a probable cause. Owen hadn't heard anything since. Might be worth asking the Flight Safety interviewer about it.

Andrea wanted him to consider their future together but Owen had no idea what his future looked like, with or without her. She knew his history; Owen had made sure she did before they had sex the first time, but he'd cautioned; "I'm nearly fifty years old and never married so if that's what you're looking for, you should consider the odds. If it's sex without guilt... I'm your man." After that she'd insisted on monogamy, which was fine with Owen; one woman at a time was plenty. But now what?

Last night's little speech had sounded like an ultimatum though she hadn't said when it would go into effect. Right away? Apparently she already had the next guy picked out. Till death us do part had always seemed like an unreasonable promise to Owen though it was a twenty-year shorter commitment now than the first time it had been suggested. Maybe he was missing the commitment gene.

Andrea was great fun, no question about that, but she wasn't irreplaceable. If he had to go without for awhile? It wouldn't be the first time.

Owen noticed Susie walk out of the hanger, watched as one of the young Beech 18 pilots spotted her skinny jeans and invited her to have a look at "his" airplane. He was a handsome kid, full of the bravado that could get a young pilot in trouble but also make him a magnet for pretty girls. Another fond memory.

Owen had called the Salt Lake FAA Flight Service station to check on the weather just before he'd left for the airport.

"Hot and dry in central Utah, jet stream out of the south-west bringing moisture up from the Gulf of Mexico, fifty percent chance of thunderstorms on a line from Grand Junction Colorado, through Aspen and into the Denver area, wind gusts in excess of sixty knots, half inch hail possible," the briefer warned. No surprises there, it was pretty much a standard forecast for a summer evening in the Rocky Mountains.

Owen thought the smartest weatherman ever was the one who had come up with the "chance of" concept. The chance of rain was never zero or one-hundred percent, even when the sky was clear for a 100 miles or the visibility had been reduced to practically nothing in heavy rain.

He had sometimes thought when making his Captain's welcome aboard announcement to say: there is 99.9% chance that you will arrive at your destination alive, an 80% chance we'll get you there on time, a 60% chance your bag will be waiting for you and a 25% chance you will never see your bag again.

Best to keep thoughts like that to yourself Owen knew. Even though the passengers rarely listened to or could understand what was said, the big airlines weren't known for their sense of humor.

2

8-15-94

Owen watched as Susie, talking now with a few of the younger Majestic pilots, heard the roar of a 727 in max reverse. Everyone watched as the nose of the landing aircraft dipped under heavy braking and slowed enough to make the 90 degree left turn onto taxiway Kilo four. It was the shortest distance to the freight ramp. FedEx did not like late.

The tugs and carts, forklifts and trucks with drivers at the ready, looked like a beehive kicked into furious activity. Susie started running toward the 99 as Owen got off the bench and headed in the same direction. The freight for the five Majestic airplanes would be off the 727 first and transferred to the outbound flights in ten minutes.

Susie, with a nod from Owen to go first, climbed the two steps of the ladder, stepped over the left seat and seemed to uncoil into the right. Standing close behind her, knowing no one could see him watching, he admired the supple way she moved. Another Pavlovian response.

Owen climbed into the cockpit, pulled the ladder up and stored it in the clips behind his seat. He gave Susie the spare headset, showed her how to put it on and adjust the boom mike, fastened the Velcro straps for his kneeboard around his right thigh to keep its notepad, maps, spare pen and small flashlight secure, pulled on his own headset, showed Susie how to turn on her audio, saying "can you hear me?" When she just nodded Owen said; "It's ok to talk, we're on the intercom, no one else can hear you."

Susie smiled, said, "ok," in a whisper, then In a normal voice, "OK." And smiled more broadly.

Owen tuned the number two radio to the ATIS (airport terminal information service; a recorded message with airport weather, temperature, altimeter setting, wind and active runway for landing and departure), then retuned the radio to clearance delivery, waited while another of the Majestic pilots read back his clearance then: "Clearance, Magic 101 with information Hotel, IFR Denver."

The response was immediate and rapid: " Magic 101, cleared to Denver as filed, maintain 7,000 feet, expect Parleys Canyon visual departure, departure control 132.5, squawk 2250."

Owen jotted the departure frequency and transponder code on his knee pad, read back the clearance at the same rapid pace it had been delivered, tuned the number two radio to the ground control frequency and the transponder to 2250 as a tug pulling a cart loaded with mail bags and boxes pulled alongside the airplane by the freight door. The driver hopped off the tug, trotted up to Owen, handed him the load manifest, then went back to the cart to help transfer the freight onto the airplane.

Owen, transcribed the numbers from the load manifest onto a Majestic weight and balance form, added the totals to find the take-off weight, then signed the bottom of the form. He heard the cargo netting latches being snapped into place, heard the cargo door latch being secured, checked that the cargo door open warning light extinguished, ripped off the top page of the triplicate form which stayed with the trip paperwork on the airplane and handed the other two pages to the lead who stepped back, removed the wheel chocks and showed them to Owen as he checked the area around both props, then shouted "Clear", showing Owen two, then one finger on his left hand, the right hand index finger swirling: cleared to start number two, then number one. Owen pulled the emergency door by his left shoulder closed, latched it with a turn of the handle, looked at Susie whose eyes were big as dinner plates, said: "It's going to get loud, for now just listen. Ok?" She just nodded.

Engines running, caution and warning lights checked and out, doors closed, lights out, Owen gave a quick salute to the lead standing off the aircraft's left side and with a short burst of throttle on the left engine and a little right brake spun the airplane 180 degrees heading for taxiway Kilo while he called ground control: "Ground, Magic 101 ready to taxi with information Hotel."

"Magic 101, north on Kilo, hold short of runway 17 Left at Kilo 9, contact the tower holding short on 118.3."

Airport taxiways worldwide are named with letters from the English phonetic alphabet; Alpha for A, Bravo for B etc. Taxiway Kilo ran parallel to runway 17 Left on its east side. Like the runway it served it was 9,500 feet, or almost 2 miles long and straight as the surveyors transit could make it. Owen let the taxi speed build to about 40 knots, there was no gauge to indicate the actual speed, then slipped the power levers aft from idle into low reverse pitch to keep the speed from building any higher. The black asphalt of the taxiway had been absorbing heat all day and was almost hot enough to melt the tires without the added heat that would be generated by using the brakes. He set the flaps to the takeoff position and scanned the before takeoff checklist to confirm the airplane was configured for departure.

Approaching Kilo 9 Owen changed the radio to the tower frequency. "Magic 101 ready for departure."

The tower answered immediately. "Magic 101 you are cleared for take off on runway 17 Left, maintain 7,000 feet, and heading 150."

Owen acknowledged the tower's instructions while steering around the taxiway corner and lining up on the runway centerline. He glanced at Susie who had a little grin on her face, asked "You ready?" When she nodded he advanced the throttles toward takeoff power while keeping a close eye on the ITT (inter turbine) temperature gauges. The redline on the gauges face indicated the engine's maximum available power on this overheated evening. The pilot who exceeded, or even approached that limit, did so at his peril.

It is mechanical and statistical fact that airplane engines are most likely to fail during the stress of takeoff when full power is most important. The loss of half that power immediately changes the pilot's focus from a normal climb outbound on the assigned route to an emergency struggle, limping back to the airport while avoiding all obstacles, man-made or geographic.

Owen had been taught long ago to consider every takeoff the beginning of a possible emergency and to be mentally prepared for the worst case; engine failure or fire was at the top of the list. Hydraulic failure, electrical failure, instrument/radio failure. Though the list of possible disasters was long, actual failure was rare, just something a professional pilot needed be aware, but not afraid of.

At VMC plus 10 knots, the minimum speed at which there would be enough rudder control to keep the airplane from rolling onto its back if an engine failed, Owen raised the nose gently and started them skyward.

He mentally ran through the after-takeoff checklist: gear up, flaps up, climb power set, engine instruments in the green, then responded to the tower's instruction to contact departure control as he turned to the assigned heading.

"Magic 101, out of 6,000 for 7,000, Parley's Canyon in sight."

"Roger Magic 101, altitude permitting you are cleared for the Parley's visual departure, climb to and maintain 13,000 feet."

"Altitude permitting." That was the phrase the lawyers would concentrate on if he crashed.

The federal aviation regulations, FARs, are divided into two basic parts: VFR, visual flight rules allow less experienced pilots in simpler aircraft to fly cross country with a minimum visibility of 3 miles and the clouds at least 3,000 feet above the ground but without the training, license and expensive instrumentation required by the other set of rules: IFR, instrument flight rules.

IFR is for the professionals with a schedule to keep. Its rules allow departure into clouds so low the runway disappears the moment the aircraft leaves the ground, aircraft control and navigation are accomplished solely by reference to instruments, and landings can be hand flown to a 200 foot ceiling with visibility of a 1/2 mile.

All IFR operations are coordinated through airport and en-route traffic control centers. A flight plan is filed and must be adhered to unless both controller and pilot agree that deviation is safe or necessary.

Departure control couldn't clear Owen eastbound until he was at 13,000 feet, the legal minimum altitude required to clear the mountain peaks east of the airport, unless he accepted the responsibility for terrain avoidance. 6,000 feet put him 1,500 feet above the valley floor as he pointed the nose toward the base of Parley's Canyon. Following Interstate 80 up the canyon instead of heading south until he was at the required altitude would shave ten minutes off the trip. He wouldn't have the required 2,000 foot clearance the rules required in mountainous terrain but he'd be close, and departure wouldn't care. They wanted him out of the way of the much faster airliners taking off behind him.

The mountain peaks above them were bathed in the russet glow of the setting sun, the canyon walls already in shadow, as Owen, hugging the right side and turning with the serpentine path of the interstate, climbed upward.

"Can I say something?" Susie asked, glancing at him for permission then back out the windshield. "Sure."

"This is so cool," forgetting herself for the moment. "This is just amazing." Owen nodded agreement. "It is indeed seriously cool," he said, perhaps enjoying her reactions as much as she was enjoying the view.

She was a tall girl but Owen had her adjust her seat to its top setting giving her an even better view.

"You want to give it a try?" Owen watched her eyes get even wider.

"Me?, I don't know how to fly." There was an added note of excitement or maybe fear in her voice.

"Don't worry, I'll show you. Put your right hand on the wheel," Owen instructed. When she did he took his hand off and placed it in his lap.

"Please don't do that. My dad said you didn't do crazy stuff like the young guys."

Owen had to laugh at that. "This isn't crazy," he assured her. "See how the canyon is bending to the left? We want to follow that curve. Turn the wheel to the left a little and watch what the airplane does."

Susie turned the wheel a tiny bit, not enough, and Owen said, "keep your hand on the wheel and feel what I do," cranking the airplane into a thirty degree bank.

As the airplane came around the curve Owen instructed, "turn the wheel to the right until the wings are level." And she did.

"Now back to the right, keep us on the right side of the canyon."

Susie had both hands on the wheel now, concentrating on following the canyon's steep right side. "What about up and down? How does that work?"

"For now we just want to keep going up," Owen pointed to her altimeter which showed them leaving 10,000 feet. "We'll level off at 13,000."

Should an engine fail while they were in the canyon an immediate course reversal would be necessary since one engine wouldn't provide enough power to continue the climb and avoid the terrain. Sticking to the canyon's right side would allow the most room for the turn. Owen would readily admit it wasn't the ten minutes saved that led him up this path. It was as much fun for him as it was for Susie. The same as the Porsche on a mountain road but in three dimensions. That it might be slightly illegal was, for him, a bonus.

Little bit of a scofflaw, Owen admitted to himself with a mental shrug as the airplane popped out of the valley smog and he spotted Summit park, the small subdivision on the south side of the interstate. FWE he thought, flying while exuberant, telling Susie to keep her hand on the wheel then pressing it forward, stopping the climb at 13,000 feet and accelerating to cruise speed as he trimmed the aircraft and set the throttles for level flight. He let Susie try her hand at altitude control but that was more than she could manage though she didn't want to let go of the wheel. The sun was gone and with it a visible horizon. "Instrument flight is more difficult than visual flight," Owen explained. "A lot of private pilots never master it." Reluctantly she released the wheel, the disappointment obvious.

"I do the return flight around 6:00am Tuesday through Saturday if that works with your plans. Just tell your dad to let me know."

"Saturday," Susie said without hesitation. "I'll be at the airport at 5:00. Count me in."

Unable to see much out the windows Susie turned her curiosity to the cockpit; she had the same set of instruments in front of her that Owen did. "There's an awful lot of dials," she said, "how do you know what to look at?"

"Instrument aircraft have the basic flight instruments across the top of the panel," Owen explained, pointing to the left of her panel and working to the right; "airspeed indicator, artificial horizon, altimeter. Next row down. vertical speed, horizontal situation indicator for heading and navigation..."

"Ok, ok, I get the idea but which ONE do you look at, what are you looking at right now."

That drew a smile. "At the moment we're in level flight, maintaining 13,000 feet. The rules only allow 100 feet of deviation so I have to keep an eye on the altimeter. Our heading is 90 degrees, at least at the moment, and if we want to end up in Denver east is the direction to go. If you watch the horizon and the HSI..." Owen turned the wheel, rolling the aircraft into a 15 degree bank to the right.

"Look out the window," he instructed, "and you get the sensation that we're turning, but hard to tell how much. If you look at the artificial horizon you can see the bank we're in while the compass will show the turn; 95 degrees...100...105..."

Owen rolled the wheel back to the left, turning them back to a 90 degree heading then leveling the wings as Susie watched closely. "So... you're mostly looking at the horizon and the compass and keeping track of the altimeter. That doesn't seem too hard, I mean you don't seem to be moving the controls much,"

"Nothing to it," Owen agreed, still smiling and placing both hands in his lap. "You want to try?"

"There you go with the hands in the lap, again." Susie didn't put her hand on the wheel but she was staring at the instruments. After 30 seconds of watching she said: "Nothing's changing," sounding like it was her accomplishment.

"The airplane's pretty well trimmed," Owen agreed, "just give it another moment." On cue the vertical speed indicator showed the beginning of a descent and the altimeter needle followed along.

"Now what?" they were already 100 feet low.

"You have to raise the nose, climb back to 13,000." She pulled, but too hard, and they soared past 13,000 on the way up. Owen put his hand back on the wheel, instructing Susie to leave her's where it was. "Don't push or pull so much as pressure the wheel," he instructed as he reversed the climb, put them back at 13,000, held them there for a moment then placed his hand back in his lap.

"It's just possible this is more difficult than it looks," Susie admitted when, after 30 seconds, the airplane was again surging up and down to her enthusiastic attempts at control. "Maybe you're right; I'm not ready for instrument flight."

"If they gave the same calculus problem to both of us, who do you think would get the answer first?"

"Calculus? That's so totally high school," Susie started then stopped. "Ahh... Ok... smart girl slowly learns her lesson. I may have a degree in math, but you have a PHD in aviation." She put her hands back in her lap. "And since we're in an airplane not a classroom maybe you should do the flying."

"Excellent strategy, knows when to delegate, definitely CEO material," putting his hand back on the wheel just as departure control instructed them to contact Salt Lake center.

Salt Lake cleared them direct to Myton VOR, a navigation facility that would show bearing and distance on the cockpit instruments. Going direct would keep them south of King's Peak in the Uinta Range, a good idea since the peak was the highest point in Utah at 13,500' and invisible on this dark night. A minute later center added: "Climb to and maintain 17,000 feet, pilots discretion," the altitude necessary to clear the Front Range of the Rockies just west of Denver.

Owen acknowledged the new altitude but stayed at 13,000 where he could get by without using oxygen. The 99 was not pressurized. The rules required the pilot to use oxygen if he would be between 10,000 and 13,000 feet for more than thirty minutes, though Owen had gone without for much longer and not felt the onset of hypoxia. Each pilot's seat had a cannula hanging by a strap within easy reach. A replica of the throwaway plastic tubes they stuck under your nose in the hospital when your lungs couldn't take in enough oxygen, both were connected to a supply tank behind Owen's seat.

Instead of oxygen, Owen chose nicotine, asking first if it would bother Susie, then lighting a Chesterfield, tapping the ash into a plastic cup with an inch of water in the bottom he'd stuck in the hole where an ashtray once lived back when smoking in the cockpit was legal. As a precaution he placed the cannula around his neck where it would be readily available when needed and showed Susie where hers was and how to put it on. Owen explained that her supply could be turned on at any time and she should tell him if she felt lightheaded or dizzy.

Being surrounded by blackness with just occasional pinpoints of light from the towns, houses, ranches and cars below, with the constant roar of engines and wind, had disoriented and frightened some of Owen's first time passengers.

Susie seemed completely at ease, either oblivious or unconcerned about the hazards of night flight over mountainous terrain. Obviously curious, she asked permission first, then fired away with a stream of questions.

"How do you know where we are now?"

Owen pulled his map out and gave her a flashlight. Both overhead map lights had quit working a month ago and her dad had been unable to fix the problem. It was annoying but legal, at least according to the Chief Pilot's interpretation of the rule, which only required "sufficient" available illumination. "Use the cockpit fluorescent," he'd recommended, apparently not concerned with the ten minutes of night blindness that would follow when they were switched off.

Owen's solution was an extra flashlight and some industrial strength rubber bands which he used to fasten the light to the sliding sun visor positioned by his left shoulder and focused on the chart clipped on the yoke. Rube Goldberg though that might be, it was enough light to read the charts when necessary and, since there was no Autopilot, left both hands free to maneuver the controls and throttles.

Owen showed Susie the symbol and frequency for Myton indicated on the map, then pointed to the navigation radio in the panel where it was entered, the single needle that pointed to its location and the counter that showed the mileage.

"Where do we go next? She asked, moving the flashlight around the map.

"Meeker next, 113.2, then Kremling, 113.8, but that's the easy part." Owen handed her his book of approach plates. A red three ring binder, like a grade school student would carry, it contained all the approach and departure charts for Salt Lake and Denver, doubled in size on the office copier to be readable by flashlight.

"There's no instrument approach for runway 26 Right. It's the shorter of the parallel runways, the one the smaller aircraft use, and if the weather is visual it's what we'll get tonight. If the weather requires an instrument approach, it will be for 26 Left." Owen showed her the title line at the top of each page and challenged her to find the plate for 26 Left.

Susie found the section for Denver then started leafing through the pages. "You telling me you memorized all this?" She said, with an obvious note of skepticism.

"Find the ILS 26 left chart yet?" Owen was not bothered by the confident tone, remembering what he had been like at her age as a newly certificated pilot. When she nodded Owen continued, "The frequency is 110.5, heading inbound 262 degrees and if you look at the bottom of the page you'll see the altitude profile. The final approach fix is named Elway and is to be crossed at 6,950 feet."

"Ok," she said "very impressive, but what about all the rest of these?" pointing at the dozen other numbers on the chart.

"Lots of stuff on there you don't need, but the book will be open and available when we start the approach, just in case."

"And all the rest of these charts for Denver? You memorized all of these?"

"Naw, 95% of the time the landing at night in Denver is west. Tomorrow morning in Salt Lake the landing will be south on runway 17 Left. Unlike a math test there's not that much to remember."

They seemed to be the only airplane on the Salt Lake Center frequency. There was no radio chatter, the air was smooth, an overcast high above blanked out any light from the moon or stars. Peaceful. Owen pointed out the traffic below on US highway 40, the lights of the small towns and cities as they slid by: Heber, Duschene, Myton. He retuned the number one NAV to Mecker, 100 miles to the east, and tuned the number two COM (communication) radio to the Salt Lake Flight Service station frequency and requested the latest Denver weather.

" Have a special report for 2140: overcast at 20,000 feet, visibility greater than 50 miles, temperature 70, dew point 48, wind calm, landing two-six Left and Right. Remarks, Lightning distant south through north-west, cloud to cloud and cloud to ground."

Thinking Cheyenne, to the north of Denver, might be a safe alternate in case one was needed Owen requested their weather. "Cheyenne at the moment has a 1/2 mile visibility in heavy rain, sky obscured, lightning cloud to cloud and cloud to ground, thunderstorm overhead, rain began 21:30. Colorado Springs is also reporting a thunderstorm at the field," the controller said, reading Owen's mind, "My radar shows some gaps in the line to the north of Denver. You might be able to pick your way through with your radar." The computer flight plan that Majestic filed automatically showed that the 99 had weather radar. It did, but it hadn't worked for months. When Owen complained at the beginning of the summer thunderstorm season the chief pilot quoted the paragraph in the regulations stipulating that only aircraft carrying paying passengers required radar. "The FAA doesn't appear to care if freight pilots live or die."

"My radar isn't showing any precipitation at the moment and I can already see lightning distant north through south," Owen danced around the truth with the controller. He hadn't turned the set on.

"Precipitation is over the Front Range at the moment," the controller confirmed, "Eagle and Steamboat to the west are clear. The line appears to be stationary and building. Have had top reports above 40,000 feet. Anything else I can help you with?"

Owen said no and thanked the man just as Salt Lake Center told him to call Denver Center. The Denver controller confirmed the thunderstorm reports Owen had just gotten. He said that traffic from the west had been crossing the Front Range inbound about 40 miles to the north of the airport and seemed to be getting through a hole in the line of thunderstorms. When Owen reported his radar inop the controller offered vectors, "as soon as I've got you in radar contact."

Owen knew he had to be at 17,000' before that would happen so he reported, "out of 13 for 17," and slipped the oxygen cannula strap around his head, instructing Susie to do the same, then reached for the valve behind his seat and turned it on. He could see Susie's expression change as the oxygen began to flow.

Owen advanced the throttles to climb power and started up. The lightning, though still distant, began to resemble a fireworks display spanning the horizon from left to right. Beautiful without question, but an indication of the enormous power lurking.

Susie, who had been sitting silently for several minutes, apparently fascinated by the now almost continuous lightning flashes directly ahead, decided to share a story. "Three college friends and I were hiking over Guardsman's Pass in May before graduation, you know? Kind of a rite of passage thing. My dad dropped us off where the road turns to dirt outside of Park City. The idea was to take a couple of days and end up at Brighton then one of the other dads would come and get us."

Owen knew the route she was talking about. It began where his afternoon walks turned around and headed downhill, back toward civilization. He had on occasion driven the dirt road in the all-wheel-drive Subaru, no way would he take the Porsche, and remembered the steepness of the grade, both up then down into Brighton at the head of Big Cottonwood canyon. He also remembered the remoteness of the terrain and that there were no conveniences; no motel, restaurant, store, or telephone.

Owen thought about that for a moment. He had been a Boy Scout in his youth. He'd done the camping trips, put up the tent, lit the fire with flint and steel and got the merit badges, but sleeping on the ground no longer appealed to him nor did two days of walking in the middle of nowhere with the possibility of an inadvertent meeting with creatures who did not have his best interests at heart. Cougars, snakes, bears? He appreciated the middle of nowhere as long as you could drive there, but at day's end wanted hot water, iced vodka and a weatherproof space with a bed. It suddenly occurred to him she had said May?

"The road isn't even open in May. The snow doesn't usually melt until the first week of June, at the earliest."

Susie had paused for a moment as a particularly brilliant series of horizontal flashes lit the sky. They were close enough now to distinguish individual thunderheads. Seemingly lit from within and tightly packed together; the tops towered above them.

"Wow, that was really bright," she said, sounding awed, her voice now with a hint of fear as she began to realize there didn't appear to be a way around them. She continued her story.

"Yeah, there was still some snow but not a lot if you stayed on the road. Middle of the week, no one up there, really pretty cool. There are forest service cabins at the summit and we stopped for the night, built a fire, opened the bottle of champagne we had brought and had just taken the first sip when we heard thunder. Thunderstorms were not in the forecast, our parents had really checked that cause they were kind of worried about letting their little girls wander around the mountains by ourselves."

Susie looked at him then with a disbelieving shake of her head at the foolishness of parents. "Little girl? Twenty-three years old and about to graduate college, I've been hiking that mountain since I was in grade school, could've walked in and out blindfolded but it's nice to know they care, I guess." She stopped talking, lost in her own thoughts for a moment.

"Thunderstorm?" Owen prodded.

"Thunderstorm," she continued. "It had gotten dark and we were sitting by the fire at the front of the cabin. All of a sudden a big gust of wind blew up, seriously cold wind, then without warning hail started falling, big hail stones, almost golf ball size. We jumped back into the cabin and watched from the door opening. It was really, really loud on the roof. There was a giant flash and almost immediately an enormous cracking sound. Lightning had hit a tree not fifty feet from where we were standing and it just exploded. BOOM," Susie used her hands to emphasize the volume. "Chunks of the tree flew in every direction. There was the ozone smell, then the hail quit and it starting pouring, rained really hard, drowned the fire, lasted maybe ten minutes then quit, just stopped, and we watched the thunderstorm move off to the east, lightning flashing out the bottom every couple of minutes. Scary, very scary, and it was just one storm, not a whole bunch like what's in front of us, and my question is: if lightning can explode a huge pine tree, don't you worry about what would it do to this little airplane?"

"I've been hit half a dozen times in big airplanes but I've never had a lightning strike in this one," Owen admitted.

"And what? Obviously you didn't die but what happens when you do get a strike? This possibility hadn't occurred to me before I decided to come along and I have to admit I'm a bit worried, feeling a bit trapped even. Doesn't this kind of thing scare you just a little? I don't mean to be pushy. My dad says I've been developing an attitude lately," did the quote thing with her fingers at the word 'attitude', "but college, if it teaches you anything, it's the importance of facts and logic, big tree BOOM, little airplane...what?"

When he glanced her way, even in the darkness of the cockpit, Owen could tell by her body language that she was indeed scared, her smile was gone and her hands were clasped tightly in her lap. Owen had dealt with frightened passengers before, but not seated next to him in the cockpit. He didn't want to scare Susie any more than she was scaring herself.

"Ok, facts: this airplane was originally designed for the military and has the same defense against lightning that an airliner has. A strike usually hits the nose or a wing tip, maybe punch a little hole at the entry site then flows across the skin until it finds an exit point it likes. Might leave some burn marks but nothing catastrophic. Pilots need to respect thunderstorms because there is no instrument on the ground or in the cockpit that defines the danger level, but can't be afraid of them or they'd never go to work. They can be exciting, I will admit that."

Owen could tell she wasn't buying. "Excuse me, but I have to make an announcement to calm the passengers," Owen said as he reached behind the throttle console and pulled the small plastic PA microphone off its hook. For some reason the system hadn't been de-activated. Owen positioned the switches that would feed the mike's output into their headsets.

"Ladies and gentleman...this is your captain speaking," using his hushed, unflappable, Captain's voice. "I know those gigantic thunderstorms and all the lightning on the right side of the airplane looks really scary, just be glad you can't see what's in front of us. Our First Officer will explain why you have nothing to worry about," and hand-ed the mike to her.

"And people call me a smart ass," she said, taking the mike, but she was smiling again.

"Ladies and gentleman," she tried to imitate his voice but failed. She tried again. "Ladies and gentleman, well, I'll have to start smok-ing if I'm going to sound like the Captain. He claims there's nothing to worry about because he's a hundred years old, has been flying since he was a kid, has been hit by lightning dozens of times and yet, though it's hard to believe, it appears he's still alive. But, and maybe the Captain thought I wouldn't notice, he never answered my ques-tion so I'll repeat it: Captain, doesn't this scare you, not even a little?"

"Were you scared during the takeoff and climb up Parley's canyon?"

"No," she admitted, "that was fun, but it was light. I could see where we were going and there wasn't any lightning."

"Well, since you're a mathematician and you understand statistics, statistically we were in more danger then than now. Besides, You are much more likely to get hurt or killed driving from Salt Lake to Denver than flying, even if there are some thunderstorms. You aren't scared when you drive a car, are you?"

"Of course not, but that's an everyday experience."

"Ok, for me this is an everyday experience. It doesn't scare me any more that driving a car scares you and just like you would be more careful driving in heavy traffic or on snow and ice, flying in this kind of weather makes me pay a little more attention."

"If you say so, but you don't seem any more alert." She apologized immediately. "Sorry, I don't know what I expected. Maybe to see your nose pressed against the windshield looking out, as if that would do any good."

"Actually, that's one way way to get through a line of storms at night. The lightning does illuminate the edges of the cells, sometimes better than radar. The problem is the flash can temporarily blind you, that's why..." Owen reached without looking and placed his right hand on a switch on the overhead panel..."it's important that I can find this switch for the fluorescent lights without looking. They would provide enough light for me to see the instruments until I got my normal vision back."

He thought about explaining that the real danger was hail and turbulence and radar wouldn't help you identify either, then decided against it. She didn't need more to worry about.

3

They were just crossing the Kremmling VOR when the center called." Magic 101, squawk ident." Owen pressed the button on the transponder that would light up their image on the controller's radar screen.

"Magic 101 is in radar contact. I'd suggest a heading of 060 to get you pointed at the gap in the weather the other inbounds are using."

"Magic 101 turning to 060."

Susie, her chin so far forward it was nearly touching the glare shield said: "I don't know what he's talking about, I don't see any gap, just lightning and I don't see any other airplanes."

"Magic 101 you have traffic, a United 757, 6 o'clock, 3 miles, descending to flight level one-eight-zero, you'll be following him into Denver," the controller explained.

Susie thought about that. "Wait a minute, if he's at 6 o'clock he's behind us. Why should we follow him if we're in front?"

Well, the fear seems to be gone, for now at least, Owen thought, "He's probably 100 knots faster than we are, so he'll pass us in a couple of minutes. We want him in front. Odds are he has radar and if he gets into anything he doesn't like he'll complain, and we'll know what's coming."

"Denver Center, United 510 out of flight level one-nine-zero for one-eight-zero. Traffic in sight at 12 o'clock."

Susie was surprised. "The United Captain is a woman?"

"We don't know if she's the Captain," Owen explained, "pilots alternate duties on two man crews; one handles the controls, the other handles the radios. She could be in either seat."

Susie thought about that for a moment. "Still, that must tick you off just a little. You flying this little mail plane and she's flying something bigger and faster...probably getting more money to do it."

"I see what your dad meant about your "attitude," Owen said, taking his hands off the control wheel to do the four fingered quote move, "but the fact that she's a woman doesn't bother me. It's the way airline seniority works. The Captain isn't necessarily the most experienced or talented pilot in the cockpit, just the most senior. All the airlines are the same."

They were approaching the back side of the thunderstorm line with most of the electrical activity now between their noon and three o'clock position. The hole Center was steering them toward should be visible soon. Several thin layers of cloud streamed just above and below their altitude, changing the visual sense from being suspended unmoving in blank space, to one of rapid forward motion. Suddenly, a series of flickering strobe flashes directly above them, like a bunch of press photographers capturing a night crime scene, caused Susie to jump. "Whoa, what the...?"

Owen laughed, "go ahead and say it, I won't tell your parents. It's United," Owen explained, "wingtip strobes reflecting off the cloud layer, not to worry, we should be able to see him in a minute."

"See her you mean, see her In a minute, and if you're referring to the expletive: WHAT THE FUCK, my dad already knows I use it when appropriate. It's my mom that thinks it's unladylike," the confidence back as though a switch had been thrown.

"Denver, United 510's radar is showing a hole in the line of precipitation ahead about 20 miles. A heading of 090 should get us through but it's not very wide, has anyone gone through recently?"

"United 510, It's been about 15 minutes and the gap is closing but it's the only one I see unless you go north of Cheyenne."

"Wow, there she is," Susie exclaimed, "they're almost right on top of us." She was looking up through her side window, head tilted to the right, touching the glass. The strobes reflection bouncing off the clouds made the interior of their cockpit look like a disco. It would be disorienting for the moment, but gone quickly, the difference in their speeds guaranteed that. The similar tracks they were on was creating another issue.

"Magic 101, United 510 now at your 12:30, 1,000 feet above your altitude, caution wake turbulence."

Caution indeed. 757s put out a wake like a battleship at warp speed. It was invisible, and therefore potentially treacherous to any smaller craft trailing behind. In smooth air, wake turbulence could last for many minutes, flowing away and down from the creating aircraft. Rough air tore it apart.

Although out of sight below them, Owen knew they were approaching the peaks of Rocky Mountain National Park. With the presence of all this thunderstorm activity, the smooth air they had been enjoying wouldn't last much longer and, most likely, neither would the wake turbulence.

United confirmed it: "Center, United 510, experiencing some moderate chop here." The word moderate sounded like someone had whacked the speaker in the gut; mod-erate.

"That didn't sound very promising," Susie said, sounding pretty unsure herself.

"It will be bumpy for awhile, not dangerous, just uncomfortable,"

Owen assured her, while wondering if there was any space left between these two cells. There had been a number of cloud to cloud strikes just ahead of their position, but higher.

"Magic 101, copy the moderate chop report?"

"Affirmative,"

"Magic 101, turn right heading 090, your discretion, that should take you through the thinnest part of the weather."

Thinnest? Not a hole anymore, "Snug up your seatbelt" Owen cautioned, then turned on the inlet heaters and pulled the ice vane control handles to prevent sudden ice accumulation from choking off the engines' airflow. There was the possibility of supercooled moisture in the vertical currents of a thunderstorm causing ice to form rapidly on the leading edges of the wing, engines and props. Best to be prepared.

It started gently enough, like someone smacking the base of your seat with a willow branch, but built rapidly into 50 miles an hour down a washboard dirt road, the kind of abuse that would inflict 10,000 miles of wear on a car's suspension in 10 minutes. Owen leaned closer to the windshield. They were skimming near the top of a layer of cloud that resembled a grey plate of scrambled eggs with every little tuft giving them a thump. It had been six minutes since United had passed them.

"Denver, chance Magic 101 could get a block between 17 and 17-5? Pretty rough here."

As soon as the center approved his request Owen eased the nose up; 100, 200, as they climbed above 17,300 feet the bumps moderated then stopped and the St. Elmo's began.

Susie, who had been tensely gripping both armrests through the bumps, looked at him, eyes wide again, but before she could speak Owen said:

"I know... WHAT THE FUCK!!" That got her laughing.

"Called St. Elmo's fire," Owen explained, "static electricity, harmless for the most part."

"For the most part? You have to stop making statements like that."

They were skimming along in the top of a layer of mist. Pull up 50 feet and be above it or sink back down, smooth either way, but when they slipped below the surface the St Elmo's would start on the windshield; dancing little fingers of electricity. Susie was fascinated but still held tight to her armrests. Owen let them sink a little lower and the tips of the props started to glow with a circle of fire. Climb back above the mist and the St. Elmo's disappeared.

"What's that?" Susie asked, pointing to two thin parallel white cloud streams just above them.

"United 510 would be my guess."

"I see her," Susie exclaimed, the 757 now distant and small, the wingtip strobes plainly visible in the dark alley between the two knotted whorls of grey cloud on either side that stretched forward toward infinity, towering above them. The lightning, at least for the last few minutes, had been contained within the clouds making them look like they were being lit by swarms of angry, gigantic fireflies.

Suddenly, a bolt snaked out of the right hand cloud and lit up the United 757, flickering and dancing around the exterior for a long couple of seconds before it retreated into the cloud it had come from.

"Holy shit," Susie exclaimed, "now what happens?"

After 15 seconds of silence: "Denver, United 510, just took a lightning strike on the right wing, doesn't appear to be any damage and we're proceeding on course but you might caution the traffic behind us," like she was making a hair appointment.

Owen responded; "Magic 101 we copy, thanks."

"Is she cool, or what?" Susie enthused.

"Impressive," Owen admitted, having heard any number of male voices under similar circumstances pitch up a couple of octaves.

It didn't take Susie five seconds to figure out their next problem; "So, now what are we going to do?"

"We? You have a suggestion?"

"Well, we can't just keep going. Won't we get hit by lightning?"

"Possibly."

"There you go again, possibly? Couldn't you work up something a little more definitive?"

"Not really. I don't know whether we can squeeze through this hole without getting hit but don't see any alternative. Do you?"

"Do I? I'm the math major, you're the pilot." She thought for a monument. "Couldn't we just turn around? I know the mail must get through, and all that crap, but if we crash and burn nobody's getting their damn mail anyway."

"Turn around? Okay, you check the rear view mirror to make sure it's clear, make sure the thunderstorms haven't closed in behind us."

"Rear view mirror, ha, ha. Very funny. It's obvious we can't see what's behind us. Why don't you ask the Center guy?"

"That would be the same Center guy that told us there was a hole we could get through?"

"Look, my family used to hike in Southern Utah?" Susie said, in what appeared to be another total change of direction though her grip on the armrests hadn't lessened. "Canyonlands, Bryce?

"There are dry washes: old stream beds cut into the sandstone with walls maybe fifty feet high, they're really neat to walk in, but there's always a sign at the start of the path down that says;

"DO NOT ENTER IF YOU SEE ANY CLOUDS ON THE HORIZON"

"When you get in the gully you see big pieces of trees that have been carried for miles by the flash floods and a high water mark twenty feet above your head. A few times a year some fools don't heed that sign and get caught, beaten against the rocks and drowned," she paused for emphasis, "and I'm more frightened now than I was walking in those gullies because sitting in this seat I'm just along for the ride. I don't doubt your experience or ability and I came along voluntarily, but..." She stopped there.

"As a math major, you would have taken at least one course in statistics, right?"

"I took a lot of statistics courses but here's the thing; sitting in the classroom or writing a thesis about the probability of dying in an airplane crash is an exercise completely removed from being in an airplane contemplating your own mortality. I know the odds are in my favor but logic isn't helping at the moment."

Owen tried to ease her fear. "We'll be on the ground in twenty minutes and you'll have a great story to tell your friends."

"By on the ground you mean at the airport, on the runway, not into the side of Rocky Mountain Park."

"Probably."

He got the thinnest of smiles as a response but Susie didn't release her grip on the armrests.

The center called: "United 510, need you to slow to 250 knots. When slowed, descend to and maintain 10,000 feet. Magic 101 need you to keep your speed up. You'll follow United 510 to the airport." They both acknowledged the clearance.

United had been reduced to just the flashing strobes, the plane itself was no longer visible. The walls of the tunnel they were flying through seemed to tighten, the clouds still lit by their internal fire, nothing visible but dark cloud, no ground or sky could be seen. No lightning strikes now, Owen worried. One might be enough to tip Susie over the edge, but he was out of ideas on how to ease her fears.

The lights of Boulder started to peek through beneath them, then, like a curtain being drawn, appeared like a sparkling black blanket.

"Magic 101 descend to and maintain 10,000 feet, right turn heading 120."

Owen lowered the nose and banked to the right, letting the speed build to the redline before he eased the throttles to maintain 1,000 feet per minute rate of descent and rolled them out on the assigned heading. The air was silky smooth again, not a ripple, but off to their right was the line of thunderstorms they had just flown through. It appeared to extend well south of the city and from this distance seemed even more intimidating then when they had been in it, with nearly constant lightning. Susie noticed. "Uh oh, is that over the airport?"

Owen tuned in the ATIS frequency: "Denver airport information Tango at 2250, sky clear, visibility west of the airport 2 miles in rain, visibility east greater than 10 miles, temperature 72, dew point 45, wind 250 at 12, gusting to 20, thunderstorms southwest through northwest, frequent lightning cloud to cloud and cloud to ground, rain began at 2230, inbound aircraft expect an ILS to runway 26 Left, runway 26 Right is closed.

"So south through north, the airport is surrounded by thunderstorms? Can we land in a thunderstorm?" Susie's hands were back gripping the armrests, her momentary relief gone.

"The simple answer is yes, a thunderstorm doesn't prevent a landing. Visibility is the limiting factor. I need to be able to see the runway to land. In geometric terms think of a line that starts 5 miles from and 1500 feet above the runway."

"Elway?" Susie remembered.

"Elway is correct. The flight instruments allow me to follow that line to a point 200 feet above and a 1/2 mile from the approach end of the runway. At that point, if I can see the runway I can land."

"That sounds too simple, like you're telling the truth, just not all of it because you don't want to scare me."

"I'm not trying to scare you but there's not enough time for a more complete answer. From what little I remember about math there are equations that can't be solved, too many unknowns, a thunderstorm is like that. It constantly changes shape, power, direction across the ground, rainfall amount and wind velocity to name a few variables. Timing has a lot to do with it also; one plane lands safely, the next, only two minutes behind gets to 200 feet, can't see the runway and has to go around."

"Magic 101 contact Denver approach on 128.7, have a good evening.

Owen changed frequencies and called: "Denver approach Magic 101 with Tango leaving 11 for 10,000 feet heading 120."

"Magic 101 Denver approach, radar contact, descend to 7,000 feet, 7 miles in trail with a United 757, landing 26 Left, caution wake turbulence, expect vectors for an visual approach to runway 26 Left, report traffic or runway in sight."

"How are you supposed to spot another airplane or the airport with all these other lights? Do you see them.?" Susie was staring straight ahead.

"Turn your head to the right a bit, look between the nose and the right engine for a flashing green then white rotating beacon...there, green...in thirty seconds it will flash white."

"That's it, that's the only light on the airport?" Sounding worried again.

"No. When we're close to lined up on final approach you'll see the runway sequence flashers and edge lights."

"Magic 101 heading 180, do you have the runway or traffic in sight?"

"Negative on the runway or traffic but Magic 101 has the airport in sight."

"Magic 101, cleared for the visual approach runway 26 Left, keep the speed up, traffic to follow you for the left side, your traffic now 12 o'clock, 6 miles, just turning onto the approach."

"There she is," Susie said, enthusiastic again, "right in front of us."

"Good eyes," Owen complimented. "Approach, Magic 101 has the traffic at 12 o'clock," and went back to tracking their position relative to the airport. This intercept heading would require a 90 degree turn to final about 5 miles from the runway. Not a problem for a visual approach. It was how the approach played out most nights, the runway lights swinging into view the visual clue needed to begin the turn. Owen, looking off to his right, realized the brightly lit downtown area northwest of the airport, visible just a few minutes before, had disappeared. Not a positive development.

Susie came to the same conclusion: "Uh oh, what happened to downtown? How come I can't see it anymore? That can't be good." To punctuate her concern a bright flash of lightning, bright even though muted by the cloud it descended from, then, almost immediately, two more just as bright.

"I'd guess those three just hit some of the taller targets downtown," Owen theorized. "If the storm stays there we'll be...," Before he could finish the thought two more hit, one west of the airport beacon, one to the south. The airport beacon? He stared into the darkness for thirty seconds. There was no flash.

Approach called: "United 510, contact the tower on 118.7.

Owen had already tuned their second radio to the tower frequency. When he turned the volume up he heard: "Tower, United 510, passing Elway inbound for runway 26 Left."

"United 510, Denver tower, visibility 2 miles with moderate rain, 400 feet scattered, 700 broken, 1,200 overcast, wind 240 at 25, gusts to 40, frequent lightning cloud to cloud and cloud to ground, braking action fair reported by a 727 two minutes ago, cleared to land runway 26 Left."

"Roger, United 510 cleared to land runway 26 Left."

Owen called; "Denver Approach Magic 101 no longer has the airport in sight."

"Copy that magic 101, you're now on a vector for an ILS to runway 26 Left."

Susie blurted out a question. "Braking action fair? What does that mean? How's anybody stop their airplane if there's no braking,?" Susie's hands once again using her armrests for support.

"Ok, that's gotta be the last question, this is one of those times we talked about where I have to pay a little more attention. Braking has four values; good, fair, poor and nil. They're not determined by scientific method. There's no indicator. It's the same today as it was for the Wright brothers, a seat of the pants thing for the pilot, his level of fear as he slides toward the end of the runway without slowing that determines what braking action he'll report. If it's really slippery reverse thrust is what stops you anyway, not the brakes. Don't worry about the braking report, the runway's five times longer than we need. It's the least of our problems."

If he hadn't requested her silence Owen knew Susie would have been all over that last bit. "Magic 101, Denver approach, maintain 7,000 feet, turn right heading 220, on that heading intercept the localizer runway 26 Left, upon interception you are cleared for the ILS approach, maintain best forward speed, contact the tower 118.7 passing Elway."

Owen already had the number one NAV (navigation radio) tuned to the proper frequency and the inbound course set on his HSI (horizontal situation indicator). He completed the before-landing checklist down to flaps and gear. The maximum flap speed was 170 knots, gear 150. When the DME counter (mileage to selected NAV station) showed six miles Owen reduced the power to idle, as the airplane slowed below 160 he extended the flaps, then at an indicated 145 he put the gear handle down, watching as the indicator lights went first red, then green.

Owen began the right turn as the localizer moved off its left peg and began to center, the glide slope indicator centering just as the blue lights on both marker beacons began to flash. He set the throttles to maintain 120 knots and changed the transmit switch to call the tower but before he could, two lightning flashes in quick succession struck directly in front of them.

"Wow," was all a suddenly overwhelmed Susie could manage to whisper.

"Denver tower, Magic 101, Elway inbound on the ILS 26 Left." Owen waited but there was no answer. After 30 seconds he tried again. Still nothing.

They were 4 miles from the end of the runway, 2 minutes at this speed, and could see the roll cloud at the leading edge of the thunderstorm they were about to fly into. The rain started; lightly at first, just a few drops on the windshield, rapidly escalating from light to moderate to deluge, creating a roaring sound louder than the engines, beating against the aluminum skin and turning the aircraft's interior into a timpani.

"Magic 101, this is United 510, we just landed, saw 2 lightning strikes hit the tower, looked like they hit the antennas, I think the controllers have bailed." Trying to help, Owen knew, but even if there was no one in the tower the odds were their conversation was being recorded. It wouldn't sound good in a court of law.

"Copy that," Owen said,"have you cleared 26 Left?"

"510's cleared the runway, very heavy rain now, we broke out at 200 feet, braking action was poor."

Illegal to land without permission, Owen knew, and switched back to the approach frequency. The controller, struggling to sequence six inbound aircraft behind them, was dealing with VHF radio's most difficult flaw; two aircraft transmitting simultaneously would generate a loud squeal. It would be heard by everyone on the frequency except the two who had keyed their mikes. They wouldn't know their message hadn't been received creating confusion, at a minimum, or worse.

They were 3 miles from the runway. 90 seconds to a decision point: land or go around. Without a controller's permission Owen could not know the potential for collision with an airplane crossing the runway or sitting in position waiting for departure. A missed approach would take them straight into the maw of the thunderstorm. A question not of the better choice available, but the lesser of evils.

With numerous possibilities to consider and little time available Owen chose. He retuned the transponder to 7600, the world wide code for loss of communication, retuned the radio to 121.5, the international emergency/distress frequency and sought help.

"Denver approach, Magic 101 on guard, unable to contact the tower, on a 3 mile final 26 Left, need landing clearance." After what seemed an infinitely long silence a different controller responded:

"Magic 101, Denver approach on guard, you are cleared to land on runway 26 Left. The airport weather reporting system is out so can't provide field conditions, visibility or ceiling. Advise clear of the runway on this frequency."

"Roger that and understand Magic 101 cleared to land."

They had been immersed in benevolent grey cloud, nothing outside the cockpit visible, the ride smooth, when suddenly the bottom dropped out, like being in an elevator when the cable broke and it plunged downward. The sinking sensation elicited a long groan from Susie: "Ohoo...

They had flown into the storm's center, the downburst, a vertical column of descending cold air that could reach velocities greater than most aircraft could counter.

Power was the answer. Owen knew from previous experience that power, lots of power, provided the only hope of escape. He pushed the throttles forward, watching as the ITT surged toward the redline, pulling the nose up to counter the unwanted descent and keep them on the glide path, watching as the airspeed deteriorated; 120,115,110,100... Mother Nature was winning this tug of war.

2 miles from and 600 feet above the runway, still in the cloud, the power at max when the elevator changed direction and started up. Owen pushed the nose forward as the airspeed began to climb; 110,115, retarding the power and continuing the descent; 500 feet, 400 feet, the sequence flashers now dimly visible through the thinning cloud; 300 feet, 200 feet, suddenly brilliant white light reflecting off the rain drenched windshield as they dropped below the base of the clouds and left the last of the sequence flashers behind.

The runway stretched out before them like a blurry grey ribbon, defined by its white edge lights. Owen turned on the windshield wipers knowing they wouldn't help much. He'd used them before.

Owen had always found it odd that even with all the technological advances that made their descent through the clouds to this exact point in space possible, a successful landing was dependent on the fifty year old mechanical contraption that was now attempting to sweep water from the windshield.

Sight of the runway had changed Susie from panicked to concerned spectator; had restored a belief that she might indeed survive this craziness. "Can you see alright?" she asked.

The bumps had gotten stronger as they approached the runway, gusts from the left tossing the 99 like an abandoned styrofoam cup on a windy ocean swell. Fifty feet from touchdown, the altimeter not accurate enough to be much help, success dependent now on visual acuity and learned reflex. Owen, looking through the windshield at the runway, gauging the sink rate, watched in amazement as the left wiper, his wiper, disappeared. Swipe, swipe...Gone. Not just the blade, the whole arm assembly. As blurred as the view had been, this was worse, much worse.

Owen had been pointing the nose of the aircraft to the left, into the crosswind, Susie's wiper was still functional and through her window he could see the runway's right edge lights. The 99's wingspan was 48 feet, the runway 150 feet wide; if he hugged the right edge, kept the wingtip 10 feet inside the single string of lights they'd be fine. The new difficulty: dark night and a dark runway offered little in the way of depth perception. One string of lights instead of two made it even more of a challenge.

Easing the throttles to idle he held the upwind wing down with the ailerons, straightened their path with the rudder as they touched down gently and pulled the throttles into reverse.

As they slowed Owen tried the brakes. Susie's idol, the lady United pilot, hadn't been joking. There was little, if any, reduction in speed. More reverse, max now, and as the airplane slowed, the props threw a sheet of water forward, the crosswind slinging it onto the windshield, reducing the visibility even more.

Down to walking speed, idle reverse, Owen searched for a high speed taxiway on their right, blue edge lights instead of white, spotted one, made the turn to clear the runway and stopped. Called approach:

"Magic 101 on guard, clear of 26 Left and holding on Yankee.

"Magic 101, right turn on Alpha to the freight ramp, caution for other taxing aircraft, ground control frequency out of service."

"Right on Alpha to the freight ramp," Owen acknowledged, "500 feet on final experienced a 30 knot airspeed loss, 26 Left braking is poor."

The controller rogered Owen's report as he made the right turn onto Alpha, a semicircular taxiway around the perimeter of the passenger terminals, creeping along, still blind on his left side.

Taxiway Alpha terminated in the freight ramp, a mostly empty macadam pad with enough space for thirty 747s. On its west edge, large signs identified a line of storage and transfer hangers; US postal service, FedEx, UPS, and a dozen smaller, little known outfits. A series of geometric painted white lines and numbers directed traffic and identified parking spots. Majestic was handled by FedEx.

A yellow-rain-suit clad figure with white flashlight wands darted out of the building as they approached, waving them straight ahead then into a 180 degree turn to the right, crossed wands to indicate their spot, followed by a throat slash to indicate engine shut down. The ramp coordinator pulled back the hood on his rain jacket and Owen realized the rain had stopped.

They were parked facing east and could see three sets of landing lights in line on the approach. With five miles of separation the visibility was back up to fifteen miles. Owen checked his watch, eight minutes had passed since they had landed in the fury of the thunderstorm. It must have retreated back toward the mountains, leaving the approach path to the runway in the clear, at least for the moment. No windshield wipers for them. "Timing, an essential key to happiness," he muttered, making sure the ITT temps had stabilized before pulling both fuel controls to cutoff.

With the dying turbine whine Owen removed his headset and set it on top of the glare shield, pulled the oxygen cannula over his head and placed it on its storage hook, turned off the fuel pumps, navigation lights, rotating beacon, instrument lights and turned on the cockpit fluorescents.

Susie mimicked his actions with her headset and cannula then heaved a big sigh, looked at him, said: "Sorry... I'd guess I'm probably the worst passenger you've ever had."

Owen just smiled, shook his head, said, "no, nope, not even close," and told her about the passenger in Miami, young girl about her age. The weather was similar to what they had just flown through with thunder and lightning all quadrants. About ready to push back from the gate when he'd heard a high pitched scream and a moment later the girl was in the cockpit, standing between the copilot and himself, hanging onto their seat backs as the flight attendant tried to pull her back into the cabin, crying uncontrollably, sobbing, and begging him not to leave the gate. She'd had a vision, she claimed, and if he took off they would crash, and everyone would be killed; all of this loud enough to be heard halfway back in the cabin.

"No shit? That really happened? What'd you do?"

"Made a calming announcement," Owen smiling at the memory, collecting his stuff, kneeboard and headphones stuffed into his bag, "We need to get inside before it starts to rain again, and you have to call your father."

"There's got to be more to that story," Susie insisted.

"There's plenty of stories, but I'm not kidding, I promised your dad I'd get you to phone as soon as we landed."

"Ok, ok," climbing down, waiting while Owen closed and secured the door, put the control locks on then followed him into the hanger and an empty office with a phone on the desk.

"Get the operator first," he instructed, "it will have to be a collect call."

Owen listened to her excited explanation, no mention of fear or concern. When she hung up he said: " give me a second, I need to call the hotel, have them send the van, then I'll walk you out."

"We could give you a ride to the hotel," Susie volunteered, "my cousin Samantha is picking me up. You'd like her, she's like me only ten years older, so a little more mature, if that's your thing. We could buy you a drink and you could tell the rest of that story and maybe about tonight's flight, Sam will never believe me otherwise."

Long, lean, smart and ten years older, half his age plus seven. What could be bad about that?

4

8-16-94

5:30am the next morning, Owen watched the sun begin its rise over the eastern Colorado horizon. The air was cool and clean, washed by last night's thunderstorms. Standing outside the airport hotel with his go-cup of coffee, waiting for the van to take him to the airport, Owen thought about the challenge of landing in the heart of a storm, the dawning day, and how much fun the return trip was going to be.

He was paid $120 for the round trip. Owen preferred to think of the $120 as his earnings for the flight last night in the darkness and weather. The return he would do for free.

Owen had learned to fly at a small grass strip airport in New York State, just north of Newburgh. As a neophyte pilot he was taught to rely on visual cues as well as the basic flight instruments, to see where you were heading as well as remember where you'd been, to memorize the terrain and landmarks surrounding your home airport so you could find your way back. Light airplanes don't leave a trail of breadcrumbs and IFR to the private pilot means I follow roads, railroads or rivers instead of instrument flight rules. It is the most basic type of navigation, has the fewest rules and was, for Owen, the most fun.

The liquid brilliance of a Rocky Mountain morning glistened on the still wet skin of the 99 as Owen opened the cockpit door and tossed his bag inside, did a quick walk around and removed the control locks. A Fed Ex ramp foreman approached as he was stepping up the ladder. "No freight this morning," he said.

Owen had yet to carry a single envelope on the return to Salt Lake in the three months he had been flying the route. Bit of a worry. No freight, no money for Majestic, and eventually no job, again, but it was too pretty a morning for worry.

He called clearance delivery, requested they cancel the IFR and get him a visual departure clearance westbound. Short taxi to runway 34, finishing the checklists as he rounded the corner and advanced the power. Airplanes like cool dense air; less strain on the engines, more lift for the wings.

Holding the nose down to accelerate rapidly, 50 feet above the runway, gear and flaps up, then let her loose. 1,500 horsepower in the palm of his right hand, the visceral thrill had not gotten old. Owen headed for the crease in the Front Range just south of Rocky Mountain Park.

Light airplane with no freight plus minimum fuel allowed a 2,000 feet per minute climb rate. Not quite fighter performance, but as close as Owen was likely to get. He bid the tower good morning and re-tuned the radio to the ATC area frequency, just in case, but no need to call. Set the transponder to 1200, the VFR code, so all the ATC radar would see was an unidentifiable target with no altitude readout. Stealth mode.

Drifting mist was rising out of the trees as he climbed the slope, no people here, no civilization at all, his space to explore. North of Steamboat Springs and the towns along US40, heading west along the spine of the Uinta mountains looking for his waterfall. There, there it was, straight ahead, maybe 200 feet from the top of the cliff to the pond below, a thin string of diamonds flashing in the morning sun. A temporary glory, created by the previous night's rainfall overfilling the hollow at the top of the cliff, it would be gone by late morning.

Pushing the nose down and letting the speed build to the redline Owen aimed at the pond at the base of the cliff. Close, closer, now pull...hard, adding power as he started up the cliff face, close as he dared, over the top and push the nose down to stay 50 feet above the flat topped mesa. A real life, high speed, three dimensional arcade game with the potential for disaster an eye blink away. Hard not to smile.

There was the rain-filled pond that fed the stream, scrub trees clinging to the rocks, and; uh oh, knee deep in the pond stood a couple, bare ass naked, locked together in passionate embrace. They heard him now, coming up behind them, looking up as he zoomed past 50 feet above their heads. What a sight, for him...and them. Owen felt a sudden pang of guilt for the interruption, but quickly realized it would be a momentary intrusion; they'd be back at it before he was out of sight. After expending the effort required to climb to that spot they wouldn't relinquish it easily.

He wasn't worried that they would turn him in. Even if they wanted to their odds of being successful were slim. The airplane had the required N numbers on both sides of the fuselage near the tail. Only 6 inches tall, the absolute minimum, there was no way they could be seen well enough to identify the aircraft as it roared overhead and past. The previous owners logo had been painted over and there was no "Majestic" signage. It was a generic turboprop aircraft doing something illegal at low altitude but would be hard to report without a positive ID. The temptation to circle back was strong but momentary. He did dumb things occasionally but tried to avoid the blatantly stupid, thinking he'd have to stay away from the waterfall for awhile. Maybe tell Susie's cousin Sam. She had indicated an interest in getting together and had seemed to enjoy his company and stories last night. Probably another dumb idea; Susie's cousin, George's niece, a little too close to home.

Owen headed for Heber then Park City, climbing to 10,000 feet to avoid the half-dozen hot air balloons sure to be aloft in the still of this summer morning, called Salt Lake approach while heading down Immigration Canyon in his airborne Porsche at 225 knots, crossing the Eastern edge of the city with the engines at idle to keep noise complaints to a minimum, bleeding the speed and altitude in a 60 degree banked turn as he approached the runway and landed, shutting down both engines as he exited on the high speed taxiway and coasted to the freight ramp. Quiet as a whisper.

Pointless to rush home since the overnight package he was expecting from Flight Safety wouldn't arrive until about 9:30 Owen decided on breakfast. Back up Emigration Canyon road. to Ruth's diner and a seat in the shade on the back terrace under a copse of aspen for a plate of house made corn beef hash and eggs accompanied by an ice cold bottle of Heineken.

After breakfast Owen ambled back up I-80 to his condo thinking about the couple he'd seen on top of the mesa. Long way to go for sex, even if it would provide a spectacular mountain view. Why would you need a mountain to look at? A change of scenery or because your partner's beauty had become routine from too much observation? He had been in that situation before but had changed partners rather than scenery. Had been accused of being callous. Wondered why a woman would want him around when the magic was gone, for her as well as him. Callous or rational? Try as he might, it was nearly impossible to exit that painful situation without looking like the bad guy. Still, he didn't see faking attraction as a viable path to conjugal bliss, with or without the wedding.

The FedEx envelope was leaning against his door. Owen opened another Heineken, sat at his kitchen table and pulled out the contents. The cover letter, with a Flight Safety logo, confirmed a few of the details the secretary had given him yesterday and added a few new ones; The airline was to be based in Clear River, Missouri, wherever that was. A lease arrangement had been reached for 5 ex-USAir

737-200 series aircraft with more to follow. 737-200? Identical to the United aircraft that crashed in Colorado Springs. 30 year old aircraft? The airline was starting out on the cheap.

Talk about cheap, the second paragraph was the real stunner. Applicants would have to possess a 737 type rating or pay to get one. Owen had three airline type ratings. He had never been in the cockpit of a 737.

A deal had been arranged with Flight Safety; ten grand plus cover your own living expenses in Long Beach, California, for the four to six weeks the training would take. Fifteen grand to get the job? Owen sped through the rest of the bullshit to the important page, pay scale. Captains would be paid $4,000 a month although the amount of work, or hours flown was not defined. Didn't sound good. Less then half of what he made at Eastern and fifteen grand to get the job? He'd heard this song before.

Owen had enquired about a pilot job with Southwest several years earlier. He was told he needed to have a 737 type rating to apply but having one was no guarantee of being hired. If their training schedule permitted, Southwest would put you through their school and get you the rating. If you were hired the cost would be deducted from your pay. If not, you had to fork over $20,000. Not a deal worthy of consideration since at the time Southwest wasn't hiring, nor was anyone else who flew the 737.

If No-Name airline lasted four months he would have covered his training costs, have the rating, and could apply with Southwest when they did start hiring. A Southwest copilot made nearly twice what No-Name was proposing to pay their Captains and they would almost certainly be in business long enough for him to reach the age 60 mandatory retirement.

Work for Southwest? Start over as a junior copilot flying with Captains who had been in kindergarten when Owen had begun his airline career. Move to Dallas, their junior base, be on reserve sitting in a cheap apartment waiting for the phone to ring.

It was depressing to contemplate. He would be going back to the beginning, except now he was fifty years old, not twenty-three. He needed a job that had more of a future than Majestic, and flying was the only career he'd known. As big a question mark as a future with No-Name represented, he knew he had little choice.

He would need a few days off. It never occurred to him to lie about the reason. Although none of the other Majestic pilots had mentioned the ad, Owen was sure all of them knew, including the Chief Pilot. No way to hide his intent but all the pilots, especially the Chief Pilot, would quit Majestic in a heartbeat to fly for a different airline.

He picked a travel agent out of the phone book and was told that round trip airfare Salt Lake-St. Louis was $399 if he left on a Thursday and returned Saturday. Flight Safety's info packet included a list of nearby hotels that gave a discount, $150 for two nights including van service to the training center and nearby restaurants so he wouldn't need a car. Still, nearly a week's pay to apply. Had to take the risk or he'd be locked in the air freight hauling business and getting no-where. Pointless to make the trip unless he intended to take the job, if offered. He gave the travel agent his credit card information and asked her to set it up for the Thursday after next.

Owen hadn't been to a real job interview, the kind you had to dress for, in decades. He didn't own a suit, had one sport coat, one pair of dress khakis, one tie, one blue dress shirt, and a pair of boat shoes that would do if he spent an hour with polish and brush. The info packet said the process would include several aviation and general knowledge tests, an interview, and twenty minutes in a DC9 simulator.

Knowledge tests? At this point in his career if he didn't possess the knowledge to get an airplane from A to B he was never going to learn. DC9 simulator? It had been seven years since Owen had flown a "9" but he had nearly 10,000 hours combined right and left seat time in that model. At the beginning of his last Captain's simulator check ride the bored instructor had placed the sim at 10,000 feet over the Miami airport, ran the "weather" to zero-zero and failed both engines.

Owen had started the APU (auxiliary power unit to provide electric and hydraulic power), slowed to 180 knots with the slats extended, did a rapid series of mental gymnastics to calculate the rate of descent and distance from the runway he would need to begin the approach, circled to lose altitude then glided to a blind landing. They were only 10 minutes into the required 2 hour session but the instructor had seen enough. "You pass," he said, "let's go get a drink." The simulator wouldn't be an issue.

He would need to hide his ever present lack of respect for authority but he'd managed that for years.

8-26-94

Owen's sim partner was a young good looking kid; red-blond hair and blue eyed, he could have been Owen's son. He addressed Owen as "sir", said his name was Josh Logan and he'd been flying left seat in a Lear for 3 years. Would Owen mind if he occupied the left seat for the ride. "I'll be more comfortable there" Josh said, and although Owen hadn't flown from the copilot seat in 15 years he readily agreed. Josh had struck him as a likable young man and seemed a bit nervous. They agreed, at Owen's suggestion, that Owen should fly first. That would allow Josh to get used to the simulator which was, Owen explained, very different from a Lear.

Owen didn't have any problems, the muscle memory implanted through his thousands of hours in the cockpit of a DC9 was firmly entrenched. When it was Josh's turn Owen helped him with subtle cues; putting his hand on the gear and flap levers when it was time for their extension, picking up the paper checklist when it was time for that.

Josh sat for the interview first, came out of the office with a big smile. "I got the job," he said, "I got the job and I owe you for that. I was shaking like a leaf when we got in the sim and watching you really calmed me down. Drinks are on me."

The Flight Safety instructor conducting the interview, Alan Brandis, scanning Owen's paperwork said: "Your sim instructor put in his remarks that you could have easily passed a Captain's check ride and that's what they're looking for. He also noticed that you were instructing your sim partner."

Owen began to protest but Alan waved it aside, "Josh's a great kid and he did score well on the tests. He'll start as a First Officer but I'd guess he'll be ready to move to the left seat quickly. Did you instruct or do any Check Airman work at Eastern?"

Owen shook his head. "Too much politics, too complicated. By comparison flying a trip was simple, without drama. Fly your trip and the Captain gets to set the tone. I like easygoing. Didn't want to give that up."

"Ok with me but I'd guess you'll get asked again. If you can make it, you'll be in the first class with Josh. There will be 10 First Officers and 10 Captains. We don't have a confirmed start date yet because they're still finishing the paperwork for the operating certificate but I would guess that will be completed in about a month. You'll get a two week notice and class and simulator training will be at Flight Safety's Long Beach facility. That sound ok so far or do you have doubts, maybe some questions?"

Owen smiled, couldn't help himself, though he knew it probably wasn't the surest way to employment; this was meant to be serious business. "Questions? Sure I've got questions, but I don't think the answers are available just yet. Got to be honest here, the choice of aircraft is a bit of a worry. I have some experience with aging aircraft, none of it good, and the 737/200? United crashed one in C Springs almost 3 years ago and I haven't seen a probable cause from the NTSB. Have you heard anything about that?"

Allen just shook his head, "Not a word and there are a lot of that model flying worldwide. I haven't heard of another crash caused by a loss of control. There have been some incidents of rudder problems but Boeing claims they were caused by a malfunctioning yaw damper. Replacing the yaw damper has solved the problem each time. Does that answer your question?"

"I'm a tad skeptical. I've not flown a 737 but the 727 has a yaw damper switch. If you're having problems with the yaw damper you turn it off. I don't believe it has enough authority to cause a loss of control but what do I know?"

"Anything else?" Alan asked.

"Well, there's the timing; I wouldn't want to write a check to Flight Safety for ten grand before the airline had a certificate and a name."

"Understandable," Alan agreed. "Shouldn't be a problem, Flight Safety won't schedule a class until there is a certificate. They don't care about a name but they do care about a corporate bank account."

Josh was waiting when Owen walked out of the office. "And the answer is?" He said with a tentative smile.

Owen smiled back. "Let's drink," he said.

A month later Owen got a letter from Alpha Airlines inviting him to pilot training class number one to start in two weeks.

Alpha? Interesting name. Dominant member of a group... but in a group of airlines? Seemed a bit presumptuous for a startup with four ancient aircraft. Well, Owen thought, at least they would appear before American in the telephone directory if anyone bought their airline ticket that way anymore.

The last aircraft type rating class Owen had attended was for the 757 six years ago when Eastern Airlines was still in business. In those days pilots were paid their normal salary for training, which included the two weeks of ground school plus 7 simulator periods, including the check ride, to get the FAA certificate. Hotel and meal expense were also covered. Fail the check ride and you'd get more training then try again. ALPA, the airline pilot association, had been there to protect you. It was hard to get fired. Times had changed.

The FAA requires the specific type rating for the pilot in command (Captain) of any "large" aircraft; want to be an airline Captain, you need the type rating. This class was going to be different. Owen would be paying for his education, protected only by his ability. There was no safety net.

The Porsche had to go. He had no rational choice. Owen had made a risky aviation bet once before, borrowing $5,000 thirty years ago to pay for his pilot training with no idea if he would ever get a flying job. That bet had paid off handsomely but in 1964 he hadn't had an option. Now he had his version of a four-wheeled savings account. He sold the Porsche for $15,000 to the dentist who kept his Alfa Spider in the adjacent storage garage. Owen thought about asking for visiting privileges but decided the dentist wouldn't go for that.

He was sorry to see her go, another love story disaster, but knew it was time to move on. If this worked out he could buy another one, newer maybe, or another motorcycle. He wasn't finished with motorized entertainment forever, but he was for now. Owen loaded the Subaru early Saturday morning and headed for Long Beach, ready to begin part two of his airline pilot career.

He checked into the Holiday Inn that Flight Safety had recommended, arriving in time for a late cocktail hour and dinner. Josh wouldn't check in until the next afternoon.

Sunday morning Owen slept in, had a big breakfast, and drove the four blocks to the Flight Safety building at the airport. Like the major air carriers, Flight Safety's training operation was pretty much 24/7. A secretary checked his name off the Alpha class list, gave him a parking pass, a name tag that had Alpha Airlines across the top with his name underneath, a 737 aircraft manual, the flight operations procedure manual and a receipt for his check. $10,000. Owen went back to his room, put the manuals on the desk and started to read.

The aircraft manual was a hard cover, loose-leaf tome some 400 pages long. It covered every dimension, weight, pressure, temperature, and mechanical system of the 737. Normal, non-normal and emergency procedures for before engine start, after start, taxi, takeoff, climb, cruise, descent, landing, after landing and engine shut down with a checklist for each.

There were diagrams and photos showing the cockpit layout and procedures for the pilots to monitor and operate the myriad dials, switches, caution and warning lights for the engines, electrical, hydraulic, pressurization, fuel, fire warning and extinguishing systems along with schematic diagrams for each. Instructions on how to adjust the pilot's seat, turn on the lights, the radar, the radios; even the location of the fire ax on the bulkhead behind the Captain's seat showing the warning label indicating it was illegal to leave the gate without it.

Separate chapters in the manual were devoted to the cabin layout, the galleys, the lavatories, the location of emergency equipment including medical oxygen, and cockpit and cabin fire extinguishers both foam and H2O.

Owen had 3,500 hours in the 727, had flown it as First Officer and Captain, and was familiar with Boeing's methodology which would give him a head start, but there would still be a lot of studying to do.

At 5:30 Owen walked through the swinging doors into the bar and spotted Josh sitting at a cocktail table with the airplane manual open in front of him, his nose buried, his beer sitting untouched.

"Beer for cocktail hour? Not this boy," Owen said and ordered his Absolut with olives and twist. Watching the bartender pour he said, "Better make it a double please, I don't have to be sober until 8:00 tomorrow morning." $6 dollars for the drink. Owen put a $10 on the bar and left the change. If this was going to be his home bar for a month he wanted the bartender on his side.

Josh looked worried. "Man, there are a shitload of numbers in here," he said waving at the book and taking a big gulp of the beer. I may have to take up drinking vodka."

"I can recommend the vodka but not the worry. It always looks impossible at first, worse after the first week when all the numbers seem to run together but then it starts to get better. At the end of three weeks you'll have learned enough to pass the oral and check ride. After a month on the line you'll have forgotten half of what you learned. When it's time for the six month check ride you'll have to learn it all over again but after a couple of years you won't have to study much to pass a check ride. I've never understood why they make you memorize the numbers. They're not really necessary. Every gauge has a normal range marked in green with the limits marked by a red line. Green good, red bad, it's really that simple."

"You sound like you've done this before."

"Once or twice," Owen laughed, "and it is always the same. When you start, it feels like trying to take a sip from a fire hose"

Three weeks later, sitting at the same table, Josh proposed a toast as they tapped their glasses together: "Goodby ground school, hello simulator. Man am I ready for the change, fly instead of read. Any helpful hints about getting through the simulator?"

Owen took a sip of his vodka and thought about the question for a moment. "I try to visualize each procedure, see myself in the seat, then think about where the information I'll need will be presented, which gauge to look at, how the sequence of events will unfold, how to recognize it, control it and resolve it.

"We'll be training to pass the check ride which is a choreographed sequence that hasn't changed since my first attempt 30 years ago. I passed that one and every one since." They were to be paired in the sim. "Don't worry," Owen assured him, "we'll have fun."

"Easy for you to say," Josh thought. Like Owen thirty years earlier he had borrowed the ten grand to pay for the training and he didn't have a Porsche to sell if it didn't go well. The Lear job wouldn't cover his costs if this didn't work out. Still, he thought, the risk was worth the potential upside. He could be an airline Captain in a year; even if no one had ever heard of the airline.

Josh did have fun in the simulator. The 737 was 60 tons heavier than the Lear 24 he had flown but the simulator required the same delicate touch to fly it well.

It became a contest between them, an anything you can do... entertainment. Both men had a competitive streak. They were just about equal in their ability to control the sim but Owen was much more experienced in the check ride game. He was better able to guess what disaster the instructor was going to throw at them next, always a half step ahead of his younger partner but he made sure that Josh looked good even if he finished a half step behind. They worked well as a team. Owen enjoyed helping Josh figure it all out. Enjoyed seeing him relax and gain confidence. Enjoyed a shared sense of accomplishment when the last simulator ride was complete and both had passed with ease.

One drink into the graduation party the bartender handed Owen the phone.

"Captain Swift? My name's Andrew Rossi. I've just been hired as the VP flight operations for Alpha and your name came up when I asked the Flight Safety instructors if they could recommend a few candidates for the Check Airman positions. You were their first recommendation but they said you had not expressed interest in the position. I'm at the Flight Safety building, could I stop in and buy you a drink, maybe talk to you about considering the position? Check Airman first then once we get the airline a little better organized put you in the Chief Pilot's office. You'd be helping me out. I'm going to need someone with your level of experience and you'd be helping yourself too, Chief Pilot experience looks good on a resume in case Alpha doesn't exist for long. You'd also have a chance to help train young guys like Josh."

"Yet to meet me and already has me figured out," Owen thought, "That's a bit of a worry." Rossi was right about at least one thing; Chief Pilot would be an attention getting item on his resume.

An hour later Owen rejoined Josh at the hotel bar. "And, the answer is?" Josh greeted him. He had ordered a fresh drink for Owen and pushed it toward him. "You going to be a Check Airman?"

"Looks that way,". Owen raised his glass to toast with Josh, "Check Airman, and if I don't fuck that up too badly, Chief Pilot."

"Really? Chief Pilot? I can see you doing the Check Airman thing, you're a great instructor, but Chief Pilot? That's an office job. You want to spend your days behind a desk?"

"Not really sure. For awhile anyway, see what it's like. I'll still be a Check Airman so I'll get to fly, just not every day. Honestly, I'm not really sure what a Chief Pilot does all day. Rossi said in an airline this small he wasn't sure either. Said we'd make it up as we went along. Kinda hard to tell in an hour and I've been fooled before but he seems like a decent guy." Owen shrugged, "Look at it this way. If neither one of us fucks up, in a couple of years I'll be the Chief Pilot, and you'll be the Check Airman.

"What could be bad about that?"

5

Airline statistics indicate that you could fly 24 hours a day, 365 days a year for 50 years before dying in an air carrier plane crash. Passenger surveys reveal, however, that nearly half of all adult airline passengers suffer from some level of trepidation, 10 % are deathly afraid, avoid the experience if possible, and if not possible require alcohol, drugs, or some combination thereof to keep from lapsing into a psychotic state.

Big airplanes have at least two of every important system; electrical, hydraulic, navigational, and at least two engines. There are also two pilots with thousands of hours of experience, usually, who are well trained, then tested every six months for a Captain, yearly for the First Officer. Big airplanes are safe, little airplanes less so, though the fault is more often the pilot's than the airplane's.

The pilot of 3585MD, Dr. Peter Hawthorne, was an emergency room doc; bright, articulate, with skills honed through decades of practice. In the operating room he had faced all manor of medical emergencies and brought his patient through. The nurses, talking among themselves, readily admitted he was good, as well as good looking, but thought his giant ego would eventually get him into trouble. No one bothered to tell him. They knew he would dismiss their opinions as unworthy of consideration.

The doctor had been a three sport athlete both in high school and college but medical school allowed time for only one thing... medicine. The internship and surgical residency was even more intense with little time for outside activities. He was about to slide into his forties when he realized that although he had a doctor's house and car, a lovely wife and two smart kids, he hadn't yet bought himself a doctor's toy. Golf was ok...and tennis provided some aerobic activity but neither was thrilling. Wanting more, he decided to learn to fly.

Hooked in the first 10 minutes of the introductory ride by the pucker factor and physical thrill of command in three dimensions, the good doctor went balls-to-the-wall, a term he learned from his aviation reading that was attributed to the Air Force in the 60's, and referred to the ball traditionally at the business end of the throttles when pushed as far forward as they would go. Maximum power. Maximum speed.

Dr. Hawthorne signed up for two lessons a week. Weather permitting he flew more when he could, attacking the task as he would any other in his search for perfection. He soloed quickly, after only fifteen hours of instruction; not the fastest ever, but quick.

Talk about exciting. The ER could get pretty intense with its rapid fire life and death decisions, but there were other doctors to confer with and all his previous experience to fall back on. Not true in an airplane on his first solo. There was no instructor to save his ass. It was your own life on the line. Fuck up and you die, not some patient you'd never seen before. The doctor loved the feeling of independence and self reliance, disconnected from the ordinary.

Proud of himself he pressed on and got his private license. With that replacing the student certificate in his wallet, he could legally carry a passenger. His took his wife up first.

Jo-Ann Hawthorne was one good looking woman. Not school smart but shrewd, she'd figured out early on that college wouldn't advance her prospects any faster than a good secretarial course and getting that stunner of a body where it could be spotted by the "right" man. By "right", she was thinking "professional"... doctor, lawyer, banker, like that. Hired as a temp in the doctor's newly opened office it was game over the moment they met. She ran just fast enough to guarantee getting caught, then made herself indispensable. Now, fifteen years into the marriage when her husband proclaimed his desire to purchase an airplane, she agreed readily. It was that or he'd be skirt chasing. An airplane would be less dangerous, she thought. She was wrong.

In the OR Dr. Hawthorne was the consummate professional. In an airplane he was a rank amateur, had reached that tipping point in a pilot's life where he begins to believe he can do no wrong, has enough experience to try most anything, sure he can get away with it.

The doctor had accumulated almost 200 hours in fixed gear, small single engine airplanes, since getting his private license seven years ago. He had only 14 hours in the much faster, more complex, retractable gear Beech Bonanza he had recently purchased, and was flying this morning to a meeting in Chicago.

Dr. Hawthorne had worked on getting his instrument rating for six months before he bought the Bonanza. He read all the books, watched the instructional video tapes, and got thirty hours of instruction in his home airport's rental instrument trainer, a Cessna 172. He had passed the written then taken the flight check with the local FAA examiner.

The examiner had seen a number of really smart professionals, from fields other than flying but used to being in charge, get themselves into situations they couldn't escape because their egos took control of the decision making process. He knew the Bonanza to be a much faster airplane than the Cessna the doctor had been flying and taken his test in. He cautioned the doctor on the potential hazards. Doctor Hawthorne didn't heed this advice.

When the doctor got the Bonanza home he went flying every chance he got, and shot practice approaches, one after the other. He loved the repeatable precision of it, turning onto the final approach outside the outer marker, about 6 miles from the runway, and maintaining 90 knots of airspeed. Each approach an exact duplicate of the last. He was getting good at this, he thought. His home airport had one runway, one ILS (instrument landing system) approach, no approach control to alter his plan, no tower to get landing permission from and little other traffic to worry about.

He had studied the approach plates for Midway airport in Chicago but there were 15 of them for the 4 instrument runways, plus the airport diagram, which showed the 10 visual approach runways and looked like a maze. There were taxiways everywhere. He should have heard warning bells clanging. Lansing or Gary would have been much simpler and were only about 20 miles farther from his morning meeting. The doctor was accustomed to complicated medical problems and ignored the signals. He knew he was a smart guy and was sure he could handle whatever problems Midway might present. From Midway he would be a 10 minute taxi ride to his meeting, as opposed to a rental car and 20 miles in Chicago's morning rush hour, then the return trip in the evening's crush. He didn't want to waste that much time. After all, this was exactly the sort of trip he was thinking about when he decided to get his pilot license. He was a little nervous, but doing well, until approach control asked him to maintain maximum forward speed, they had a line of 737 airliners behind him, then cleared him for an ILS to runway 31 Center with a sidestep to 31 Left. He wasn't sure what that meant but was too embarrassed to ask. A sidestep had not been covered in the video, though he was sure he had heard of it, or read of it, before. He thought 180 knots indicated should be fast enough, indeed it was the same speed as the 737 that was following him, but double the approach speed he was used to, making decisions necessary in half the time he was accustomed to. The extra speed didn't allow him to extend the landing gear where he normally would, at the outer marker, because the gear limit speed was 120 knots, and rushing now, when approach control told him to contact the tower, he misdialed the radio.

When no one answered his call, he tried going back to the approach control frequency but it was so busy he couldn't get a word in. This required him to look up the tower frequency on the approach plate, whose small print required him to fish for his glasses in order to read it.   Still going 100 knots and 2 miles from the airport when the tower cleared him to land on 31 Left he pulled the throttle to idle and tried to figure out which of the 5 strips of concrete and blacktop, 3 runways and 2 taxiways, he was supposed to land on while completely unaware that the warning horn, which was supposed to sound when the throttle was closed and the gear was not down and locked, wasn't working.   In his confusion he had completely forgotten that most important item on the before-landing checklist.

The doctor discovered his error as the first of the 3 blades of the prop struck the surface of the runway.   Although the Bonanza did originally touch down on runway 31 Left, it slid sideways and stopped at the intersection of 31 Center and 22 Left, blocking both and effectively closing the airport to airline traffic. The tower controller, when questioned later, admitted that he was focused on two 737s on final approach that no longer had the required minimum separation and that he had failed to notice the lack of gear extension on the Bonanza.

The loud TWANG of the first prop blade hitting concrete came as such a surprise to the doctor that he gave up being the pilot in command and became just a passenger, along for the ride. The descent rate was slow enough that there was time for all 3 blades of the prop to make contact with the runway and bend backward at a 90 degree angle before the body of the airplane touched gently and began to slide. The prop would never recover from this abuse.   The engine didn't fare much better. The sudden stop twisted the crankshaft and destined the rest of the engine's mechanicals to a cheap used parts bin.

Physically, the doctor was fine.   It was his confidence that had crashed along with the airplane. His ego, like the prop and engine, would never completely recover. He made a deal with the insurance company the next week, getting 70% of his purchase price back in return for signing over the remains of the Bonanza. He never piloted another airplane.

Alpha flight 50 was on an 8 mile final for runway 31Center, had the airport in sight, and had been cleared for the visual approach when Approach Control gave them the bad news, along with holding instructions at the outer marker, finishing up with "indefinite delay."

"First fly the airplane," recently certified Check Captain Josh Logan mumbled to himself, caught off guard by the new instructions and startling Dan Stern, the First Officer sitting next to him who was on his initial 737 trip. It was the beginning of his IOE (initial operating experience). He had received 20 hours of simulator instruction but this was his first time in the airplane.

Dan had done well in ground school, studying hard, and had excelled in the simulator training program but he had never flown anything bigger than a King Air, and the 737 was a much larger bird. He was confident he could make the transition but didn't welcome a surprise on his first flight. One thing he knew for certain; surprises in aviation were not a good thing.

"Just thinking out loud," Captain Logan eased his First Officer's concerns, then explained what he was thinking. "Holding speed will be 180 knots, right turn when we cross the marker which is 5.2 miles on the ILS/DME (instrument landing system with distance measuring equipment). Dan looked at his paper copy of the approach plate that he had clipped to his control wheel and agreed.

Josh glanced at the fuel gauges to confirm what he already knew. Fuel, or the lack of it, was going to be a problem. They were down to 4,500 pounds of fuel on board. 45 minutes before their 737 would go silent, would turn into a glider. "Shit," he swore a quiet curse, causing Dan to look at him again with alarm. "We can only stay here 10 minutes max, then we'll have to find someplace we can get fuel." The weather had been good enough that morning that no alternate airport had been required and none had been named on the dispatch release. Good weather reduces the FAA fuel reserve requirement to trip fuel burn plus 45 minutes, the amount Josh had agreed to depart Clear River with.

Less fuel, lower aircraft weight, lower fuel burn, lower cost. That mantra had been delivered by the VP of flight operations, Andrew Rossi, at the recent Check Airman meeting. Owen Swift, the Chief Pilot, pointed out what he saw as the fallacy in that claim; one diversion to an alternate airport for whatever reason would consume more than the fuel saved by mandating minimum fuel for a year, but the VP was the boss in these decisions.

Still, there was some good news. From their present position there were several airfields within a 100 mile radius that were suitable for a 737. Suitable meant a runway at least a mile long and weather above the landing minimums. The weather shouldn't be a problem yet, since the area had partly cloudy skies and good visibility. Josh knew, having watched the weather channel before he had left home this morning, that the cold front that might give them some trouble later in the day was, at the moment, still west of Minneapolis.

There were other things to consider. Once his flight is airborne an airline Captain has the authority to land at any airport for any of a number of reasons including, a disruptive or ill passenger, a mechanical problem that threatens the safety of flight, weather unsuitable for landing at the destination or lack of sufficient fuel to reach that destination. In this case landing would not be the issue, departing would. You cannot depart without a new dispatch release but that only requires a phone and a fax machine. Buying two thousand gallons of jet A at an airport where no credit arrangements exist can get complicated. Josh needed the dispatcher to pick an airport and make the arrangements for him to get fuel once they landed. He knew his credit card wouldn't cover the expense.

"We are at the marker, 5.2 miles," Dan reminded him, and Josh rolled them into the right turn, thankful that the autopilot was working and his first officer a quick study. He wondered if he should let Dan monitor the aircraft while he tried to figure out what to do next.

"When Approach stops for a breath see if you can get us 10 mile legs," Josh requested. There were 6 inbound aircraft behind them and the Approach Controller had his hands full getting them all turned around and moved to different altitudes. "6 miles Alpha 50 is the best I can do right now," was his response to Dan's request and without waiting for a reply said, "Southwest 210 give me your best right turn to 080 and best climb rate to 5,000 feet."

"Why don't you fly the airplane while I try and come up with a plan," Josh made up his mind. "There's not much wind so a heading of 130 should work, turn at 11 miles, 3,000 pounds of fuel flow a side for starters, little less straight and level, little more in the turns."

Since the autopilot was on and holding heading and altitude there wasn't much for Dan to do other than announce, "I've got the airplane."

Josh took a deep breath then let it out slowly. "You monitor Approach Control, I'm going off number one and see if I can raise the company on number three."

Josh switched the number three radio to Alpha's Ops frequency on the ground at Midway. They responded immediately to his call. "Hey flight 50, Chicago Ops, understand on the ground, we're waiting for you at gate 6." The operations office was in a cubbyhole behind the gate and didn't have a window.

"Negative on the ground, we're holding at the outer marker, indefinite delay, airport closed."

"Airport closed? We are unaware of any airport closure."

"Now you know. Need you to call dispatch, have them pick an alternate where we can get fuel and make the arrangements. We only have 4,500 pounds onboard so need a decision pretty quickly."

Josh glanced at his instruments; 2,000 feet, 180 knots, and 9 miles from the airport. He decided to give Dan a chance and 40 seconds later Dan announced: "11 miles, starting the right turn," and using the control yoke rolled smoothly into a 30 degree bank, then bumped the throttles up a few hundred pounds. "Glad I've got good help today," Josh complemented, though he would still keep one eye on his first officer.

Just as Dan was rolling out of the turn the cockpit door popped open and Tracy stepped in, closing the door behind her. Petite and trim with a natural sparkle, she made the uniform of dark blue slacks, white oxford blouse and blue blazer look like a made for tv advertisement for Alpha Airlines. Tracy glanced out the window, looked at her watch, and demanded "what the hell are you guys doing, practicing turns? You don't get us on the ground pretty quick we won't have time to get some ham and egg bagels, and you know how cranky I get when I'm hungry." Then she laughed.

When Josh told her about the airport's closure she looked quickly at the fuel gauges. "4,000 pounds? Shit, where are we going?"

"I don't know yet," Josh admitted, "I'm waiting to hear from dispatch."

"Great," she laughed again, "only 9:30 in the morning and already turning into an Alpha day." She opened the cockpit door. "You better make an announcement. These people have already figured out that you're flying them in circles and they would like to know why." She stepped out, closing the door behind her.

Josh did as he was told, explaining the situation to the passengers and promising more information when it was available. Chicago Ops called just as he was hanging up the PA mike. "Dispatch says to add amendment number one to your release, Milwaukee is the alternate, 70 miles, time en route 14 minutes, fuel burn 1,500 pounds, initials A A, Archie says he's already called the fueler, they'll be ready when you get there. Let us know if you're leaving." Josh had to smile. Archie the dispatcher was on top of things as usual.

Dan was looking at him. "Milwaukee," Josh said, knowing that Dan couldn't hear the other end of the conversation on the number three radio. "Has Approach given out any more information?"

"They're looking for a flatbed truck or trailer to put the Bonanza on," Dan said, there's no time estimate yet."

They both looked at the fuel gauges; 3,800 pounds, time to go. Josh called approach; "Approach, Alpha 50 needs to divert to Milwaukee, Mike, Kilo, Echo."

The runways at Midway were cleared and the airport open to traffic 30 minutes later but Alpha flight 50 was already on the ground in Milwaukee.

It had been a very busy 30 minutes for the flight crew. Neither pilot had ever been to Milwaukee, though Josh had studied the alternate list for Midway and knew Milwaukee's general location to be north and a little west of Chicago on the shore of lake Michigan. Midway approach turned flight 50 over to departure control who issued a heading of 080, out over the lake, and a climb to 10,000 feet. Josh took exception with both instructions.

"Tell them we are in a fuel critical situation," he instructed Dan.

"Alpha flight 50 are you declaring an emergency?" approach asked.

Josh thought about that. No pilot likes to declare an emergency, although it can be a very useful tool. He could declare and land at O'Hare, only 15 miles away. By declaring, the Captain frees himself of all rules and regulations. He could demand and expect the shortest route to Milwaukee, or any other airport, at whatever altitude he deemed most efficient. Once safely on the ground the only requirement was the completion of a one-page form, explaining why you declared, and what rules you broke. The form was then sent to the FAA, and that's what worried Josh. What he had seconds to decide, the FAA could take months to dissect. Josh had tangled with the FAA years before, and lost. He wasn't eager to take that risk a second time.

Dan was looking at him, the mike in his hand. An 80 degree heading would be 75 degrees from the direct heading to Milwaukee, and having to climb would increase the fuel flow from 6,000 pounds per hour to 12,000, if only for a few minutes. The controller helped him with the decision.

"Alpha 50, I need you at 10,000 to get you over the outbound O'hare traffic. As soon as you are level I can clear you direct to Milwaukee."

"Tell him we're out of 2 for 10," Josh said, watching the fuel flow increase as he pushed the throttles forward. 3,600 pounds remained in the tanks.

With so much to think about Josh completely forgot his promise to advise Chicago Ops they were diverting to Milwaukee. It didn't occur to him until Dan asked what the frequency was for Alpha Ops in Milwaukee.

"I can't find Milwaukee on the alternate airport list." Dan said. They had already descended to five 5,000 feet, and were only 20 miles from the airport, but the line of sight VHF radio had only Lake Michigan to cross and no hills to scale. Dan was able to relay the message to Chicago Ops that they were about to land in Milwaukee.

It was 9:55. The Ops agent had guessed that flight 50 was on its way to Milwaukee but he didn't want to publicize that information until it had been confirmed. Nora Fields was the gate agent working the flight. In response to her pleas, all he could suggest was patience.

"Easy for you to say," she thought, facing the 70 or so people waiting in the gate area. "You're sitting by yourself in your private office." She turned her back on the audience to make these calls, but still felt the animosity. On the manual sign board above her head she had placed a delayed notice next to flight 50's arrival time. What else did they want?

She repeated the announcement made earlier; the airport was closed to all traffic due to an accident. When she had more information she would pass it along. Just as she was finishing this statement, through the large plate glass window, a few members of the crowd spotted a Southwest 737, just about to land.

"Airport closed my ass," thought Dawn Fox, the stage name she had taken when she started dancing nude at the age of nineteen, then kept after gravity had taken its toll and men would no longer pay to see her naked. Now the only screaming she heard at work was for another cocktail. She was leaning against the back wall of the gate area sipping her second bloody mary of the morning. Her anger increased with each perceived lie, each passing minute. She hadn't gotten off shift till three am, and was going on four hours of sleep instead of her usual ten.

Dawn was waiting for Scott, her supposed boyfriend, who had been in Clear River for a week looking for a supposed job, when she knew perfectly well he was boinking his god damn ex wife. She needed a cigarette real bad, but they wouldn't even let you smoke in the airport bar. She would have to go outside the terminal, then go through security all over again. The last time through they had made her empty her purse, then rummaged through it for ten minutes, finding nothing, and not even apologizing. Dawn was certain that as soon as she left the gate area the airplane would show up and Scott would be pissed because she was not there to greet him, give him a big kiss.

Just then a cell phone started ringing. Half a dozen people grabbed their own before Dawn realized it was hers making the noise. She walked away from the crowd to take the call. "Hello," she tried, and heard some response that she couldn't make out. It was a terrible connection. She tried again; "Hello?" It was Scott's voice.

"Where are you?" Dawn asked, suddenly suspicious. It would not be unlike Scott to have changed his plans and neglected to inform her.

She could barely make out his reply. "You're where?" not believing she'd heard him correctly. "Milwaukee?, the one in Wisconsin? What the hell are you doing there?" Knowing for certain that Scott was up to his old tricks, wondering why she even bothered trying, but that was another story.

"I'm on the airplane with the other passengers you idiot. The pilot said Chicago was closed and we were running out of gas so we had to land and get more." Scott doing a little wondering of his own, the sex wasn't even that great.

"You calling me an idiot?" yelling into her phone now, "I didn't almost run out of gas. It sounds like the pilot's the idiot and you can tell him I said so."

"I'll be sure and pass that along," Scott already thinking up a new plan, "as soon as he asks my opinion. The idiot pilot also said that we'd be here for a half hour, then it would take another half hour to get back to Chicago, so it's at least an hour before we get there." Scott paused, knowing he could get an easier ride home with one more phone call, he decided to try the good guy routine. "Hey, why don't you go on home instead of waiting. I can grab a cab or get Eddie to pick me up."

Dawn didn't buy it but she didn't let on, thinking she could call her friend Rose and wake her up. They could have a few bloodies and some brunch then she'd catch a nap before she had to go back to work. It would be a lot more fun then listening to Scott's bull. "Good idea," she told him, "I'm beat anyway," washing her hands of the whole thing on the spot. "Good luck getting home." Dawn stabbed the end button on her phone and marched up to the ticket counter.

"Hey," she shouted at a startled Nora, who would remember her when questioned by the FBI, "you're damn airplane's in Milwaukee, which you probably already knew but didn't want to admit. I just got a call from my boy... my friend that's on it. They damn near ran out of gas.". She spun on her heel and marched off, digging in her purse for a cigarette.

"Milwaukee wasn't on the alternate airport list," Josh had explained to Dan, because "we've been trying to update the list but there never seems to be enough time. When we get on the ground I'll use my cell phone to call Dispatch."

"Are you in Milwaukee, Captain Logan?" was the first thing Archie asked when he answered the phone. Archie had been a dispatcher for 20 years at a major airline before deregulation killed it. He had been with Alpha since its inception and worried about his young captains.

They had landed then taxied to the terminal at the direction of the airport ground controller, who seemed to know where they should park. The gate was used by a number of airlines for the same reason that Alpha needed it that morning: failure to get into Chicago for whatever reason and needing someplace nearby to get some fuel.

"You do a walk-around," Josh instructed Dan after finishing his conversation with Archie, "but don't find anything wrong," kidding him, "I don't know if we have a contract mechanic here who is qualified on the 737. I'll go inside and try to locate a fax machine so we can get a new dispatch release."

Josh and Archie had discussed the fuel load on the phone. Both were embarrassed by the diversion though minimum fuel was the order of the day, as expressed in a note to the flight department from their VP. Fuel loads and amount burned was tracked by the computer and totals were kept for each Captain. Nobody wanted to be at the top of the list for highest fuel cost per mile.

Archie reminded Captain Logan that it would cost 25 cents more per gallon to buy fuel in Milwaukee than Chicago. Josh said he didn't care, one unscheduled stop a day was enough. For that matter, one every five years was plenty. Josh remembered Owen telling his Captain upgrade class to "carry enough fuel to make yourself comfortable, anybody wants to argue, tell them to call me."

The argument had started with the new CEO who had stated within the first week of his arrival that Alpha's fuel costs were too high. VP of flight operations Andrew Rossi liked his title, so he didn't argue with his superiors, he left that task to his Chief Pilot, who didn't seem to care who he argued with. By taking more fuel Josh wouldn't get Owen into any more trouble than he got into by himself.

The dispatch computer had calculated a fuel burn of 2,000 pounds for the flight back to Chicago. Josh reminded Archie that they would have to get around O'Hare again, which would likely require climbing to a higher altitude than the 3,000 feet the computer had based its calculation on. Archie recommended 8,000 pounds, but Josh said he wanted 12,000 and Archie readily agreed. Both were jointly responsible for the flight's safety. Normally the flight dispatcher recommended a fuel load, but the Captain had final say.

Archie was happy. Without the restriction placed on him by the VP he would have recommended 12,000 pounds to begin with. It was a lot more difficult to predict a fuel burn on a short flight, especially in as busy an area as Chicago. It would cost Alpha an extra $150, but both men knew Owen would argue their case. "We have young captains and old airplanes," one of the Chief Pilot's standard lines, "and extra fuel is the cheapest insurance we can buy."

The fueler had pointed Josh toward a door at the ramp level of the terminal that led to an office where he thought there might be a fax machine. Once inside Josh wandered around until he found a receptionist who presented him with a stack of paperwork. Archie had already sent the dispatch release and weather. A window in the office looked out on the ramp and Josh could see the fueler already hooked up and pumping. "Great," he thought, hopefully, "maybe we can get out of here in 30 minutes." He had barely finished that thought when Dan walked into the office. "Hydraulic leak," was all he said.

6

The 737 has three hydraulic systems: A, B, and standby. There are 5 hydraulic pumps; 1 powered by each engine for system A, 2 electric pumps to power system B, and 1 electric pump for the standby system. The 3 electric pumps, 3 reservoirs plus associated piping are located in the right wheel well area, and that is where Dan led Josh.

Pinkish fluid was dripping off the bottom of the wheel well door. "I told you not to find anything wrong," Josh chided his First Officer. Dan just shrugged.

"You're the boss," Dan replied, "if you think it's ok to go then we'll go," Even with no experience in the 737 he knew they wouldn't be going anywhere until this problem was fixed.

Josh borrowed a rag from the fueler and wiped down the area that was dripping. It started to drip again almost immediately. "A lot of our airplanes have some hydraulic fluid in the wheel well, but this is certainly more than normal," he said. Using Dan's flashlight he peered into the wheel well then found and released the latch that let the door drop open. The whole area was wet with the same fluid. "We're going to need a mechanic," Josh said, agreeing with his First Officer's assessment.

Alpha's dispatch "office" was grouped with 5 other airline functions in an old brick building on the outskirts of the airport in Clear River. Dispatch, maintenance control, system control, crew scheduling, and a customer representative were put in the same room because a problem in any one area would affect them all. This way there were no busy signals or voice mails. If you needed someone's attention all you had to do was yell. The group thought of themselves as the heart and brains of the airline. Some of the employees saw it a little differently and referred to the group collectively as the asshole. They claimed that most of the daily shit that occurred originated there.

This particular morning was not going well. Aircraft 407 had not made it out of Dallas yet. It had been scheduled to depart at 6:00am and connect with the 8:00am flight to Chicago, but maintenance issues had kept it grounded. The 25 connecting passengers had been shifted to the noon Chicago, but that was Captain Logan's aircraft, which was now in Milwaukee. Everyone in the room knew what a diversion to an off-line station could mean: no telling when that airplane would be heading back to Clear River.

Then Archie got Josh's call and transferred it to Harvey in maintenance control. The other four people in the room tried to listen in. Two aircraft down out of nine total would require some creativity, and would still piss off a lot of passengers.

Working in the Alpha Operations Room in Clear River could create a certain negativity in a personality. Normally carefree individuals could turn into skeptical disbelievers requiring, at shift's end, copious amounts of alcohol and bitching to regain their happy frame of mind. They lost a lot of battles but there was the rare occasion when they won.

Harvey's call to the commuter airline's maintenance office in Milwaukee was answered by a retired TWA mechanic who was working for the commuter part time to keep from being home all day and driving his wife crazy. He had never worked on a 737 but had spent thirty years working on its big Boeing brother the 727, and the hydraulic systems were similar.

The mechanic called back an hour later. He had sprayed down the wheel well with a cleaner, then wiped it with some rags. Turning on the electric B pumps yielded no leaks, but when the interconnect was opened, pressurizing the A system, he found the leak in a cracked fitting on a return line. The commuter had a flight leaving Clear River for Milwaukee in about thirty minutes. If Alpha had the part he needed they could give it to the Captain.

"Just tell him to toss it out the window when he gets here. I'll have your aircraft out of here thirty minutes after I get that part."

While Harvey checked with Alpha's parts department to confirm they had the part, John, the system controller, called the commuter's ramp to advise them of the plan. The new fitting was on its way to Milwaukee twenty-five minutes later.

The commuter's Milwaukee station manager agreed to help Captain Logan get his passengers off the airplane. Tracy had told them that the herd was getting restless and she would soon need a cattle prod to keep them in their seats. In all fairness they had been encapsulated for over three hours and wanted freedom, food, and nicotine, not necessarily in that order. Letting them off would be easy. Getting them back on would require some help from the locals.

Josh and the station manager sought out the security supervisor, who agreed to help. It would require marshaling his troops, who were on break, to screen the passengers before they could re-board. When this had been arranged, Josh stopped at the coffee shop and purchased five ham, egg, and cheese bagels for his crew.

In Clear River the system controller, after conferring with the passenger service rep, decided to send captain Logan and crew to Minneapolis, once they made it to Chicago, instead of back to Clear River. This would cover a flight that the broken aircraft in Dallas was supposed to have operated. Once in Minneapolis they would fly a round trip to Clear River. This decision was based mostly on cost. It was much cheaper for Alpha to transport misplaced passengers on Southwest to Chicago than on Northwest to Minneapolis. As an added bonus getting Captain Logan's crew to Minneapolis by 6:30

would keep them legal for their trip the next morning, a trip that crew scheduling said they would have been unable to cover otherwise. "This is the plan of the moment," Archie reminded Josh, "keep your cell phone on." Two hours later they deposited their fifty passengers in Chicago, five hours late. Thirty minutes to refuel and reload and they were on their way to Minneapolis.

Dawn Fox had indeed awakened her friend Rose and they were parked in a back booth at Tilly's, an upscale strip club on Grand Avenue where both had once performed, knew the bartender, and could get their bloodies at half price. Rose had been telling Dawn about her one misadventure with Alpha; Chicago to Clear River, three hours late and then they had lost her carry-on bag, which they had made her check in the first place. The bag was never found. As compensation Alpha gave Rose a hundred and fifty bucks. She had one outfit in her bag that cost more than that. "Scott should have asked me," she maintained, "I'm never getting on one of their airplanes again." Rose wanted revenge, but how did you get revenge against a corporation?

"You have to cost them money," Dawn replied, "time and money, that's what they cost us." The team ordered another round to help solve the problem.

Alpha's reservation center was in a rundown business park in a suburb of Clear River. There were two large rooms housing twenty-five computer stations that had been purchased, at auction, from an out of business insurance company. The equipment was a perfect match for Alpha's fleet of aircraft; something was always broken. Ginny Adams had been working with this dilapidated bunch of junk for six months when she took the call.

"There's a bomb on one of your airplanes."

All the reservation agents had received training for this situation when they started work. Ginny hadn't given it much thought since. She did, however, remember to hit the record button. It was a woman's voice. She sounded drunk, and when Ginny asked her to repeat herself the woman got angry.

"Listen up," she shouted into the phone, "I'm not going to repeat this. There is a bomb on one of your airplanes. The goddamn airplane that was so late to Chicago this morning. You cost us money and time, so it's your turn to pay now, teach you a goddamn lesson." The line went dead. Ginny stood and yelled for her supervisor.

Ginny's supervisor had been in the airline res business a long time. She knew exactly what to do. She questioned Ginny quickly; male or female, drunk or sober, calm, excited, angry, making a mental note of Ginny's first impressions, popped the audio cassette out of the computer console, ran to her office, and called dispatch.

Archie took the call. He stood up at his desk while still listening, put his hand over the mouthpiece, and said in a clear, calm voice. "We have a bomb threat against one of our aircraft." The room went dead silent. Archie continued listening to the supervisor while he motioned for John to get the operations manual open to the section that covered bomb threats. The only way he could hear the tape was if the supervisor played it on her portable recorder while holding the phone to the speaker. As weak as the transmission was, he agreed that the caller was female and drunk. "We have to contact Captain Logan," he said, "and John, find Andrew Rossi."

The VP of operations had accompanied the new CEO to a Chamber of Commerce luncheon meeting being held downtown. The whole bomb business would be over before he could get back to the airport. Andrew Rossi could hear the tension building in Archie's voice. "Captain Swift is interviewing and should be in his office," he said, "get him to come to Operations, and have him call me when he gets there."

Eight minutes later Owen was standing by Archie's desk. The room was filling up. The System Controller had put out an executive page for managers and VPs. Three were in the room already as very interested bystanders along with the Director of Safety, a newly created position mandated by the FAA, and occupied at Alpha by a very pleasant young man who had never held a similar position or flown an airplane.

Archie, not interested in center stage, kept his voice low as he offered his opinion that it was aircraft 401, Captain Logan, who had departed Chicago fifteen minutes ago en route to Minneapolis. They had already called AIRINC to get them to cell call the aircraft and backed that up with a call to Chicago center, asking them to advise Captain Logan about the threat and get him to call dispatch.

Owen called the reservations supervisor and listened to the tape, then asked her to play it again. When it had run the second time Owen asked her opinion, knowing she had been around the business as long as he had.

"Sounds like a crank to me," she said, without hesitation, "but it's your call."

Archie had answered his other phone and now he held it out to Owen. "It's Captain Logan on AIRINC," an air-to-ground communication system from the aircraft's number three radio to a relay station, then by normal phone lines to the dispatch office. It sounded like two tin cans and a string.

"Josh, it's Owen, how do you read?"

"About three by three," on a scale of one-to-five: Five being clearly understandable. Owen would have to chose his words carefully to make sure he was understood.

"Do you know what's happening?" Owen asked.

"Chicago Center just told us there is a bomb threat against our airplane."

"What's your position?"

"We just went by Milwaukee, we're descending to 10,000 feet and de-pressurizing the cabin so if the bomb does go off the explosion will cause less damage. I declared an emergency and am going to turn around and land there."

Archie was listening on the other phone. He pointed to the page in the manual that listed bomb threat facilities. Milwaukee wasn't listed, Minneapolis was.

"Josh, Milwaukee does not, I repeat does not, have an airport bomb team. They'll have to get an off-airport emergency team. You will probably be on the ground before they get there and may have to evacuate the aircraft using slides. Minneapolis has a bomb squad on the airport, and they will have time to prepare. They will be ready when you arrive."

"You telling me we should continue to Minneapolis?"

"Josh, this is your decision to make, I have listened to a tape of the call to reservations. I think it's a crank call, and so does the supervisor, but we can't guarantee that." Owen trying to give him all the information available, wishing he was on the jump seat, coach him through it step by step.

"All right," Josh decided, "we'll continue to Minneapolis, I hope you're right about the crank call."

"Remember, you have declared an emergency so you can break the rules, do 340 knots to 10 miles from the airport if you want, and you might consider landing on runway 27, straight in, it would save some time. Call us when you get on the ground," ending the transmission on a positive note. "Alpha Operations out," and he hung up the phone.

Owen stood. Everyone in the room was looking at him. "They're going to Minneapolis," he said, "John, I need you to call Minneapolis center and the airport. Make sure they know he's coming." John picked up his phone and started punching in numbers.

Owen looked at his watch. "They should be on the ground in twenty minutes," he said, then he called Andrew Rossi on his cell and explained the situation. "Are you sure it was a crank call," was the first question Andrew asked, knowing there was no reasonable answer, but making sure he would not be in the middle of a legal fight should there be one. It was his way of doing business; always ready to accept the credit, just not the blame.

Owen was tired of it, but unwilling to fight, at least not at this moment. "I'll let you know when we have more information," he said and ended the call.

"I'm going outside to grab a smoke," Owen patted Archie on the shoulder. "You know where to find me."

The VPs of marketing, finance, and legal followed him out of the room. When they were out of earshot of the others they stopped him in the hall. "What's going to happen if it gets in the newspapers that we flew past a perfectly good airport with a bomb on the airplane?" the VP legal wanted to know. "We could get our asses sued off."

"I wouldn't have suggested they continue if I thought the bomb threat was real," Owen explained patiently. "If they had landed in Milwaukee and had to blow the chutes, maybe broken a leg or two when the passengers jumped, it would have been news. They land safely in Minneapolis it's a non-story. The big airlines face this sort of thing all the time."

"And if you're wrong, and it wasn't a crank call?" the VP marketing wanted to know."

"Then the aircraft will blow up and we'll all be out of work," Owen called over his shoulder as he stepped through the outside door, cigarette in hand, momentarily out of patience and in need of some nicotine and an escape from all the explanations. Owen knew that if you combined the three VP's ages you wouldn't reach a hundred years, and not one of them had ever worked for an airline other than Alpha. It wasn't their fault they didn't know what to expect. It was as much a virgin experience for these three as it was for Captain Logan and his crew.

Owen felt reasonably certain that there was no bomb on the aircraft. The caller had not identified herself or a group she belonged to, hadn't identified any passenger on the aircraft, or the airplane's number or flight number. She was angry with Alpha, that was obvious, but Owen would wager she had no idea how serious a crime she had just committed. The FBI would certainly have a long list of suspects, but there was a good chance they would catch her. Still, he thought, I'll feel a lot better when the aircraft's on the ground and everyone's safe.

Twenty minutes later Archie answered the phone and almost immediately broke into a big smile. "Very good job," he said, handing the phone to Owen, then announcing to the room; Captain Logan and crew are safely on the ground in Minneapolis," creating a spontaneous cheer.

"Take a bow," Owen said to Josh when the noise subsided, "that's your applause in the background. Everything go alright?"

"Pretty much how you said it would go. We did 340 till 10 miles, then the ILS to 27, which was a good thing because all the equipment was parked right at the west end of the runway. They had stairs and busses for the passengers, took them to the HHH terminal. I sent Tracy with them because I didn't see any Alpha personnel. I'm not sure they'll let anybody around the aircraft. I've never seen so many emergency vehicles, fire, police, FBI, bomb squad in their suits, it's pretty impressive..." He paused for a breath and Owen broke in.

"Slow down some, take a couple of deep breaths," he instructed, knowing how much adrenaline twenty minutes of wondering if there is a bomb on your airplane can produce. "We need you to speak to whoever is in charge, find out how long they'll need to sweep the airplane, then let dispatch know. You'll have to stay with the aircraft until it's been cleared, then taxi it to a gate. I'll get crew schedule working on a plan, see if we can release your crew in time for happy hour."

When Owen paused, Josh spoke, his speech already returning to its normal laconic pace. "I'm glad you were there," he said, "your advice was right on. I hate to think what chaos there would have been if I had landed in Milwaukee."

"You're welcome," Owen replied, "there has to be some reason to keep us old guys around."

Barbara Morgan, Alpha's manager of in-flight services (flight attendants), was standing alongside Owen when he took the call confirming they were safely on the ground in Minneapolis. She breathed one word; vodka? Owen only nodded, knowing all in the room were convinced they were sleeping together and, for her sake, did not want to add to their suspicions. Barbara didn't seem to care. Years before, when it had first become an issue, Owen claimed gallantly that it could only enhance his reputation. Barbara had murmured that it wouldn't hurt her's either.

"A man and a woman cannot remain friends if they're having sex," Owen maintained, "at least I've never managed it," trying to treat the matter seriously.

Barbara, or B, as Owen had started calling her when they first met, teased him constantly about it. "I want to have your baby," she'd coo about halfway through her first vodka, grabbing his hand and hanging on when he tried to pull away. B was a foot shorter than Owen and 100 pounds lighter; one vodka was her rational limit, though she wasn't always rational.

They agreed to meet at the Gung Ho, Owen's home away from home. A cozy Chinese restaurant with an impressive array of jade and ivory carvings separating the five seat bar from the dining room. Owen's glass of Absolut on the rocks was waiting on the bar when they walked in, with a lemon twist and a couple of olives. B was not as predictable as Owen, as liable to have a glass of white wine as vodka, but not today. "It's been a vodka kind of day," she told Lee Chin, the youthful owner. They picked up the drinks and walked to their customary booth at the back of the smoking section. Owen acknowledged the hellos from the staff as they walked through the dining area.

B wasted no time. "Where was Andrew when this business of the bomb threat was going on?" she demanded.

"The VP was downtown with the CEO," knowing immediately where this conversation was headed, "attending a Chamber of Commerce luncheon, I believe."

"You've got to be more careful," B chided him, "you're making calls that should be his, taking responsibilities above your pay grade. You're going to end up getting yourself into trouble."

Most times, when she started on this argument, she had a valid point. Not this time. "It was Josh I was worried about, not my position in the corporate hierarchy. By the time Andrew could have gotten back to Operations, Josh would have landed in Milwaukee, blown the chutes and dumped the passengers on the pavement. Could have been ugly, but it turned out that I guessed correctly. The people in Operations know what happened. Josh knows what happened, and that's what I care about, not whether the CEO is going to give me a bonus."

Like a terrier with a rat's tail between its teeth once B got started on a topic she thought needed discussing she was hard to dissuade. Owen knew it was because she cared, but he didn't know how to convince her that none of the corporate stuff mattered to him. If Andrew Rossi fired him as Chief Pilot he would go back to being a line captain. It would mean a pay cut; it would also mean flying fifteen days a month instead of sitting in an office five days a week and being on call twenty-four/seven or going to what seemed an interminable round of pointless meetings.

Owen sat peacefully sipping on his vodka while B rattled on, slowly winding down until she stopped completely and took a big slug of vodka. "You worry me sometimes," she declared.

"You know I hate corporate politics," Owen started in, giving it one more try, "so why do we keep having this conversation? You know I don't belong in that long line of ass kissers."

"Speaking of ass kissing," she teased in her coy little girl voice, "What did you think of Cynthia's?" She watched for his reaction.

"You're slipping," Owen laughed at her, "that information is a week old," not at all surprised that B had heard. It was an intimate little family that they were a part of. There were few secrets at Alpha airlines.

"She's twenty-one years old for god's sake..."

"Twenty-three, but very mature for her..."

"Mature MY ASS," B was laughing at him now, "you expect me to believe that her long legs didn't enter into the equation? The fact that VP Rossi was hot on her tail didn't affect your decision to take advantage of that sweet young thing.?"

"Hey, you hired her, and I'm not really sure who took advantage of whom. If I thought you could keep a secret...?"

"Absolutely," B responded eagerly, crossing her heart, loving the possibility that she would be the first to hear some new gossip.

"I have no idea what happened. I wasn't even aware I had asked and she was waltzing into my apartment. Caught me completely by surprise."

"That's worthless news. Everybody already knows that she went to your apartment. There are at least a dozen flight attendants who live in that complex. Good luck hiding your love life there."

Owen just smiled at her. He already knew the word was out and knew that no one was going to be shocked. Owen needed another vodka, B switched to wine. They had met when Alpha was in its infancy. B was on the initial startup team, the group that came to the office every day for nearly six months to work on the enormous pile of paperwork the FAA requires before it allows an airline to begin operation.

They shared the same jaded view of the world, the same caustic sense of humor and an ability to laugh at themselves as readily as they would laugh at others. B had a boyfriend, a long term relationship with a man who showed up occasionally for weekends and made no promises. The arrangement suited her perfectly, she claimed, and it allowed the friendship between her and Owen to develop without the added complexity of sex.

There had been one near miss three years ago on the anniversary of Alpha's first flight. They had joined some coworkers for a Friday night imbibe and bitch session at an airport bar called "The Final Approach" and Owen had followed her back to her apartment to help with a box of books in the trunk of her car that were too heavy for her to carry.

When he placed the books on the kitchen counter and turned around she was standing right in front of him, weaving slightly to music only she could hear. She placed both hands lightly on his hips, holding him six inches away, so they were both swaying. Owen said nothing, his hands remained at his sides, but he didn't try to pull away. His intoxicated brain was swirling with possibilities. He had not had sex in a while and the proximity of all this female heat was causing his imagination to go into overdrive. He thought of all sorts of banal quips to lessen the tension but wisely remained mute. "Please tell me you are at least tempted," B said in a small resigned voice, then dropped her hands and took a step back.

"Of course I'm tempted, but you know as well as I do that's it a bad idea. It would never work."

"Maybe not, she agreed, "but what a waste." Walking to her apartment door and opening it for him to leave. The incident had not been mentioned since.

Owen's pager, which he had removed from his belt and placed on the table, started buzzing. He kept it on vibrate because he had difficulty hearing the various high pitched chirps and whistles. Now it resembled an electric shaver on the loose, humming toward B, who snatched it before Owen could. "Hmnnn," she was reading the message, "Hmnnn, you have a secret admirer, refusing to turn the pager back to Owen who was holding his hand outstretched, patiently waiting. B tossed it in the air in his direction and he caught it deftly. "Nice hands," she said, smiling now, the vodka working its magic.

Owen read. "You sexy devil, have I got a deal for you, call me." The messaging could only be activated by an Alpha computer, and the listed number was for crew scheduling. "Must be Carol," Owen said. It was obvious that B already knew. He rummaged through his jacket to find his cell phone, then punched in the number.

"Owen," Carol gushed, as soon as she heard his voice. " It's so nice of you to call." Wasting no time she began her spiel. "The crew that was stuck in Dallas this morning is going to be illegal for their Denver turn tomorrow. They can do the other three legs, but not Denver. The only available first officer available is Larry Jensen. He's still on IOE and there are no other check airman that are legal to take the trip," she paused, waiting for a reaction.

"I've got interviews all day..." Owen began, but she interrupted. "I know sweetheart, but the flight doesn't leave till 1730."

Owen generally loved to get out of the office, especially to go flying, but he would have to be in his office at 8:00am. If he took this flight he wouldn't get to return to Clear River until 9:00pm, if they were on time, and he wouldn't get home until 10:00, then back in the office at 8:00am the next morning. Another in a series of long days.

"Please, please, pleeese" Carol begged. Owen caved.

"Okay, okay, okaay, who did you say the first officer was?

"Larry Jensen, a really nice guy, you hired him."

Owen could not bring to mind a mental picture. He had hired all of the first officers and half the captains on the seniority list. Remembering names was not his forte.

"Isn't there supposed to be a snowstorm in Denver tomorrow?" B asked when he told her.

7

1-9-98

Owen was exhausted. He had startled awake from an uneasy sleep at 3:00am, his brain still awash with vodka, a light sheen of sweat covering his body, the sheets and comforter twisted into knots. It was the dream again, or some variation of it, different than before, but just as terrifying. He had rolled out of bed and staggered to the refrigerator, downing the first half of a diet coke from the can before pouring the rest into a large glass filled with ice, then opening a second can and adding it to the first. He stood in front of the sliding glass door of his apartment staring out at the low hanging cloud, the swirling mists filled with rain, the door rattling on its tracks in the gusting wind.

The LA and San Francisco flights were due in three hours. Both crews had departed the previous evening. Flying west into the winter jet stream, the flight time would have approached four hours. The three hours ground time, used to coordinate their arrival back in Clear River with the 8:00am departure bank, would be spent with the crew scattered throughout the cabin, trying to catch a nap before applying a splash of cold water and a shot of caffeine to jump start the brain for the return trip. Owen had flown both trips before. It would be a fun approach in this weather after a sleepless night. At least it wasn't snowing. That wouldn't start for a couple of days, if the weatherman was correct in his predictions.

Owen searched the coffee table for his cigarettes, shook one out of a nearly empty pack and lit it before taking another swallow of Coke. He went back to the bedroom for the comforter and, wrapping it around his shoulders, lay down on the worn sofa in the dark, staring through the slider and trying to remember the details of this latest nightmare.

He remembered being on what looked like a subway car, the plastic seats arranged along the walls in some places, facing forward in others. There were advertising posters lining the walls, glistening in the bright fluorescent light, a stainless grab rail and handles suspended from the ceiling. The car was filled with Alpha airline employees. They stood in angry little groups, some shouting, some pointing an accusing finger. He tried to look out the windows but there was nothing to see. It was pitch black.

When he looked forward he could see a cockpit, a 737 cockpit with two pilots seated there, but he didn't recognize them. There was no divider between the cockpit and the rest of the car so Owen could make out the red warning lights, a bunch of them, but couldn't tell what was wrong. He tried to tell the people around him that he had to get forward, had to help the crew, but they kept stopping him, wanting him to listen to their complaints.

These are small issues, he tried to explain, we have to fix the big problems first, but they wouldn't let him by. The more he struggled the less progress he made. Suddenly someone pointed out the window and let out a scream. When Owen looked out he could see trees, streets, city lights. They were going very fast, just above the tree tops now, and losing altitude. He yelled at the pilots, trying to get their attention, but they ignored him. He could see that the throttles were all the way back, in idle, and above the din of voices could hear the stall warning's thumping, could feel its vibration throughout the frame of the car.

"Push the throttles up, push the throttles up, pull the wheel back or you're going to kill us all," he tried to yell but no sound came. He recognized the pilots then; the new CEO Spencer Elliot and TL Bentworth, the airline's billionaire owner. You don't know anything about flying, Owen shouted, watching helplessly as they sat with their hands in their laps, apparently deaf to his concerns.

Five hours later Owen stood in the cubby hole that was the chief pilot's office gazing out the window at the seemingly endless shades of grey on this January morning in Missouri. The office was on the top floor of the passenger terminal and the window offered a wide view of the gate area and the runways in the distance. Nosed in below was an Alpha 737 being readied for departure. He checked his watch and shook his head. Less than half full, fifty passengers, no mechanicals, and already fifteen minutes late for departure. When are we going to get this right, he wondered.

He continued to watch as the ground crewman standing alongside the tug waved his arms wildly trying to get the Captain's attention, tapped both ear pieces while shaking his head no, and removed his headset. The jetway gave a rearward lunge, like a startled animal, and began to creep backward, the large steering wheels turning first one way then another, the operator confused about just what was supposed to happen. The ground crewman, now with the headset laying on the hood of the tug, raised both hands in the air with fists clenched, then unclenched them simultaneously, the brakes off request mimicked immediately by the Captain. The tug belched a copious puff of coal black smoke, gave one jerk, and began to inch forward, straining against the fifty-ton aircraft it was trying to push, its exhaust smoke boiling up in the cold prairie wind.

Owen continued watching as the aircraft was turned and stopped, the ground signalmen clenching both fists, indicating to the Captain he wanted the brakes set. Left hand raised with two fingers showing, right hand, index finger extended and swirling, cleared to start number two then number one. A wispy stream of gray smoke trailed from the left engine as it was started, but dissipated as the airplane began to taxi. This too had been a feature of aircraft number 401 for the last several months, along with the ground inter-phone problem. The engine was old and tired, Owen knew, but still willing. The inter-phone had a type of amplifier that the mechanics had never seen before. They had been unable, so far, to locate a replacement, so it got jury rigged and worked for a while before returning to its recalcitrant ways. Aircraft 401, Alpha Airline's flight 50, the daily 8:00am departure for Chicago's Midway airport, turned the corner onto runway 35 Left and trundled north, gaining speed at a leisurely pace, the nose rising gracefully, the gear just beginning to retract as the aircraft disappeared into the overcast.

When Owen opened his office door Miranda looked up from her computer and smiled. "Good morning sir," she said, all business in front of the applicants. " Miranda," Owen smiled back at her, not as concerned with appearances. She stood and handed him the applicants files.

"Everyone's already finished their test," she said. "They are ready when you are."

The four pilot applicants had risen when the door was opened, and they looked expectantly at him now. Owen held the door open and waved them in. There were four chairs crammed into the space in front of his desk and Owen gestured for them to sit. "Please get comfortable," Owen said with a smile, and looked at each one in turn. The woman was much more attractive in person than the photo she had submitted as part of the application process. Walking past him as he held the door open he caught just a hint of what? not perfume, soap maybe? or shampoo. Owen was careful not to let her have any more of his smile than the others.

Owen really enjoyed this part of his job, which was a good thing since he was forced to interview pilot applicants frequently to replace the pilots who moved on to other carriers. The majors were hiring, and practically every pilot who worked for Alpha had an application in with all of them. The result was a resignation rate that averaged

35% yearly. Alpha needed 10 pilots per airplane, 5 Captains and 5 First Officers. 9 aircraft, 90 pilots, 3 resignations per month. It had recently been decided that Alpha was going to grow to 12 aircraft in the next 4 months; 30 more pilots, plus the 12 who would resign, 42 pilots to hire. Owen was going to be very busy.

"Good morning," Owen continued to smile, and they all smiled and nodded in return. The men were nearly identical in dress; dark suit, power tie, shiny black shoes, short hair, they looked like bankers. They'll probably wear the same suit when they interview with United a year from now, Owen thought. The woman also wore a dark suit jacket with a skirt of modest length. The last chair available put her in a position where her legs were visible to Owen when she crossed them, which she did, then tugged her skirt down demurely to cover her knees. Athlete, Owen thought, swimmer maybe or distance runner, long muscled, attractive... then, somewhat reluctantly, he returned to the matter at hand.

"You will be pleased to hear that you have all passed the appearance test." Owen continued, "this is how it's going to work this morning. I'll give a brief overview of Alpha's plans for the future, and how you would fit into them, some other items that may be of interest to you, and then I'll try to answer some of your questions. After that I'll speak with each of you individually. I'll ask some operational type questions. Then we'll discuss your background and some other flying-related topics. The whole thing usually takes thirty to forty-five minutes. We are in the process of setting up a simulator period in Dallas, hopefully in the next week. If you are successful in convincing me this morning that Alpha should hire you, the next step will be to convince me all over again in the simulator. Fifteen to twenty minutes, normal take off, climb to 8,000 feet, level off, maintain 250 knots, two steep turns, return for an ILS approach to 250 feet, and land. If you get selected for the simulator we will send you a sheet that describes what is expected."

One of the men was nodding his head and when Owen looked at him, eyebrows raised and questioning, he spoke: "it's on the Internet," he said, hoping he wasn't creating trouble for himself. "That instruction sheet you're talking about, you can get it off the Internet."

"Really?" Owen was surprised. "Alpha hiring practices are on the Internet?"

"Absolutely," the three men nodded in agreement. The woman looked as though she was about to add something, then changed her mind.

He would have to ask Miranda to check this out, Owen thought, Miranda being much more adept with computers than he was. "Anyway, Owen continued, "since you already know what's coming in the Sim, I'll remind you that we charge $100 dollars for the privilege. If you demonstrate a high enough skill level, you will be offered a job. The next ground school starts February 15, lasts for 3 weeks, then simulator training which runs about 2 weeks, depending on simulator availability. Both of those are in Long Beach, California. While you are there, your hotel will be paid for and you will get $30 dollars per diem, which in California should get you a great breakfast." This last statement got a few chuckles, although Owen wasn't sure how genuine. Laugh until you are hired, then complain. "Once you've passed your check ride it's back here to Clear River for your IOE, initial operating experience, minimum of 15 hours riding with a check airman. Complete that and you report to scheduling where they will make a schedule for the remainder of the month. Then you will bid for the next month. Junior people generally end up on reserve, which has 10 days off and pays 75 hours."

All of them were looking at the info sheets they had been given by Miranda. One raised his hand. "Do you think Alpha is going to survive?"

"Good question," Owen responded, "I'll give you the simple answer. Nobody knows."

"And the complicated answer?" another one asked.

Owen shrugged. "The complicated answer," he glanced at his watch.

"I'll give you the Cliff note version of airline economics. This airline was started 7 years ago with 6 million dollars, which is a minuscule amount with which to start an airline. That meant we were basically broke the day the doors were opened. We started with 4 airplanes, and while the aircraft direct operating cost is about $1,800 dollars an hour, you can just about double that figure to cover corporate expense, salaries, ticketing, advertising, and the like. 4 airplanes flying 8 hours a day…32 fleet hours a day times $3,600 per hour," having given this speech many times Owen didn't hesitate, "$115,200…in a 30 day month, that's nearly 3.5 million dollars."

Owen paused to see what effect his statement was having. All four were watching him with interest, wanting him to continue. In a way it was their careers he was discussing and he understood their concern.

"Here's the hard part," he continued. "For Alpha to get a passenger away from a major competitor we have to lower the ticket price between 20 and 40%. If the major decides to match our price, they get the passenger, no contest. Let's look at Clear River to Chicago. Southwest has 17 flights a day and their average ticket costs $70. United and American have 8 and 9 flight respectively and their tickets run about $90. Alpha's average price over the last year has been $50…fifty dollars."

"The flight averages an 1:20 times $3,600 an hour rounds out to $5,000. At $50 a ticket you need 100 passengers to break even or a 73% load factor, which is about where the rest of the industry is. This morning's flight had 50 passengers, or a loss of $2,500." Owen's audience was silent, digesting the information. He repeated the number. "$2,500 and that's only one flight. There are 45 more to go today. You think you can lose a lot of money fast in Vegas, try betting on an airline."

"Back to the question of survival. Alpha is owned by a billionaire from Clear River. So far every time we have needed more money he's come up with it. Most 'experts' would say you need a minimum of 15 aircraft to break even. We have 9 currently with plans for 3 more in the next four months, so we're getting closer. Will our billionaire run the whole race? He says he will." Owen shrugged, "But here's the important thing for you to consider. If you get hired and complete the training you'll start adding heavy turbine time to your logbooks which will make you that much more attractive to a major. If the airline succeeds, you'll be an airline Captain within 2 years. Not many opportunities out there like that, and it's free. The first 50 pilots hired by Alpha had to pay for their type-rating, that's $15,000. Instead, you will be paid while in training. One last note on this subject. There are a lot of talented people trying to make Alpha a success. It certainly is frustrating at times, and we disagree plenty, but it is a challenge for everyone and it's fun, in a masochistic kind of way. Getting a job with Alpha is like joining a rambunctious, caring and dysfunctional family."

Owen checked his watch again. "We've got to wrap this up," he said, "I'm sure you have more questions, but I've got you 4 to interview this morning and 4 more this afternoon so we need to get going. I'm going outside for a few minutes to grab some nicotine, it doesn't matter to me what order you interview in, decide that among yourselves."

The woman spoke first. "I'd like to go last if that's ok with you guys?" Owen left them to decide. As he walked past Miranda's desk she handed him a manila folder. "A little light reading for the smoke break," she said, in a good mood this morning for no apparent reason.

Once outside, after the first big drag, Owen checked the contents. There were three identical letters of investigation, (LOI), from the FAA district office in Minneapolis, each naming a different crew, but the same aircraft, and issued by the same maintenance inspector. Owen knew all about this case. He had been trying to resolve it for a month. The inspector had contended that all three crews had left the gate with a fuel imbalance of 500 pounds, 7,500 pounds in the left wing tank, 8,000 in the right. The fuel load was supposed to be 15,500 pounds, the standard amount for a fair weather day's flight from Minneapolis to Chicago, so they were ok there.

It was the imbalance the inspector was concerned with, and the fact that in his mind all three crews had ignored the warning from the fueler when he had informed them of the discrepancy.

This was exactly the kind of make-work nonsense some of the FAA inspectors could drag you into. Had the guy called Owen, he could have explained the issue in a matter of minutes. Instead, this was the third letter, with copies going to the local office and headquarters in Washington and each requiring a response from Owen. Like the traffic cop who hadn't gotten his quota for the week, writing tickets for infractions he would ignore if it was his lunchtime, this exercise was to show his boss that the inspector was on the job.

Alpha used a contract fueler in Minneapolis and Owen had attempted to contact them to see if he could talk to the employee who had notified the FAA, but they wouldn't return his calls. He had already sent two pages of information to the inspector, one from Alpha's airplane manual that showed an allowed fuel imbalance of 1,200 pounds for taxi, takeoff, and landing. The other page was a graph that showed an allowed 5% inaccuracy in the gauge. At 7,500 pounds each side the gauges could be off by as much as 375 pounds.

In his first letter Owen had pointed out that another carrier had taken off in a 737 with one wing tank full and one empty. Other than the embarrassment, no harm came to the airplane or crew who simply flew around the pattern and landed without incident. The inspector showed no interest in this incident being a "rules are rules" kind of guy, and pressed ahead anyway.

Now it seemed that the last two pages of "evidence" Owen had sent had done the trick. Enclosed in the envelop were letters to each of the crew members involved informing them that the investigation had been completed and the letters of investigation resolved.

That must have been what Miranda was smiling about. One of the Captains named was her "main squeeze", as she called him, and Owen knew he was in the final stages of the hiring process with United. If United saw an unresolved LOI, his chance of getting the job would be greatly reduced. With the FAA, much like the IRS, you are guilty until proven innocent.

Miranda was still smiling when Owen returned to the office.

"Peter will be happy," Owen said

"He said to thank you. I just talked to him."

"Then call the others, First Officers too, tell them they are free to get on with their careers."

"Already talked to three and left messages for the other two,"

Owen was not surprised. Peter was a good Captain, but it would be harder to replace Miranda than Peter.

He glanced at the three men waiting to be interviewed. "Ok," he said, "first victim, and you can take off your jackets and loosen the ties This office is business casual and for the rest of the morning what you say is more important than how you look."

Owen hated prejudice, or as he would put it: "I dislike hate intensely." He took little pride in this trait since he had been raised to not prejudge someone on the basis of race or religion. Of late, gender and sexual preference had been added to his list. In the same way he would acknowledge the partial truth in the old saying; "clothes make the man," while disliking its meaning, he realized that it was impossible to be completely without prejudice, hard as he might try. Still, he was somewhat dismayed when he discovered he was, in fact, becoming prejudiced against military pilots.

Owen had learned to fly at a small grass strip where the rules, if not disobeyed, were certainly lightly regarded. The military was all rules. "The thing I love most about flying is that it takes place in a fluid, air," Owen would argue with the military pilots at Alpha, "and is difficult if not impossible to define." He understood that his was the minority opinion, but that had never dissuaded him from the pursuit of his convictions.

After years of the theory that the curvature of the upper wing surface caused a low pressure which produced lift, and wondering how an airplane could fly inverted, the theorists at NASA had now decided that it was the wing's angle of attack that produced lift. You could strap a tractor seat onto a couple of sheets of plywood, add a motor with a propeller, and you'd have an airplane. So while aviation is certainly part science, it is also part mystery, and part art. It is hours of approximation with minutes of exactitude required at both ends of a flight. He had found a few who agreed with him, but had never changed the minds of those who didn't. Most military pilots made perfectly competent airline pilots, but they were more in tune with the science than the art.

There was little question that the first applicant to interview that morning was the military man. Owen recognized him when he walked into his office before connecting him to the photographs Miranda had laid on his desk that morning. He sat straighter, his hair was shorter, suit better pressed, shoes shinier, shave closer, handshake firmer, and he addressed Owen as Captain Swift despite instructions to the contrary. He explained that it was habit. His name was Robert Crown and he had been in Marine Aviation for fifteen years. He had accumulated 2,300 hours in the FA-18 and achieved the rank of Major.

Major Crown had scored well on the written test Alpha administered as a precursor to the interview, but lately most of the applicants were managing that. He did not appear at all nervous, in fact gave the distinct impression that he felt the interview was something to get out of the way, so he could get on with the hiring process.

Some of Alpha's young pilots were a little on the arrogant side, especially the younger Captains, and they were a bit of a worry. "There is a fine line between confidence and arrogance," Owen would admonish, "arrogance in an airplane can get you killed."

Owen understood that flying a single seat fighter probably required more arrogance than flying a 737, but one of the criteria he used in the hire/no hire decision was how difficult the applicant would be for him to manage once he became a line pilot. Major Crown almost sealed his fate with his answer to the last of a series of questions he had been asked.

""You're at the gate here in Clear River," Owen began, "you've been in the same airplane all day, already flown to Dallas and back, and Denver and back. Everything's going great; the weather is clear, the next leg is to Minneapolis and then a layover." Major Crown, as he had been during the entire interview, was watching Owen intently, perhaps trying to read his manner, or inflection, seeing if there was a clue to the right answer. "The Captain you're with has been with Alpha since day one, seven years in the 737, and 5,000 hours. Everything he's done up to that point has been by the book."

Owen had a list of questions he had dreamed up when he first started to do the interviews but he no longer needed to refer to it. He was watching Major Crown's reactions to each sentence, watching for the point where he made up his mind, had enough information to make a decision, like a game show contestant trying to name that tune.

"You're brand new, just finished IOE, (initial operating experience) have maybe 30 hours in the airplane."

Owen saw just the trace of a smile on Crown's face. He had the answer. He was not about to allow any Captain, no matter how experienced, to include him in a departure from normal procedures. Not going to happen.

"You start to taxi and the Captain calls for flaps fifteen and the taxi checklist. You put the flap handle to the fifteen degree detent and grab the check list, notice that the flap indicator shows fifteen degrees but the light that indicates the leading edge devices are all extended is not green, as it should be."

Major Crown was ready to answer, started to speak, but Owen shook his head no, and Crown stopped.

"You look at the overhead panel, there is a pictogram description of the leading edge devices with amber and green lights showing the position of each. All are green except the number six slat, which is amber. What would you do?"

Crown leaped into the breach. "I'd tell the Captain we'd have to go back to the gate." Not the slightest hesitation, never having flown a 737 he was still convinced of the rightness of his answer.

Owen pressed on. He wanted to be sure. "The Captain looks up at the slat annunciator, then at the aircraft number, and says. "it's aircraft 401, this airplane's been doing the same thing for three years. Look out your right side window, you can see the slats, see if number six isn't down." You look, and sure enough all slats are lined up in the extended position, which you report to the Captain. He says: "then we'll go. We'll tell the crew in Minneapolis about the problem. When they get back to Clear River the aircraft sits for two hours, maintenance can adjust the proximity switch on number six then without causing a delay. Finish up the checklist." Owen paused, looking at the Major.

Major Crown was shaking his head and smiling, thinking this was a silly question. "I'm not taking off with an aircraft that has an obvious mechanical problem. It's a safety of flight issue."

"The Captain sees your hesitation and starts completing the rest of the checklist items," Owen continued, "he picks up the PA, tells the flight attendants to be seated, calls the tower and tells them you are ready for takeoff, the tower clears you to go, the Captain pushes up the throttles and is rounding the corner onto the runway..."

"I'm not going," Crown almost shouted, envisioning himself a prisoner in a doomed aircraft.

"Well, the Captain says you are. The throttles are at takeoff power and you're accelerating down the runway. What would you do?"

"I'd take control of the aircraft."

"Take control? How would you do that, the Captain's hand is on the throttles."

"I'd knock his hand off."

"Knock it off?" Owen almost laughed but held himself in check. He had asked this question dozens of times and had never gotten a response quite like this. "How, exactly would you manage that? The Captain's hand is on top of the throttles, on the knobs, he's got all the leverage."

Again there was no hesitation, a man of deeds not words, Crown demonstrated with a sweeping motion of his left hand. "Under and up," he said, repeating the motion. "Under and up."

He took Owen's stunned silence for admiration. "Take control of the aircraft and bring it to a full stop." Mission complete he sat back with satisfaction.

"You're going down the runway at 80 knots and you're going to knock the Captain's hand off the throttles and take control of the aircraft?" Owen wanted to make sure he had heard correctly. Crown nodded his agreement.

"You're going to take an airplane away from an experienced Captain, who's already explained his actions to you, who showed you the problem you think you see doesn't exist, is in fact an indicator problem." Owen wondering if he laughed, would Crown laugh with him, tell him he was just joking. "You do know that in a part 121 airline operation the Captain is, by federal law, in command of the aircraft?"

"Not if he's about to do something dangerous." Crown still sure of his actions. Not listening to the tone of Owen's voice.

"What would happen if you were coming in to land and the number six slat didn't extend with the others, was jammed in the up position?" Owen hoping the Major might learn something, do a little better on his next interview.

You could almost see the shadow spread across his face, doubt starting to wrinkle his brow. For the first time that morning Crown hesitated. "I don't know," he admitted, "I've never flown a 737."

Still trying to give him a chance Owen said "Suppose I told you that if you have a leading edge device fail to extend in flight you must apply a 10 knot penalty to the V2 landing speed. That's it, 10 knots, no other limitations, would you still try and wrest control of a moving aircraft away from its legal commander?"

The way Owen stated the question caused the major to give it some thought instead of just blurting out an answer.

"Look," Owen said gently, "I know you don't have much use for CRM in a single seat fighter. Have you heard the term? CRM, stands for crew resource management."

"Of course I've heard the term," Crown shot back, just a little indignant, "I've got my airline transport rating."

Owen tried to ignore the tone. "Well, CRM procedure requires the Captain to make use of all available resources, including an inexperienced First Officer. However, FAR 121 regulations state that the Captain is in command, and all crew members will comply with his instructions."

"Not if he's wrong. You don't have to follow orders if the Captain is wrong."

Owen had a brief image of a conversation with Crown's own Marine Commander, see what he had to say about this line of thought. He said, "you might want to reread the section about Captain's authority in the regs," standing as he spoke and extending his hand, "I appreciate you coming here to interview with us today."

Major Crown served up another manly handshake. "You'll let me know when I'm scheduled in the simulator?" he asked, no doubt in his mind about the outcome of the interview.

Owen felt a small twinge of guilt when he said, "You'll be getting the message from us shortly."

The truth was the correct answer to the question posed depended on which "expert" you asked. It was a very grey area. Alpha's manual allowed an airplane to depart the gate with an improper slat indication as long as the position was verified visually. United's manual might not.

The Captain's command authority, however, was spelled out in the rules governing US airline (part 121) operation: "The pilot in command of an aircraft is directly responsible for, and is the final authority as to, the operation of that aircraft". No grey area at all in the regulation.

Owen had a grading sheet he completed after each interview. He sat thinking with one in front of him now. He filled in Crown's name, the date, and his name as interviewer, then started down the list. Test score: one hundred percent, but all four applicants had achieved the same perfect score. The test was probably available on the internet now he thought. Appearance fine, Owen gave him a perfect ten. Only once had an applicant shown up looking like he had slept in his clothes and he had a good excuse; Alpha had lost his suitcase on the flight into Clear River. He was now a First Officer, about to check out as Captain, and had been a model employee. The truth was, it was all subjective.

While Owen agonized over these decisions he did not have the luxury of turning down an applicant who could fly. That was the real bottom line, the most important quality. If you wore a clean shirt and tie, didn't flunk the written, had the required minimum flight experience and a good excuse for any accidents, incidents or violations, you would most likely get an invitation to demonstrate your ability in the sim. Alpha was upgrading First Officers to Captain in less than two years. Owen had little choice.

Given this year's probable scenario Alpha intended to grow to at least twelve aircraft, preferably fifteen, by year's end. "That is, unless we go broke first," the new CEO had advised at his first staff meeting. Six more aircraft, one every two months.

Owen had decided not to interview any pilot who had less than 1,000 hours as pilot in command in a turbine aircraft. He had instructed Miranda to sort the incoming resumes by that minimum. Those without the minimum were sent a polite letter advising of the deficiency, thanking them for their interest, and told to reapply when they met the requirements.

Miranda had sent interview invitations to each of the 95 applicants who met the requirements. So far only 72 had responded. Of the 30 pilots he was scheduled to interview this week about 25 would actually show up. Owen would have two simulator periods of 4 hours each to work with. He could test 3 pilots an hour, so he invited 26, guessing that at least 2 wouldn't appear, though lately he was lucky to get 22. Of the 22, Owen would really like maybe 6; well spoken, well dressed, good test scores, good attitude, and they would do well in the sim.

To fill the class, and have 2 alternates, Owen chose primarily by attitude. "You can teach anyone to fly if they have the right attitude, they try really hard, and they're willing to listen. This way it's more of a challenge for you," Owen would tell Chuck Bert, the director of flight training.

"Just being an employee here is all the challenge I can handle," was Chuck's standard retort.

Owen put Major Crown's file in a folder marked with a big question mark and went out for another smoke. Crown would be a pain in the ass as an employee, but he might get the job anyway.

The next two interviews were much more satisfying for Owen. Both pilots had corporate experience in small jets, and both wanted to escape the tether that corporate flying cinched around the ankle. Both were invited to the simulator at the conclusion of their interview. Owen enjoyed their smiles and sighs of relief. He did like giving out good news.

The first issue Owen faced with the next applicant was whether to close the door to his office. He had been advised by the VP Legal that closing the door while interviewing a female was a risky proposition.

If he wanted the door closed he should find a female manager to sit in with him but none were available. He treated the problem with his normal disregard for convention, asking Ms. Long if she would be disturbed by a closed door and explaining the reason for the lawyer's concern. "No," she said, "it's not a problem, and please call me Anna."

Short of a past murder conviction Owen already knew he would offer Anna the simulator check. It was nearly impossible for an airline like Alpha to attract a female pilot since the majors would hire her with half the experience Owen required. In the four years Owen had been in charge of hiring pilots not one female had applied. Anna would not get away easily.

"You got a 100% on the test," he started, and paused when she smiled.

"It's on the internet," they said in unison. Both laughed.

Owen looked over her application. "No incidents, accidents, or violations?" he asked. "No DUI's, DWI's, no misdemeanors or felony convictions?"

"No, nothing like that," Anna said, A few speeding tickets a long time ago. The occasional parking ticket but that's about it."

She was secure enough not to bother with her natural beauty. If she wore lipstick or eye makeup it was barely discernible. Her black hair, trimmed short, showed traces of grey. Her movements were more athletic than feminine.

"You have almost 3,000 hours," Owen continued, "that's fine, but just 1,000 turbine pilot-in-command?"

"1,017.5, 17.5 since I applied. I've been flying a Citation for a medical group, sort of half medevac, half golf junket, and I fly that single pilot."

And proud of it, Owen thought. "How did you get into flying?"

"My ex-husband's a pilot, flies for Northwest now, but back then he was a flight instructor. We met in college, he was in the aviation program, and for our first date he gave me a ride in a Cessna 152. I loved it. He even let me take the controls for a while. I was hooked, but I couldn't afford the lessons, and he didn't have much money either, so he got the ratings and I got my degree in Education. The deal was that once he got a real aviation job, and we could afford it, he'd teach me to fly. We got married after graduation and he got that real job, flying a Lear for a local corporation, but I got pregnant." Anna shrugged, "It was also something I wanted, just the order got reversed. Am I rambling here?"

"Not yet," Owen said, "helps me get a feel for who you are."

"I'll cut it a little shorter," she promised. "I became a mother and Jim, my ex, got a job with Northwest. He wanted to move to Minneapolis. I didn't..." she stopped in mid-sentence. "Well, anyway, we got divorced, and I got two things in the settlement. We sold the house here in Clear River, used the money to pay for my flying lessons, and he agreed to pay for our daughter's college. I got my flight instructor's rating, you know the standard route, teach till you can get a multi-engine job, then fly multi-engine, mostly night freight, till you can get into a jet." She paused "That's it really. I'm here because I want to try flying a bigger airplane, it's my dream." She seemed almost embarrassed by that last admission, not wanting to seem emotional.

"Have you applied with any of the majors," Owen asked, thinking she would almost certainly get hired and wondering why she hadn't tried.

"No," she paused, "my daughter was pretty upset about the divorce. That was five years ago and I promised we wouldn't move until she finished high school and went off to college. She's in the middle of her junior year in high school, so..."

"You have eighteen months," Owen finished the thought for her. "You know we have a training contract?"

She finished his thought. "Twelve months from the completion of IOE." It was obvious she had already done the calculation.

"All right." Owen felt he had to ask at least one operational question. Out of curiosity he chose the same question he had asked Major Crown. Anna listened carefully, hands quietly in her lap, until the aircraft was approaching the runway. When Owen paused, she was ready.

"I'd tell the Captain that I was uncomfortable going with an improper indication, but if your aircraft are anything like the Cessna 402s I flew freight in, and you had to wait until everything was working before you left the gate, you'd never get anywhere."

"Spoken like a true freight dog," Owen stood and extended his hand, "Miranda will contact you with the date and time for the sim evaluation."

"I'm going to the sim? That's great," her face relaxing into a broad unpretentious grin. "Thank you," she said, taking Owen's outstretched hand. Her grip was firm and warm.

Make sure I'm first in line for that, Owen thought, breaking into a grin of his own, sure the line had formed a long time ago.

8

1-9-98

First Officer Larry Jensen was in the crew room at 3:30, an hour before he was required to be there. He knew he was flying with the Chief Pilot and that made him nervous. Owen had asked Miranda earlier what Larry Jensen looked like and now she pointed him out, sitting on one of the shabby couches, studying his aircraft manual.

Larry didn't notice Owen's approach until he was standing beside him, looking over his shoulder at the page in the normal operations section Larry was reading so intently. Larry jumped to his feet, the manual spilling off his lap onto the floor. "Captain Swift," his voice a tiny squeak as he extended his hand, "I'm rereading the section on winter ops. It's snowing in Denver," he added, almost as an afterthought.

Owen shook the proffered hand briefly, it was damp to the touch, and tried to put the young man at ease. "Larry, good to see you, how's your IOE going?

"I've only got 10 hours so far. I guess some of the check airmen quit, that's why I'm flying with you. It's not because I've done something wrong?"

"You haven't done anything wrong," Owen soothed, "two of our check airman have decided to pursue a career with Southwest and we are a bit understaffed at the moment. This is not a test, it's a continuation of your operating experience. I'll fly to Denver, you fly back, that's all there is to it."

Larry relaxed immediately. He had a ready grin, probably one of the reasons Owen had hired him in the first place. "You'll fly to Denver, that's great," the relief obvious, "the weather's really bad there, it's snowing really hard and the visibility is only 1/2 mile, winds gusting to 40 knots, it's like a regular blizzard. I don't think you want me landing there, my landings aren't that good when it's clear and calm." The grin turned into a self-deprecating frown.

Owen did some more soothing while knowing perfectly well that at 10 hours some of the pilots he had trained were regular aces, Some it took 30 or 40 hours, and some would never get it.

"I've got two more interviews to conduct," Owen said, "the aircraft's not going to get here until 5:00, so I'll have plenty of time but I need you to get the paperwork and meet the aircraft, then get the cockpit set up, get a clearance, and start the weight and balance. I'll do the exterior walk around." Larry's mood had changed rapidly from trepidation to anticipation. Owen had a reputation as a demanding but skilled and patient instructor. All the new First Officers wanted the chance to fly with him.

Owen stepped outside for a smoke. He thought about the two Check Airmen who had been hired by Southwest. They were good guys, good pilots, but neither had flown for an airline before Alpha. Check Airmen were part of the training department and while they asked his opinion, Owen didn't get to choose. There wasn't that much of a choice to begin with. Alpha was seriously short of experienced Captains.

The director of training, Chuck Bert, was an ex-Navy pilot who'd had no airline experience before he came to work for Alpha. Chuck was an earnest and hard working young man and Owen liked him a lot, but he was also a book man, who believed a Captain needed to know the book, and a Check Airman needed to know the book well enough to be able to teach it.

Owen didn't agree, but there was not much he could do about it. The attitude was prevalent not only in the military but in the airlines as well. Owen knew he was the odd man out, but was loath to change. He had too much respect for the Captains he had learned from decades ago. Owen readily admitted to the need for standardized procedures so a two man crew could function the first time they shared a cockpit, but he preferred logical explanations to rote memorization.

A Check Airman at Alpha made an additional 10% override on his paycheck. $5.00 an hour wasn't much of a motivator for accepting the responsibility of having your name on the training form that certified a pilot's abilities. A lot of the guys did it because it looked good on their resume and Owen couldn't really blame them. The Chief Pilot was considered to be at the top of the pilot heap. Having worked for two failed airlines Owen was aware of the sudden, and potentially disastrous, career consequences of corporate failure. He kept his own updated list of pilot positions that would suit him, just in case.

At 5:00 on the dot Owen shook the hand of the last pilot interviewee, grabbed his worn black flight bag and headed down the stairs to gate 32. He had dressed this morning in his black uniform pants, the white shirt with epaulets, and black tie, so he didn't have to change. He walked to the head of the line for security, about 20 people, and politely cut in front of an elderly woman. She looked him over carefully.

"You the pilot for Denver?" she asked. When Owen indicated that he was indeed going to Denver, she nodded her head. "Good," she said, you look like you've been doing this a while. Some of your pilots look like they haven't started shaving yet."

The woman laughed and Owen laughed with her.

"The weather is not so good in Denver?" Owen got the impression that she was testing him.

"There is a bit of snow falling," he admitted, tossing his bag on the conveyor belt for the scanner, then emptying his shirt and pants pockets; wallet, keys, cigarettes, lighter, pocket flashlight, logbook and loose change, into his leather jacket pockets and placed it on the belt behind his bag. He was stepping up to the scanner arch when he saw Doris.

Built like a bowling ball and old enough to be Owen's grandmother, she ordered people about like a prison guard. "Take off those earrings," to a little woman about her own age, "and step back through. That belt will have to come off," to the little woman's husband, who hesitated at first then complied, seven decades of male dominance caving in to the shining authority of Doris' security badge.

"Here comes trouble," Doris said in her bullhorn voice as Owen stepped up to the detector. She smiled with satisfaction as the machine gave it's telltale chirp. "Step back through," she ordered, but Owen shook his head no. They had a history of confrontation going back a month to her first day on the job. Confrontation that had repeated itself each time they met under these circumstances.

If there was one thing that got Owen's temper simmering, would get the flush creeping up his neck, put steel in his voice, it was unquestioned authority. Especially if the authority was, in his mind, undeserved.

Owen had begun flying airliners before there were security checkpoints. Then someone invented aircraft hijacking as a means of garnering publicity for their cause. It was a relatively benign activity at its inception in the early seventies, causing inconvenience and lost revenue rather than the loss of life and property. Owen would readily admit that life was more violent now, but the way airport security was operated wouldn't stop anyone bent on the destruction of an airplane. Making the flight crew go through the scanner was another of these unquestioned rules that drove him crazy.

"You think the pilot needs a weapon to destroy the aircraft?" He would argue with anyone who would listen. "I don't need a gun, all I have to do is push hard at the wrong time."

In the winter Owen wore black boots when he was in uniform.

They were waterproof and insulated, necessary armament against the slush and muck of a Midwestern winter. Unfortunately, steel nails were used to fasten the sole to the upper leather; it was these nails that set off the machine.

Owen had explained all this to Doris when it first occurred, but had made no impression, other than changing her facial expression from its normal suspicious glare, to one of utter disbelief.

"You expect me to fall for that? I don't care what you're wearing, you have to do what I say, and I say step back and go through the scanner again." She stood in front of him, hands on her hips, blocking his way.

The absurdity of the scene had made Owen smile grimly the first time it had occurred, though a sudden rush of anger was making his face red. He had felt the flush, and had to resist an almost overpowering urge to grab her fat throat and squeeze. His change in mood appeared to have little effect on Doris. Either she was too dense to notice, or, more likely, she knew she had the authority. That first confrontation had been resolved by Doris' supervisor, a gracious elderly black man named Henry, who had taken the wand from Doris' fist and run a cursory inspection, then waved Owen through. He had apologized for Doris with the explanation that it was her first day on the job. Nothing had changed since that day and at the moment Henry was nowhere in sight.

"Look," Owen said, "you know who I am, you see me practically every day, I have two photo IDs," holding them in front of her face, then stepped closer to her and whispered confidentially, "put the wand next to my boot," using the same low soothing tone he would employ with a growling dog that was blocking his path. By now everyone in the gate area was watching. She did as instructed, grudgingly. The wand gave a beep. It was the opening Owen was looking for.

"See," Owen said loudly, "it's the boots," turning away toward the conveyor before she could disagree. His flight bag and jacket were waiting and he snatched them up, moving quickly toward the gate, glad that the security guards had yet to be issued firearms. Doris would have to break into her high-speed waddle to catch him, something she didn't appear willing to attempt in public. Watch me Doris,

Owen vowed once again to himself, I'm going to get you fired. So far he had made no progress in that direction.

The gate agent handed Owen a sheet of paper as he walked past her on his way to the jetway. Ken Selby, the pm dispatcher, had faxed a copy of the latest Denver weather, along with reports for Colorado Springs and Cheyenne. Two alternate airports? Owen knew that was not a good sign. At the bottom of the page was a handwritten note requesting him to call dispatch.

The passengers waiting in line to board made room for him as he walked past them down the jetway onto the aircraft and turned to go into the cockpit. Several asked about the weather in Denver. "Snowing, windy and cold," he replied nonchalantly, "if I were you I'd be catching the flight to Miami," he joked with a pair of businessmen, but was more sincere with the worried looking older couple, recognizing them as the ones Doris had abused. "Everything is going to be fine," he assured them.

Amy was standing in the cockpit doorway and she squeezed by him, chest to chest, to make room. As she went by she gave him a peck on the cheek, explaining to the two businessman that he was her favorite captain, drawing out the A, and accenting the T with a sexy flick of her tongue, "faaavorit," much to their amusement.

"Boy, are we glad to see you," she said when Owen was in his seat. She was standing in the cockpit doorway with her back to the boarding passengers so they couldn't hear. "The last flight crew did not inspire lots of confidence."

Flight attendants judged their pilots on a number of levels. In the aircraft, it was landings that counted most, the ability to make smooth touchdowns was, in their minds, synonymous with safety and skill. A greaser, a roller, the transition from flight to a fast taxi imperceptible. Consistently smooth landings in a 737 required an understanding of the art of flying, and practice. The inbound crew hadn't had much chance to practice.

The First Officer was in his first month flying the line, the Captain had less than 100 hours in the left seat. The rules required a new Captain to make all landings until he exceeded the 100 hour minimum. Credit for the landings that Amy was referring to as less than inspiring would go to the Captain. "He did buy all the drinks in Dallas last night," Amy added, "so he's got potential."

Potential maybe, but not for this flight. A captain with less than 100 hours is a high minimum captain. He can be dispatched to an airport whose forecast weather calls for a ceiling no less than 300 hundred feet and visibility no less than 1 mile. Get past the 100 hours and the minimums drop to a 200 foot ceiling with visibility of 1/2 mile. Denver was forecast to be right at those minimums when they arrived.

Larry was already in the right seat and now he reminded Owen that dispatch wanted to talk to him. He called on the number three radio.

"Roger Alpha 190, I show a fuel minimum of 18,000 pounds using C-springs and Cheyenne as alternates. Owen was looking at the weather sheet the agent had handed him. It was snowing at both alternates, although the forecast predicted the ceiling and visibility would remain above minimums.

"Is there any place around Denver where the weather is good?" Owen inquired, "how about Pueblo?"

"Pueblo is VFR"(visual flight rules), but we'll have to add more fuel," already knowing what Owen's response would be.

"How many passengers?" Owen wanted to know.

"About 60," half-full, plenty of room for more fuel. Owen did some fast mental calculations. Flight time was 1:40, with a fuel burn of 8,500 pounds. If they went straight in they would reach the gate with 15,500 remaining, enough for the return trip. The fuel in the wings would be cold soaked by the time they arrived in Denver. If the snow was dry, it wouldn't stick to a cold wing. They might not have to deice, which would save time. If they couldn't land in Denver, and they didn't wait too long to make a decision, they would have enough fuel to return to Clear River, always a safer bet for servicing than landing at an alternate where there were no Alpha personnel. Owen had a dozen reports on file where the aircraft, passengers and crew had been stranded for hours after landing at an off-line airport, unable to get the support needed to depart.

"Let's go with 24,000 pounds, full tanks."

"24,000 it is, show it as amendment number one, we'll add it under contingency fuel, time 2300z, initials Tango Delta."

Larry was already getting out of his seat. "I'll tell the fueler before he gets away."

Amy was back in the doorway as soon as Larry had departed. "By the way," Amy said, then noticed Owen was checking the overhead panel and positioning switches. She waited until he was finished. "The other two flight attendants are Judy and..." she paused to get the full effect. Owen looked at her over his shoulder.

"Judy and ...?" Amy had a mischievous smile.

"Me, Judy and...Cynthia, you remember Cynthia don't you? Apparently she remembers you quite well, in fact she seemed to light up when your name was mentioned, although she wouldn't tell me why," her tone indicating that she thought she knew. Amy was loving this little dialogue.

It reminded Owen of high school. "Let's not get overly dramatic," he said, "ask her to come up here, please."

Amy stepped back and a moment later Cynthia was standing in the doorway. "Hi," she said extending her hand, "remember me?" smiling at him. Owen saw Amy put a hand on Cynthia's back and gently push her far enough into the cockpit so she could close the door behind her. For a moment neither spoke. Owen took her outstretched hand in his.

"You didn't call me," Cynthia said, more a statement of fact than an accusation.

"Call you? I was under the impression that our night together was a no obligation, sex for the fun of it episode. A spur of the moment one night stand, an item on your to-do list, you know, Tuesday night sex with the chief pilot. Mind you, I'm not complaining. You're a treat to look at, even with your clothes on, and sex for the fun of it has long been one of my favorite amusements."

"Ok, I will admit to active membership in the sex for the fun of it club, although not as long term a member as you, but no obligation one night stand? After all the effort it took to get you into the sack, I think I deserve at least...two nights," teasing him.

"I'd been planning this seduction since you talked to my flight attendant class a month ago. Rumor had it you went to the Gung Ho all the time. I can't tell you how much Chinese food I had to eat before you turned up. Chuck Bert talked to our class the same day you did. A lot of the girls thought he was the prize, I mean, he is young and pretty good looking, but there were a few of us who voted you the best choice for a quick fling, the fulfillment of our Oedipus fantasy. You are a lot more entertaining than either Bert or that VP, Rossi."

"A few of you? You have that list with you?"

"Maybe when I'm done with you, if there's anything left to share," she said laughing. "For now just think of yourself as another notch on my bedpost."

Larry opened the cockpit door, surprising them both. They were still holding hands and Cynthia maintained her grip when Owen tried to pull away, then loosened it so their hands slid apart slowly. Still laughing she turned and was gone, closing the door as Larry climbed into his seat.

"The flight attendants seem happy to see you," Larry said, straight faced and innocent, when he had buckled his lap and shoulder harness.

With a puzzled shake of his head Owen acknowledged the thought.

"Let's read the checklist," was his only reply.

9

The gate agent stepped into the cockpit. "Ready for some numbers?" she asked Larry, who reached for the weight and balance clipboard beside his seat. The big airlines had long ago gone to computerized weight and balance systems. They were faster and more accurate than the manual methods Alpha still employed, but expensive to purchase.

"60 passengers, three lap kids, 25 bags aft and 35 bags forward," this litany given at a pace Larry could keep up with, writing the numbers in their proper boxes on the triplicate form.

While Larry labored with the form's intricacies, Owen ran some numbers in his head. The empty weight of the airplane, in round numbers, was 76,000 pounds; adding 24,000 pounds of fuel put the weight at 100,000 pounds; 60 passengers plus the same number of bags at a rounded 200 pounds each passenger and bag combination, and their take off weight should be close to 112,000. Owen opened the plasticized flip cards that had the take-off data on one side, the landing numbers on the other, found the page for the 112,000 pound weight and propped it on the radar screen at the front of the center console where it was visible to both pilots. Larry was still calculating.

Owen knew that Larry's task required more than an estimate. Each number entered in the column required a center of gravity index to be transposed from the back of the sheet to the front, then added to the number above it in series until the zero fuel weight was identified. Adding the fuel weight to that number and subtracting the estimated taxi fuel burn would reveal the takeoff weight. The CG, or center of gravity, would appear in the column on the right side of the page. Larry would have practiced this in ground school, but not with two people looking over his shoulder, one of them tapping her foot and looking at her watch. Owen smiled. "Captain's watch says we are going to have an on-time departure," he assured her. The agent nodded her head in thanks.

As the Chief Pilot, Owen heard all the stories. He knew that some Captains wouldn't allow the gate agent in the cockpit while the First Officer was calculating the weight and balance numbers, and there were those who would record a flight departure as one minute late, if that's what their watch indicated when the tug started to move. To each his own.

"Life is an approximation," was Owen's credo, "and flying even more so."

At 112,000 pounds they would be about 18,000 pounds under their maximum calculated gross weight for take off on runway 35 Left. Those numbers were based on flight tests that had been done thirty years ago, when the aircraft had first been certified.

"That would be like asking me to carry 12-inch cinderblock all day long like I used to thirty years ago," Owen would explain to the pilots he was training. "Take the numbers in the performance book with a large dose of salt."

While the passenger count was usually close to accurate, the actual passenger weight was based on the assumption that each weighed 180 pounds, including their carry on luggage, until April 1, when the FAA said you could use 170; summer weight based on less clothing or the desire to look good in a bathing suit. Every bag placed in the bins below was assigned a weight of 25 pounds.

"Carry-on bags weigh more than 25 pounds," Owen would joke. "I can't imagine what's being tossed in the cargo bins, although if you watch the guys struggling while they're doing the loading you would get some idea."

The three fuel gauges allowable tolerance was plus or minus 3%, in this case a possible 1,500 pound swing. If they were within 2,000 pounds of the calculated weight Owen would be surprised. 2,000 pounds amounted to less than 2% of their estimated weight, a 2 knot difference in their takeoff speed. There was no instrument in the cockpit that was accurate to that degree. The needle on the airspeed indicator was 3 knots wide, the takeoff and landing speed cards in 2,000 pound increments, but the weight and balance calculations were supposed to be accurate to the pound.

"Set the stabilizer trim in the middle of the green band, set the V2 bug to135 knots, and you could fly the 737 for an entire career and not have a problem," Owen would joke with the check airmen, though he knew the attempt at accuracy was mandated by federal aviation regulations, and not to be tampered with.

"It's all based on economics; the more people, bags and freight you can stuff on an aircraft, the more money an airline can make. Besides, the numbers are all based on the loss of an engine at V1, the take off safety speed. Lose an engine before the speed is reached and, in theory, you could stop the airplane before the end of the runway. After V1, also in theory, there is enough power in the operating engine to safely continue the takeoff and climb rapidly enough to clear the obstacles in the departure path. The one good statistic: jet engines almost never quit, almost never."

Larry was ready; "Zero fuel weight is 88,000, take off gross weight, 112,400, trim 4.5 degrees," right in the middle of the green band.

When the pushback crew disconnected the tow bar, saluted, and started to back away towards the gate they had just left, Owen settled down to practice his art.

All aircraft taxi differently. Some need lots of power to start rolling, idle thrust is sufficient for others. The two hundred series seven 737 was in the latter group unless the aircraft was sufficiently heavy, the pavement soft, or there was a slope to climb. At their current weight, releasing the brakes and a little patience was all that was required. The aircraft started to roll slowly straight ahead before Owen, with his left hand on the steering tiller outboard of his left knee, coaxed them into a gentle turn. As much as they love pilots who make smooth landings, flight attendants adore smooth taxing. They're the ones standing in the isle giving the safety demonstration.

"Flaps fifteen and the taxi check," Owen requested, "if you please," his mood improving, Doris and Cynthia forgotten, the upcoming flight the sole occupant of his mind.

He flipped a switch on his audio panel that allowed him to monitor the cabin PA. Amy was almost halfway through her announcements. She had asked before they departed the gate, "runway three five left?", knowing that a short taxi would result. She would be ready in plenty of time. Larry would be another story.

One way to tell if a pilot is new to a particular aircraft is to watch how he stows the items he will need in flight. Larry had placed the weight and balance metal clipboard on the glare shield. It was the only horizontal surface available and would be a fine spot until they started the takeoff roll, when it would bounce into his lap or worse. Owen let this oversight slide, for the moment, and watched as Larry placed the flap handle to the fifteen degree detent, then sat waiting for the flaps to extend.

"What is the second item on the checklist?" Owen asked.

Larry had the checklist clipped to his control yoke and he consulted it.

"Flight controls checked," he started to apologize but Owen cut him short.

"It's ok, but remember your flows? We will be at the runway in 90 seconds. We need to be ready. This airplane costs $30 a minute so we can't afford to waste time. You need to go as fast as you can without making a mistake."

The check airman's task is not an easy one, especially with a pilot who is new to the airplane. It is necessary to allow the student to do his job or he will never learn, but you have to watch everything he does, every switch he throws, while also doing your job. Then there's the economic factor. The airline was losing tons of money. Taking extra time to teach was not, in Owen's mind, an option. They could discuss it in flight when there was little going on.

"I'm going to help you a little," Owen said, picking up the cockpit PA mike after checking that the flight attendants were no longer talking. The cockpit PA overrode the cabin PA and could interrupt the safety demo.

"Good evening ladies and gentleman. We will be next for departure in Clear River and on our way to Denver. I would ask the flight attendants to please be seated."

Owen hung up the PA mike and while rounding the next corner held the turn with the steering tiller and pressed the rudder pedals to the floor, first left, then right, to make sure they were moving freely.

Larry was checking the yoke and the ailerons for full travel then started to read the checklist; "recall...Owen had pressed the amber caution light before Larry read the item, trying to hurry him up. They were approaching the runway and Owen decided to give Larry some more help. He tuned the number one radio to the tower frequency and heard "Alpha 190 are you ready?"

Owen picked up his mike. "Alpha 190 ready in 30 seconds."

"Alpha 190 taxi into position and hold on runway 35 Left."

"Position and hold 35 Left for Alpha 190." Owen responded.

Deciding that Larry needed still more help Owen moved both engine start switches to left ignition, turned on the anti-skid system and the strobe lights.

A check list is just that; not a read-and-do list, but a check that all required items have been accomplished. It is normally read by the PNF (pilot not flying) and responded to by one or in some cases both pilots. Larry was obviously confused about how this was supposed to work, something else to explain once they got to cruise altitude. Larry read down the list until he got to "takeoff brief?"

Owen answered: "runway is 35 Left, runway heading after departure, cleared to 10,000 feet, outbound on the River Three

Departure, problems before V1 I'll reject the takeoff, after V1 I'll fly the aircraft. If we need to land we will return here to Clear River. Any questions?

"None," Larry replied, knowing that was the checklist answer, if not what he actually thought.

"Shoulder harness?" Larry's was on and he responded that way. He looked at Owen whose straps were still stowed in his seat back.

"On," Owen said with a grin. "Continue"

"Takeoff minimum fuel," Larry was stumped by this.

"15,000 was the minimum, we have 24,000, continue." The thirty seconds was almost up.

Larry finished the checklist items, reading and answering.

"Alpha 190 you're cleared for takeoff, maintain 10,000 feet and runway heading."

"You ready?" Owen asked, already pushing the throttles forward, "put that clipboard on the floor, and let's go to Denver."

Larry grabbed the clipboard and dropped it on the floor. "I feel like I'm still at the gate but you seem to know where we're going so sure, let's go to Denver."

This was the part that Owen loved; the hands-on manipulation of the aircraft, fifty-six tons of machinery responding to fingertip pressure on the controls. The 737 was not pretty to look at, nor did it possess the level of alacrity found in smaller or higher powered aircraft, but it was an airplane nonetheless, doing it's business in the three-dimensional world of flight with stodgy determination.

This particular airplane, Alpha's number 412, was getting a little long in the tooth. Originally designed with a service life of 50,000 hours she was now pushing 70,000 and had departed and returned to earth more than 55,000 times. She'd suffered her share of calamities; a leak in the forward lavatory, undetected over a period of years, had caused a cancer in the stringers and skin just below the floor, a rot so pervasive it had to be surgically removed with a torch then replaced with a bone and skin graft, the results visible in an ugly patch just forward of the air stair door.

The wing leading edge still showed the dimpled scars from an encounter with a shaft of hail a dozen years ago. Being parked for a year at an airstrip in Southeast Asia, with its constant humidity, had turned the thousands of electrical connections so carefully assembled decades ago into just so many question marks. This evening she was behaving flawlessly; no warning or caution lights, real or imagined, she lumbered down the runway, raising her nose in response to Owen's urging, and took flight one more time.

They entered a solid but benign overcast at 500 feet above the runway. It was flat layered and smooth, without bumps or precipitation but an obliteration of the outside world that was complete and absolute. With easy concentration on his flight instruments, Owen followed the instructions given by departure control; a turn toward the northwest then another turn westbound to intercept the outbound course on the standard instrument departure, cleared now to 23,000 feet. In the back of the aircraft the only thing missing was a view, like sitting in your fog bound living room with no sensation of motion.

As they climbed through 9,000 feet their surroundings began to lighten, slowly at first, then with increasing rapidity, until they burst into a sun flooded sky, blue replacing grey as the dominate color. Most of Alpha's pilots would have turned on the autopilot shortly after takeoff; Owen continued to hand fly the aircraft, guiding with light pressures and an occasional flick with his thumb on the electric trim switches on the side of the yoke.

It was obvious that Larry had a question and Owen encouraged him to speak. The rules required that there be no conversation below 10,000 feet unless it concerned the safety of the flight, but they were well above that altitude now, the after-takeoff checklist had been completed, and there would be little to do until they started the descent into Denver.

"You flew with one of my roommates a few months ago," Larry began, "and he told me you didn't wear your shoulder harness for takeoff," this said somewhat tentatively, Larry not to sure of himself or the ground he was treading.

There were a number of approaches Owen could employ here. Ignore the question; Larry was a new hire and beholden to him for his very existence at Alpha. There was no way Larry could hurt him even if he wanted to but the need for truth was deeply ingrained in Owen's psyche. He liked the purity of it, the feeling it generated knowing he was being honest. He would laugh this off by saying that it was the fault of a failing memory, he had enough trouble remembering what had actually occurred without fabricating a different story then trying to remember Version Two. This trait may have made him a better person, but in the corporate environment at Alpha it had proven to be a liability.

"One of my problems is that I've been in this business too long," Owen began. "When I started flying there were no shoulder harnesses in transport aircraft. When they were first installed, wearing them was optional. Then some freight Captain had a heart attack on short final going into LA, he slouched forward into the yoke, the First Officer couldn't pull back against his weight and they crashed. It wasn't a big deal in the press because nobody died, but after the investigation the FAA decided that crews should wear the shoulder straps during takeoff and landing so it wouldn't happen again. But here's my problem with the rule." Owen pulled both shoulder straps out of their holder in the seat back, then fastened them to the lap belt with a solid click. "Sounds good but watch this." He began his imitation of a man having a heart attack, making choking noises then clutching at his heart and slowly falling forward against the yoke. The shoulder harness didn't stop him. "They're on an inertial reel, they won't stop you if you slump forward slowly, you need to hit a brick wall." Owen shrugged. "The only difference then would be an open or shut casket."

Owen glanced out the window. They were at 35,000 feet, the auto pilot on and holding them perfectly level. The true airspeed was 420 knots, a compromise between speed and fuel efficiency. The air was smooth, the cloud deck far below, the sun sinking slowly behind some distant cumulous clouds. Owen switched his navigation radio from the station behind them to the next one on their assigned route,160 miles away, and turned the aircraft a few degrees to the right to stay on course. There was little else to do. Owen thought his position on rules needed more explanation.

"You ever exceed the speed limit when you're driving?"

"Sometimes," Larry readily admitted.

"Ok, most people, myself included, do. Let's say you're going down the interstate at 75 miles an hour, 5 miles over the limit, and it starts pouring down rain. Would you slow down?"

"Sure, if the visibility was reduced or it was getting slippery, sure I would slow down. Common sense thing to do."

"Ah, common sense, there's a concept for you. The law doesn't say you have to slow down, the speed limit's 70 whether it's clear and dry or the road's covered with ice and snow, but most people with half a brain do slow down because it makes sense. Thirty years ago the book of rules governing aviation was this big," indicating a 2 inch space between his thumb and forefinger. "Now it's like this," his hands measuring a trophy fish. "There are those who would tell you flying is safer, and it is, but it's because of the jet engine's reliability compared to its piston predecessor, and improved navigation technology, not more rules. Common sense," Owen snorted.

"On my very first check ride for my private license, I only had 40 hours total time but I knew I was hot, aviation had never seen a talent this great, and the FAA inspector was this old stodgy guy who had asked me all the memory questions he could think of. I knew all the answers, including the clear of cloud criteria. I had a memory in those days.

"The ride was about over. I had already aced all the mandatory maneuvers. We were returning to the field from the practice area, one more landing and I would have my license. There was a little deck of stratus cloud above us and I asked the inspector how you could tell when you were 500 feet below a cloud. If I remember correctly that's what the rule is for visual flight; 500 below, 1,000 feet above and 1 mile horizontal clearance of all clouds. I mean really, how can you define the edge of a cloud and how are you to know if you are closer than the law allows? There is no gauge in the cockpit to measure it.

"Why couldn't the rule say, if you are on a visual flight plan stay out of the clouds and you'll know if you're in one because you'll no longer be able to see out the window.

"The inspector was speechless. He told me years later that he had been tempted to fail me because of my arrogance, but on that day he said that the rules were there for my protection, were created by people who knew more about aviation than I would ever know, and I should follow them to the letter. Never answered the question because there is no answer that makes any more sense than the rule does.

"You know why you can't have a conversation below 10,000 feet unless it concerns the safety of flight?" Owen continued without waiting for Larry's response, warming to his subject. "Because twenty years ago the FAA conducted a survey and found that 99% of all aviation accidents occur below 10,000 feet. They reasoned that if pilots would just pay more attention below ten, the number of accidents would decrease."

"What nonsense. I mean, duh? Unless airplanes run into each other, what else have they got to run into but the ground. And to add insult to stupidity it's not 10,000 feet above the ground, it's just 10,000 feet, so in Denver you can talk until you're 5,000 feet above the ground. I have to believe that these rules are written by lawyers who have no aviation experience. How else could they come up with this drivel?"

"Wow," Larry said, mouth agape and eyes wide, "I didn't mean to get you all riled up."

Owen burst out laughing. "Yeah, sorry about that, I'm getting old and cranky I guess and that makes me less tolerant of bullshit. All this crap used to just wash over me and I paid no attention. It's just that now there's no escape, there is so much of it that it seems endless. I just had a conversation with our POI (principal operations inspector) about the new duty regulations that the government has just approved.

"It used to be that you could fly 8 hours in 24, period. Now they have instituted a sliding scale where you look back 24 hours to see how much rest is required and the max hours were increased to 10. I asked him an operational question, you know, a what if, and he said he couldn't answer because the rule hadn't been to court yet. Gone to court? Why couldn't they write a rule that said if you're too tired to fly, if you are starting to make stupid mistakes, land somewhere and get some rest.

"Pilots have had to stop worrying about how safe something is and start worrying about how legal. Most of it is absurd, has absolutely nothing to do with safety, and that used to make me laugh. Not anymore. I'm having trouble laughing nowadays. Chuck Bert probably summed it up best a while back when we were arguing about the need for one rule or another and he called me an aging hippy with a little bit of anarchist thrown in."

At the beginning of his airline career Owen had spent 10 years as a First Officer for a major airline. It was written in the first page of the "BIG" book that the Captain's word was law. Every crew member did what the Captain said, without hesitation. What other job, Owen thought, was your boss seated 2 feet away, watching your every move. When he finally became a Captain, Owen tried to take the best attributes of the hundreds of Captains he had flown with and incorporate them into his own style, without becoming as autocratic as those few who had driven him crazy.

When Alpha was in its infancy the V/P of operations had asked Owen to become a Check Airman. There had been very few pilots hired at that point who had enough large aircraft or airline experience to placate the FAA in general, and the airline's first POI in particular. Owen had at first resisted. The Check Airman position at Eastern Airlines had included a lot of political maneuvering, with the job not always going to the most qualified. He had declined the position then, and felt the same way at Alpha until the V/P said simply;

"I need your help." Owen liked the man for his honesty and he took the job.

He was surprised to discover just how much he enjoyed it. Though most of Alpha's new-hire pilots had a reasonable amount of flight time, few had flown in an airline environment. Owen put his years of experience to good use. He believed what the old Captains he had flown with had told him: thinking was the key to long term survival in this business, not learning the manual word for word. Tired of arguing with the director of training whose military mind could only handle rules and procedures, Owen waited until he was on the aircraft, or in a bar, to preach his own brand of aviation intelligence Not all the trainees were interested. There were a fair number, larger than Owen wanted to admit, who agreed with the training department that flying was a science and could be learned from a book. They had no interest in flying as an art form. Owen persisted, singling out those whose passion for perfection matched his own and encouraging them to pursue it.

Larry had a long way to go before he could think of the 737 as a canvas for his art, but he was eager to learn, and peppered Owen with questions until they were 100 miles from Denver. Owen had tuned in the ATIS on the number two radio, and they both listened, Larry scribbling furiously to get the information on paper.

10

1-9-98

"**D**enver International Airport information Xray, 1800 special report, wind 310 degrees at 22 knots gusting to 42, visibility 1/2 mile in snow and blowing snow, ceiling 200 feet overcast, temperature 28, dew point 26, braking action on runway 35 Left was reported as poor by a 737 at 1730 local, numerous pilot reports of moderate to severe turbulence below flight level two-four-zero..." As soon as Owen heard the turbulence report he stopped listening and rang the flight attendant call button. Amy was in the cockpit 30 seconds later.

"Good news or bad?" she wanted to know.

"Bumps," Owen said, "maybe some big ones. Can you get picked up and seated in 5 minutes?"

"Probably quicker, we're about done anyway. We going to get into Denver?"

"Weather is above minimums at the moment. If it stays that way and they don't close the airport for plowing we'll be on the ground in 20 minutes. I'll make an announcement. Ring us when you're seated."

Amy spun on her heel and was gone.

Because the airport was on the downwind side of the Rocky Mountains, moderate turbulence on the descent into Denver was not all that unusual, Severe turbulence however, that was something else again. Severe turbulence meant inability of the pilot to control the aircraft, extreme changes in heading, altitude, airspeed, and a good possibility of aircraft upset, structural damage or both. There was no quantifiable measurement. No G meter, (measure of the force of gravity acting on the airplane) in the cockpit. It was open to interpretation by the pilots, like the braking action report, and there was a wide range of opinion amongst the pilot community about when the turbulence went from moderate to severe, the braking action from poor to nil.

The turbulence penetration speed recommended by Boeing was 280 knots indicated. Owen would slow to that speed before descending into those innocent looking cloud wisps, making sure the flight attendants and passengers were seated and belted, knowing that Amy would have closed and locked all the galley doors and made sure all lose items were stowed.

The braking action? Well, the runways at Denver were 12,000 feet long, long enough that Owen almost never needed the brakes after landing. Reverse thrust was generally enough to slow the aircraft to taxi speed and the accumulated snow on the runway would just add more drag, initially slowing them faster than on a dry runway. Stopping wouldn't be the issue, but keeping the airplane from sliding off the side of the runway as they slowed? That might be a problem. A 40 knot gust striking the vertical stabilizer at a 40 degree angle from the left would turn their seven 737 into a 50 ton weathervane.

Owen thought of his ongoing disagreement with the training department. He had pointed out that when the 737 had been certificated a dry runway had been used. Test pilots, new tires and brakes, no reverse thrust allowed. The measured stopping distance increased by 50% to come up with the theoretical distance required in slippery conditions. No definition of slippery supplied. To Owen's knowledge no real world tests had ever been tried.

There was a friction measuring device available. A small wheel mounted on a vertical shock absorber then installed on the back of a pickup truck. Owen was sure its use had never been adopted because an exact measure of the stopping power available to a departing or landing aircraft would most likely restrict the amount of weight the aircraft could carry. Restricting weight meant restricting earning potential. The airlines wouldn't like that.

Stop a 737 in these conditions without using reverse thrust while using less than 4,000 feet of runway. Not likely. "It's the kind of information new Captains should have," Owen argued, to no avail, but he made sure the Captains he trained knew.

Owen wondered if he would attempt this approach in Midway where the runway was half as long. Glancing at the fuel gauges and noting they had enough fuel to make it to Pueblo, he thought briefly of the consequences that decision would have, maybe buy all the passengers a drink, call the VP of flight ops from the bar, tell him he just didn't feel like landing in a blizzard tonight.

Denver Center interrupted Owen's wandering mind. "Alpha 190, you're cleared to descend to and maintain flight level two-four-zero, pilot's discretion."

Larry read back the clearance then looked at Owen; "Should I tell him we're out of three-five-zero?"

"What would you do?" Owen turned the question back.

Larry didn't hesitate; "Well, the other check airman I flew with said to use a three to one ratio, so from three-five-zero we should have started down at 105 miles." They were 95 miles from the airport.

"That works great if there is no wind, "Owen countered, "What is our ground speed?"

"I can't find the ground speed readout?" Larry admitted, "I've been looking for it for a while."

Owen laughed and shook his head. "Two things," he said, "first, please do not hesitate to ask a question because there is no such thing in this cockpit as a stupid question. Second, you can't find a ground speed readout because we don't have one in this aircraft, in fact only one of our aircraft has one. We do things the old fashioned way." He tapped the clock mounted in the lower left corner of his instrument panel.

"Just like in a little Piper, number of miles flown in one minute times 60 for a ground speed. We have been averaging about 360, 6 miles a minute with a 60 knot headwind."

It was Larry's turn to shake his head. "The last little Piper I flew had a ground speed readout and that's in an airplane that seats 4, not 137, costs thousands not millions, and goes 2 miles a minute not 7."

"Nobody claimed that Alpha was state-of-the-art," Owen shot back, "Our motto is cross the plains in a day. Tell Center were starting our descent and let's get back to the problem. We're 90 miles from the airport, landing straight in. To be on the glide slope we need to be at 10,000 feet and 250 knots 30 miles from the airport, how would you plan your descent?"

Larry was silent. Owen had taken the auto pilot off altitude hold and was gently pressing the yoke forward with his left hand, his right on the throttles pulling them slowly back to the idle stop. He lowered the nose until their descent rate approached 3,000 feet a minute, the airspeed indicator stabilized at 320 knots. He looked at Larry who just shrugged.

"I don't think I follow what you want, I don't really know how you are planning this approach," Larry said, somewhat embarrassed by his ignorance.

"Not to worry, I do this a little differently than the other check airmen and I don't expect you to know my way, but you need to figure out how to make efficient descents. We want to be at 10,000 feet and 250 knots at 30 miles, we're 60 miles from that point so we have about 10 minutes before we get there and 25,000 feet to lose. With the engines at idle and the airspeed at 320 we'll average about a 3,000 foot a minute rate of descent. That gives us a little fudge room to slow for the turbulence we are bound to encounter and for the 250 knot max speed below 10,000 feet. Also in the bank is the fact that Denver is 5,000 feet high, 5,000 feet we don't have to lose, which saves us a couple of minutes."

"I think the three to one rule sounds easier," Larry protested, "I can't quite get what you're telling me."

"You will," Owen assured him, "you will. The problem with any rule, is they don't always apply. If you had a 100 knot headwind and you use the three to one rule you'll be way early on your descent, a tailwind like that and you'd have to use the flight spoilers to get down in time. Ideally, you would put the engines in idle when you leave cruise altitude and leave them there until you are 1,000 feet above the runway on final approach. That would burn the least fuel, and fuel is expensive. We'll work on it some more on the way back to Clear River. For now, why don't you call our station in Denver, tell them we'll be on the ground in 20 minutes, and see if you can find out about the conditions in front of the gate. Then we'll do the descent check list."

"There is about 6 inches of snow, the taxi way has been plowed down the center line and that's left a bit of a drift in front of the gate that you'll have to taxi through, but it doesn't seem too slippery by the gate itself," the ground agent in Denver responded to Larry's query. "We'll see you in 20 minutes at gate Charlie 42."

Larry relayed the information to Owen then began the descent checklist. Amy stuck her head in the door, "We're all buttoned up back here, do a good job now honey," patting Owen on the shoulder then closing and locking the cockpit door.

As they descended through 26,000 feet Owen raised the nose gradually, letting the speed bleed back to 280 knots, then lowered it to continue the descent. The cloud deck was clearly visible a few thousand feet below, the dim moonlight making the surface look like the top of a meringue that had been shaped with a blow dryer.

"Let's turn on the engine anti-ice," Owen instructed. "Ignition first", he cautioned when Larry reached for the anti ice switches, "always ignition first."

As they descended into the topmost wisps of cloud the aircraft seemed to pause, as if taking a deep breath, then gave one violent shake and dropped belly first, as though it had suddenly lost all interest in flying. The airspeed went from 280 to 250 in a blink.

"30 knot loss," Larry said, after clearing his nervous throat.

"Got it," Owen responded and clicked off the autopilot, preferring to hand-fly the aircraft in these circumstances. "Autopilot's off, they don't handle turbulence that well. See if you can get us lower than 24."

The Center cleared them to flight level one-eight-zero and told them to call Denver approach.

Denver approach control replied to Larry's call. "Roger Alpha 190, turn left heading 320 and intercept the runway 35 Left localizer, cleared to 12,000 feet, slow to 250 knots, Yankee is now current, advise when you have it."

Larry acknowledged their clearance and retuned the number two radio to the ATIS frequency. "Everything's pretty much the same," he reported to Owen, "200 over, 1/2 mile visibility, the peak gust was 45 knots about 10 minutes ago. Now they're saying that 35 Left has 5 inches of snow on it."

"Did they say wet or dry?"

"They didn't say, want me to ask?"

"No," Owen replied, "we don't want to know."

Larry had just been reading this chapter in his manual and he realized why. "If it was wet snow we couldn't land," he said, proud that he remembered.

"Not that we couldn't," Owen corrected, "but according to our manual it would be illegal. That is an important difference."

"Legal in 1 inch of wet snow, 6 inches of dry," Larry quoting the book.

"You know the difference between wet and dry snow according to the FAA?" Owen asked, "it's very technical."

Larry admitted that he hadn't seen that in the book.

"Snowballs," Owen pronounced, "if you can make a snowball the snow is wet, no snowball means dry snow. I love that definition. It's possibly the most logical in all of aviation. Of course, how you can tell that there is 5 inches of snow on the runway when the wind is blowing 40 is a mystery to me."

Owen made a quick PA announcement.

"Sorry for all the bumps ladies and gentleman but there is no way to get into Denver this evening without them. Weather is what you see out the window: cloudy, windy, snowy and cold with a temperature of 28 degrees. We are 40 miles from the airport, should be on the ground in 10 minutes. Thanks for flying with Alpha."

After the initial precipitous drop the aircraft had settled into a continuous series of convulsions; up, down, left, right, in no particular order. The airspeed jumped up 10, then down 15, then returned to 250. Owen didn't touch the throttles, didn't chase the airspeed knowing that for each negative there would be an almost immediate positive. If the left wing dropped he would use opposite aileron to stop the fall, then just a little bit more to start the wing back toward level. Left hand lightly gripping the yoke, the right resting on the throttles he coaxed and cajoled rather then demanded.

"Localizer's alive," Larry called, and indeed it had moved off of the left edge of the instrument and started toward the centered position that would indicate the middle of the localizer beam, and by extension, the runway now 30 miles distant. The flight director V bars called for an immediate right turn but Owen held his heading, knowing that with this much crosswind it would take at least a 15 degree correction to keep them aligned with the localizer. A moment later the flight director agreed with him and commanded a return to the heading he was maintaining. Larry had watched this with interest.

"Not much of a flight director," he commented.

"It should work ok now," Owen said, "they're not that good at intercepts. Old and tired, I guess, like the rest of this airplane."

Once they were tracking the localizer and centered on its beam Owen tried turning on the autopilot. He had a choice to make. If the autopilot would work he could have Larry monitor its function. In that way, when they got to 200 feet, he would be the one looking out the window, the one that made the decision to try to land or to miss the approach. If he had to hand-fly the approach then Larry would be looking out the window. At 200 feet if Larry called "runway" Owen would have to transition from instrument to visual flight, hoping that Larry had made the correct call.

There wouldn't be much to see no matter who was looking. Landing lights on an aircraft have the same effect in heavy snowfall as a car's headlights, the reflection making them virtually useless. Owen had already decided to leave them off. The runway edge lights were white and mounted on two foot stalks to keep them clear of most snow conditions. If the runway's surface was clear, there were also threshold and centerline lights to help the pilot identify the grey concrete runway he was trying to land on. If the runway was snow covered, it was difficult to separate it from its snow covered surroundings.

The pilot manual procedures were quite clear. The pilot flying would focus on the instruments until the pilot not flying called runway in sight. The pilot flying would at that point look up and declare either "landing", if he could see enough to accomplish that task or he would call "going around", and execute the missed approach procedure. At 200 feet they would be 16 seconds from touchdown, crossing the ground at a 150 miles an hour. Plenty of time to make a mistake.

The turbulence was more than the autopilot could handle. As soon as Owen turned it on it began jerking the aircraft around like a misbehaving dog on the leash of its angry owner. There was a turbulence mode available but it wouldn't execute an approach. Owen clicked the autopilot off.

He explained his dilemma to Larry. "We have two choices here; you shoot the approach and if I see the runway I'll take the controls and land the airplane, or, I'll shoot the approach and you'll make the runway in sight call, if you see enough of the runway that you think it would be safe to land."

Denver approach gave them new instructions. "Alpha 190 slow to 180 knots, maintain that speed to Diamond, you are cleared for the ILS approach to runway 35 Left, contact the tower at Diamond (an imaginary point indicated on the approach chart at 6 miles from the end of the runway).

Owen eased the throttles to idle and as the speed dropped below 220 knots called for flaps 5. Larry, who had been watching Owen's manipulation of the controls was already shaking his head no. "I think we'd be better off if you flew the approach," he admitted.

"Have you landed in conditions like this before?" Owen asked, "I mean in blowing snow with this much of a cross wind?"

Just a negative shake of the head which Owen caught in his peripheral vision. It was taking most of his attention to keep them centered on the localizer.

"When we break out," Owen instructed, "the runway won't be straight ahead, it's taking twenty degrees of crosswind correction to keep us on the localizer so the runway will look like it's off to the right. I need you to describe what you see. I like a running commentary, so when you see the ground, call out ground contact, approach lights, hopefully runway. Just describe what you can see. It will help me make the decision whether to land or go around."

The glide slope pointer wiggled once and bounced off the top of its scale.

"Glide slope's alive," Larry called.

They were 12 miles from the end of the runway, the altimeter indicating 9,000 feet, 3,500 hundred feet above the snow-swept plain invisible below, enveloped in angry grey cloud, trapped in an elevator gone mad, going up for several seconds before changing its mind and reversing direction.

When the pointer indicated they were on the glide slope Owen started down to follow it, pulling the throttles toward idle to maintain the 180 knots requested by approach. They were following a United 757 which was an aircraft type Owen had flown. He had a brief mental picture of the United pilots watching their glass screens, the autopilot doing the flying. Autopilot, autoland, auto spoilers, auto brakes, all the crew would have to do was taxi to the gate and they were getting paid three times as much as he and Larry. Owen was jealous for just a moment before he told himself he was having more fun then they. Sure he was.

At 7 miles, Owen called for gear down, flaps 15 and the landing check, easing the throttles toward idle to begin the reduction to approach speed and pushing forward on the yoke to counter the balloon effect the flaps would have, adjusting the power to maintain 150 knots, 20 knots above the speed he would use in smooth air, then called for flaps 30. Larry told the tower they had passed Diamond.

"Alpha 190 you are cleared to land on runway 35 Left. You are 5 miles in trail with a 757, caution wake turbulence, wind is 310 at 30 gusting to 38, runway is snow covered with depths up to 6 inches, braking action reported as poor by a 737."

"Wake turbulence?" Larry asked.

"Wake turbulence wouldn't last 10 seconds in air this disturbed," Owen assured him, "it's the least of our worries, just standard phraseology for ATC."

"500 feet," Larry called out, "flaps are 30, gear down with three greens and we're cleared to land." He was looking out the window; "I can't see anything."

"United 400," the tower called, "advise clear of the runway." With the visibility limited to 1/2 mile the tower operator, located in the middle of the airport a mile from the landing runway's end, was unable to see a landing aircraft's position on the runway. He couldn't permit a second aircraft to land until the first had exited the runway.

"I think we can make the turn onto Mike 7," the United responded.

"Shit," Owen swore, "don't think, just get off the fucking runway."

At 300 feet Owen called; "100 above minimums."

At 250 feet Larry said; "I see the rabbit."

The tower said, "Alpha 190 stand by to go around."

Owen could sense the sequence flashers flowing below them, the "rabbit," leading them toward the approach end of the runway. It looked like an emergency vehicle passing underneath them at 5 times their speed, the brilliant white lights shrouded by the cloud they were descending through. The runway invisible. Larry said nothing.

"United 400 is clear," the United pilot said.

"Alpha 190 cleared to land," the tower said immediately.

"We're cleared to land," Larry repeated.

"Heard that, what can you see?"

Owen had already decided that if Larry had said nothing at 200 feet he would sneak a quick peek before initiating a go-around. If the United 757 that had just landed was using their auto-land system they wouldn't need to see the runway although Owen thought the cross-wind was too strong for that system to be used. Even if they were hand flying they might be good to Cat 2 (category 2) minimums; 100 feet above the runway because of the 757's more advanced instrumenta-tion. Alpha, with their 35 year old 737's, was a Cat 1 airline, restricted to a 200 foot decision height. Owen wasn't sure that would be low enough to see the runway. He had the approach wired at the moment. If it stayed that way he might have to cheat a little to get on the ground.

At almost the same moment Owen said "minimums," Larry an-nounced; "runway in sight, it's off to the right."

As Owen looked up Larry said, "It's gone."

Back to the gauges. The glide slope and localizer pointers were locked on center. 150 feet. Time to go, Owen thought but before he could advance the throttles Larry said, "Runway," sounding triumphant.

This time when Owen looked up he saw what he needed.

Looking out the window it was hard to believe they were less than 40 miles from the largest city in Colorado. They might have been in the middle of the Great Plains, the snowy landscape devoid of any sign of human habitation. The 1/2 mile visibility allowed only the approach end of the runway to be seen, the red light bar marking the runway's beginning seemed to be floating on a sea of white, the runway edge lights barely visible, the rest of the airport complex invisible in the darkness and blowing snow. The quarter-ing wind from their left made it appear that the earth was sliding sideways beneath them.

Owen quickly checked his instruments. They were aligned with the runway's centerline, it just didn't look that way. He held the nose of the aircraft where it was, pointed into the crosswind to hold their track, his eyes going from instrument panel to outside and back, airspeed, rate of descent, glance at the runway. Localizer, glideslope, runway.

They passed over the runway's end, Owen's control movements firmer now, demanding compliance from his machine. Larry called the radar altimeter heights; "100, 50, 40, 30."

At Larry's call of "20 feet," Owen lowered the left wing a few degrees, then used the right rudder pedal to align the aircraft with the runway, raising the nose to stop the descent and retarding the throttles, holding against the crosswind now and feeling for the ground.

The left main wheel touched lightly first, followed by the right. Owen lowered the nose wheel to the snow-covered pavement, pulled the ground spoiler handle and deployed both engine reversers to the idle position.

A gust caught the tail and slewed the aircraft sideways. At 120 knots the big rudder was still effective and Owen used it now, easing them back in alignment with the runway. He could hear tentative applause from the cabin, a spontaneous response from grateful passengers for being returned safely to earth. Another gust, stronger than the last, and they were sideways again. The rudder was becoming less effective as they slowed, it no longer had enough authority to keep them straight.

Owen could feel the nose wheel scrubbing across the snow. He increased the reverse on the right engine and that solved the problem, straightening their path once again. There were runway distance markers alongside the runway. Painted and unlit they were impossible to read. Owen had no idea how far down the runway they were. The lead-off lights buried in the pavement and now covered with snow gave no clues to taxiway location.

"Alpha 190 report clear of the runway," the tower requested.

Owen tried the brakes. They were going slowly now, maybe 20 knots, he guessed. There was no instrument that indicated taxi speed and no change in their apparent velocity. He understood why the United crew had difficulty clearing the runway.

"This braking action is more like nil than poor," he reported to Larry, who had his face pressed against the windshield to cut out the glare from the instrument lights.

"That look like tire tracks?" Larry asked pointing off to their left.

"Yeah," Owen said, "and some blue lights," easing the nose wheel to the left to steer them in that direction. "Tell the tower we're clear of the runway."

Owen thought they had exited the runway on taxiway Mike 7, following in United's tracks, but he wasn't sure. Fortunately, he did know that when you turned west off runway 35 Left you would have to taxi past the terminal complex before you came across another runway. Not being sure of your position on a taxiway didn't have the same potential for disaster that crossing a runway with airplanes landing and departing on it did. They came to a taxiway that was parallel to the runway they had just landed on and Owen turned onto it, heading north. He turned on the taxi lights. Through the swirling snow he could barely make out the lettering on the sign. "This must be Mike," he said.

Larry had the airport diagram pulled out of his chart book and was staring at it, tracing their route with his finger. The snow had started to melt on the heated front panels of the windshield and Owen ran the wipers through one cycle to clear it. The side windows had no means of cleaning available. Trying to look through them was like staring at a Rorschach test that had been smeared with baby oil. The 8 X 14 inch arc of the wiper blade was the only portal to look through. Owen leaned forward, his chin almost on the edge of the glare shield, to get the best angle he could.

"Alpha 190 are you northbound on Mike?" the tower inquired

When Larry confirmed their position the tower instructed, "north on Mike, left on Charlie North, call Ramp Control on 119.45 when you are on Charlie North."

The cockpit door opened and closed quickly. "Boy, that was great for me, how was it for you guys?"

Owen could smell Amy's perfume as she put her face down next to his and looked out the tiny patch of clear window. "Jesus," she swore, "can you see where we're going?"

Owen laughed. "Just looking for a road sign, tell us which way to I-70, get us to downtown Denver."

They crossed another taxiway. "That's Echo Charlie," Larry announced, getting the hang of this drill. "Should cross Mike 9 then Mike 10, then left on Charlie North. I'll tell the gate we're on the ground."

"Tell them we need about twenty sick sacks," Amy requested, "and whatever cleaning equipment they have and some extra large garbage bags. The cabin's a wreck."

When Larry's radio call was complete Owen reminded him about the after landing checklist. "Do the whole thing, just leave the flaps at 5 degrees. If there is slush on the flap drives that should prevent any damage from occurring."

They were approaching Charlie North. Limited visibility and snow- covered taxiways made the upcoming left turn guesswork. Owen grabbed the handle on his sliding side window and levered it open. A blast of cold air and snow flakes invaded the cockpit but he could see to make the turn.

"Open cockpit 737," Owen joked once they had negotiated the downhill S turn at the east end of Charlie North, an obvious surveying error in 15 square miles of straight lines and 90 degree corners. He left the window open until they had made another left turn to approach gate 42 head on. The wintery air was clean and smelled of pine forests.

When they had parked and shut down the engines Owen left his seat and opened the cockpit door. It was his custom to say goodby to the passengers, and he stood in the doorway smiling and thanking them for choosing Alpha. He got mixed revues.

A woman carrying a small child stopped right in front of him. "That was the worst flight I have ever been on," she declared. "You might have got us all killed."

"I'm sorry you feel that way," Owen said, trying an apology to see if that worked. "We weren't actually in any danger, but I know it was uncomfortable."

She cut him off. "Uncomfortable?" she mocked, "this is uncomfortable." With her free hand she tugged on a corner of her blouse, which appeared to be soaked through. "You don't look like anybody puked on you." Her child began to cry and she marched off the airplane and up the jetway. "I'm writing a letter to the FAA," she announced as a parting shot.

Go ahead and write, Owen thought to himself, as he turned to face the next passenger, knowing that any letter would find its way to the POI who would call him up and they would laugh about it after Owen had told him the story.

The two businessmen Amy had been joking with in Clear River were next. They were laughing as they stumbled forward. "Don't listen to her," one said, shaking Owen's hand, "that was the best roller coaster ride I've ever been on. Only problem was you closed the bar a little early."

Amy, who was standing in the galley next to Owen rolled her eyes as they made their way up the jetway. "They had five beers apiece and wanted to keep drinking," she said, "then one tried to get up to use the john when we were about five minutes from landing. I told him that if he couldn't hold it for ten minutes he was going to have to pee his pants. I did let him get up when we were taxing," she admitted. "I know what a smooth taxier you are."

Owen put his fingers in his ears and started humming. "I can't hear you," he clowned. They both knew all passengers had to be seated and belted when the airplane was in motion. They both knew he wasn't going to do anything about it. Owen trusted Amy's judgment with the passengers as much as she trusted him with the aircraft.

Last off the airplane were the older couple who had been hassled by Doris at security in Clear River. The woman was walking a little unsteadily. She took Owen's hand in both of hers and shook it once.

"I'm sure you did a fine job," she said, "but that was quite a frighten-ing ride."

When Owen apologized she shook her head no. "It's not your fault I'm sure," she said, "I just wish they would tell you about this sort of thing when you make the reservation."

11

Part of Alpha's plan to keep costs down was to get maximum utilization from their aircraft and personnel. Modeled after Southwest's operational philosophy, the original schedule called for twenty minute turns; scheduled to arrive on the hour, deplane, fuel, board, bags swapped and depart the gate twenty minutes later. It didn't work.

Southwest has made "turning" an aircraft into a science in the same way that McDonalds has made serving a hamburger into a science. Southwest has experienced workers and functional equipment. Alpha had neither. Southwest did all their own underwing servicing; baggage, fuel, catering, pushback crew, all were Southwest employees who were well paid, well trained and highly motivated. Alpha's underwing services were contracted out; different stations, different contractors, no continuity, no control. The scheduled ground times were stretched to thirty minutes. It helped some, but not much.

If an Alpha airplane was still on time by midday it was cause for celebration, by days end it was considered a miracle. Owen had parked at the gate fifteen minutes late, but he instructed Larry to enter fourteen minutes in the aircraft log. Anything less than fifteen minutes was considered an on time arrival by the same government rule maker who provided the flexibility in the definition of the all beef hot dog.

Alpha crews were accustomed to being rushed. As the engines spooled down in Denver they had 15 minutes to deplane the passengers, clean the cabin, board the outbound passengers, close the door and start the pushback. They wouldn't need fuel, and they could only hope that the baggage crew could offload the 60 inbound bags and get the outbound bags stowed and the bin doors closed in time for an on time departure. It was a never ending contest. In this race the biggest hurdle was going to be cleaning the cabin.

As the little old couple disappeared up the jetway, Judy and Cynthia were walking up the isle toward Owen and Amy, each dragging a large garbage bag.

"I've never collected this many sick sacks," Judy proclaimed, if the ride back is going to be as much fun we're going to need more than we have left onboard. Row twenty, seats D, E and F, is a total mess.

Cynthia, who was right behind her, looked like she had lost all enthusiasm for flying. She had been seated on the aft jump seat, between the lavs, with nothing to look at except the backs of heads bent forward in the regurgitate position. "Everyone was ok until this little girl started to throw up, her mother wasn't quick enough with the bag, and it kind of went everywhere. Then the people across the aisle got sick, and it spread like a disease. I came pretty close myself. It smells awful back there."

The gate agent, who was listening to this conversation, said immediately, "We have nothing to clean with except the little mechanical sweeper." He pointed to the alcove in the jetway and handed Owen the outbound dispatch papers, "and we only have 25 passengers checked in." He wanted them gone, never mind if the cabin smelled like the aftermath of a week long frat party.

Amy and Judy had expected this attitude, they had dealt with it before, but Cynthia was still new and she voiced her disgust. "Why don't you go back there and sit in row twenty, or even close to it, for

5 minutes. You'll be puking with the airplane still on the ground. What kind of way is that to treat your passengers?"

The gate agent looked imploringly at Owen, as did the three flight attendants. Cynthia had her hands on her hips and a stubborn look on her face. Owen thought, with some amusement, that 10 minutes before he had the lives of 65 people in his hands and now he was dealing with puke covered seats.

Owen hadn't been in Denver in months and had never met this particular gate agent. He knew it wasn't the young man's fault. All the ground personnel that worked for Alpha could look across the concourse at the competition knowing that a change of uniform would bring a 30% pay raise and the belief that the same job would be considerably easier. Most of the good ones quit Alpha within several months and Owen couldn't blame them. The employee turnover rate company wide had exceeded 50% since they had begun operations.

Every employee, from the CEO down to the lav truck driver had to work harder, do more with less, than their counterparts at the major airlines. They weren't given the tools to do the job properly so they made do until they quit. Some, like Amy and Judy stayed on, enjoying the challenge, making the passengers smile despite the handicaps. Owen wasn't too sure about Cynthia.

"You still carry that roll of duct tape?" Owen asked Amy.

In jest, she had written a request several months ago that would supply every flight attendant with their own roll. It had become the topic of some serious discussion at the weekly management meeting, then discarded as a bad example for the new employees. Owen had thought it a great idea.

"You have to have a sense of humor to work here," he had argued, but had been dismissed by the new CEO, Alpha's third in four years. Later, over cocktails, he had argued with B and some of his coworkers.

"I think we should have our logo changed to a roll of duct tape, blown up real big and put on the tail of our aircraft, let the passenger know what he gets for a $29 ticket." That declaration had come after his third vodka, when his imagination was no longer constrained by corporate convention.

Amy fished around in her oversized sack of a purse and pulled out a roll of red duct tape. "How many passengers did you say?" Owen asked the confused gate agent, "25?" Amy already knew what he was thinking.

"If we figure four per row," she said, "that way no one will have to sit in a middle seat, we'll only need seven rows. I'll go back until it starts to stink then come forward a few rows and block off the airplane from that point back." She looked at her watch. "Give us 5 minutes," she said to the agent, who was starting to get the idea, "then you can start boarding."

"Does this mean I should sit in the back of the airplane by myself?" Cynthia asked. Amy and Judy both stopped and looked at Owen. He knew that either would have taken Cynthia's junior seat at the back if he asked, it was indeed a regulation because of the rear exit door, but he didn't think it was necessary.

"Sit in the row in front of the duct tape," Owen caved like the old man had with Doris in security, but for different reasons. I should know better by now, he chastised himself, seeing Amy's knowing grin. This would haunt him eventually.

He stuck his head in the cockpit doorway. Larry was working on the weight and balance sheet. "Use 15,500 pounds for fuel," he said, glancing at the fuel gauges,"25 passengers and 25 bags, but use the head before they start boarding. Have you got a clearance?"

"Yeah, we're cleared as filed, they're using runway 34 for departure which is supposed to be plowed and sanded full length," he was already getting out of his seat, flashlight in hand. "Did the agent say we had 25 pax and bags?"

"Close enough, a couple one way or another won't matter and this way the weight and balance will be done and we can leave as soon as they finish boarding. Let me borrow that," Owen said, taking Larry's

flashlight, pulling his leather uniform jacket off its hook, and starting for the jetway's outside stairway door, "I'll do the walk around."

It was still snowing hard, the large flakes appearing then vanish-
ing in the lights and shadows of the ramp area. The metal grated jetway stairs were packed with snow, and slippery. Owen had to hold the
hand rail to keep from falling. He didn't have to look at the wings to
know there was no way they would be able to depart without de-icing,
but he did so anyway. He could see some people watching through
the large windows in the gate area as he walked to the leading edge
of the left wing and reaching high, ran his gloved hand along the
frigid aluminum. If they were passengers they might get some comfort from his actions.

He checked the left main gear and tires for inflation, and any
signs of frozen snow or ice on the brakes; the flashlight beam glint-
ing off the shiny metal of the strut. He checked the nose gear as he
went around the nose of the airplane, then the leading edge of the
right wing for confirmation. Pea-sized granules of ice were dotted
everywhere he touched. Working his way around the right wing tip
then back along the trailing edge of the flaps he looked for signs of
mechanical distress and found nothing out of the ordinary. Walking
back toward the tail he squinted upward in the driving snow. The
horizontal stabilizer had a coating of snow on it and when he turned
around and checked the top of the right wing he could see snow gathering there as well. No question, de-icing would be required.

Both cargo doors on the right side of the aircraft were already
closed. The baggage handlers, having completed their task, were
standing under the heat lamps beside the multi-million dollar auto-
mated baggage system that had failed to function from the day it had
been installed. The area it was in now served as storage for ground
vehicles and, when no one was looking, a smoking area. It was in that
direction that Owen headed.

He wasn't supposed to be there. Owen had two photo IDs, one
from Alpha Airlines, one from the Clear River airport authority

hanging around his neck from a braided lanyard and clearly visible outside his jacket. They allowed him access everywhere on the Clear River airport. Every other airport restricted his movements outside the "shadow" of the aircraft unless he was accompanied by someone with a local ID. Another stupid rule.

On a normal day he would get the gate agent to walk with him if there was time, or one of the baggage handlers, but if no one was available he went by himself. He had been questioned only once, by a security guard who looked like he hadn't been born when Owen had started flying, but he had talked his way out of trouble, claiming ignorance of the rule, and promising to never do it again.

If two ten-year background checks made him an acceptable risk in Clear River, why not in Denver, or any other airport for that matter? He did caution the line pilots who asked. If they got caught he wouldn't be able to help them. It may have been a stupid rule to him, but the FAA took it very seriously.

From where he stood Owen could see into the cockpit. He had barely lit up when he saw Larry take his seat and two puffs later the gate agent was standing in the cockpit doorway. It was time to go. The baggage handlers were watching him and when he took one last deep drag and ground the butt into powder with his boot they walked toward him as a group. They did the pushback duties as well as handling the bags and knew if he was returning to the cockpit they would be needed soon.

"In case you haven't heard, they changed the door code," the lead told him.

Owen took out his little red logbook, opening it to the last page where he kept the door codes for all the airports Alpha served. "2115," the lead said, and Owen crossed out the old code and entered the new, thanking the man.

"I feel much safer now," Owen joked, and they both laughed.

The airline was not allowed to publish these codes, which were randomly changed by some mysterious system. The crew members were usually the last to find out, and many times an embarrassed crew member would have to stand outside the door, banging on the glass until he got someone's attention. This was especially embarrassing when the passengers were standing in the jetway waiting to board, the crew member standing sheepishly on the outside, looking in.

But you had to be careful. The FAA used spies, employees who would try to penetrate the airport or airline's security. If they got through unnoticed the airline faced a heavy fine.

"If I thought it had any effect on actual security," Owen would argue with B when she cautioned him to be careful, "I would be an enthusiastic supporter of our government's feeble attempts at making flying safer. The problem is it makes no difference whatsoever. If the bad guys want to get into an airport they'll get in." He would brandish his security badge like a weapon. "How hard do you think it would be to get one of these, as if you would even need one. There's twenty miles of chain link fence securing this airport and you could cut through it with $5 shears from True Value. These rules are created by small minds, with a little authority, who have to make a lot of noise or they'll lose their jobs."

"Live with it, Babe," she said. Even B got tired of listening to him complain.

When Owen got to the top of the jetway stairs the agent was waiting. "Are you ready?" Owen asked, knowing the answer by the anxious look on the young man's face. "What time do you need?"

"Quarter after," the agent said hopefully.

Owen's watch showed nineteen past. "Quarter after it is," he said stepping onto the aircraft and peeling off his jacket. "You have everything you need?" he asked Amy as he slid into his seat.

"Now that you're here I do. We made sure every seat back pocket had a sick sack," she advised him. "Is if going to be as rough getting out of here as it was getting in?"

Owen shook his head no. "If they don't stop our climb we'll be in smooth air ten minutes after we take off. Stay seated until I tell you to get up. I'll make an announcement and explain it to the passengers."

Owen started checking the switch positions on the overhead panel as Amy closed the cockpit door. The seat belt switch was on.

"Did you turn this on?" he asked Larry.

"I did," he admitted, "I did the whole before starting engines checklist," said somewhat tentatively, "is that ok?"

"Absolutely, excellent work" Owen smiled at him. He noticed that Larry had set up his instruments for the "Plains" standard instrument departure. Larry was a fast learner.

"Call for push back clearance and let's go to Clear River, have a drink or two."

Owen heard the lead's voice over his speaker. "Ground crew is ready for pushback."

Larry called ramp control, who cleared them for pushback and asked if they would need de-icing. Owen nodded affirmation and while Larry communicated their intentions to the ramp control, Owen talked to the tug driver on the inter-phone. "Brakes released, you're cleared to push, tail east, I think we'll hold off starting the engines until pushback is complete."

"Good idea," the tug driver agreed, "the ramp is pretty slippery."

It was a big tug, probably big enough to push a 757, but there was no sense taking a chance. Even with the aircraft's engines at idle, when the tug began to turn on the snow-covered ramp they could end up jackknifed like a tractor trailer, do some damage to the nose gear or snap the tow bar.

When the pushback was complete Owen set the brakes and on command from the ground crew started both engines. Ramp control told them to taxi to the west end of taxiway Charlie North and call de-icing control on 127.5.

Denver had a slick de-icing system. As they taxied, a small pickup truck with a red rotating beacon on the roof of its cab came into view. as soon as Larry tuned the radio to the frequency for de-icing they were told to follow the truck to pad J, spot five.

It was a good thing they had the truck to follow. Pad J's location was indicated on the airport diagram in the charts folder. Pad J was also covered with enough snow to obliterate the markings on the pavement. They followed the truck, although it looked like they were being led onto the plains themselves with no lights or tire tracks to indicate anyone else had passed this way. When the truck made a 90 degree turn Owen did the same, taxiing carefully, and spotted a ground crewman, lighted wands raised, waving him forward. As their aircraft approached its spot Owen slowed in concert with the wands being raised in an arc above the crewman's head and set the brakes when they crossed in an X, engines shutdown in response to a throat slashing motion from the crewman. Every motion crisp, professional. In the sudden silence Owen and Larry prepared the aircraft for de-icing.

"Air conditioning packs off," Owen requested, to keep the odor to a minimum. Larry ran the stabilizer trim full forward. "You did read the winter ops manual," Owen complimented.

The ground crewman's voice came over the inter-phone. "Good evening," he began, his voice muffled by the full face ski mask he was wearing. "We have two choices for your de-icing pleasure. First we have type two, cut 50% with boiling water, but still very effective for snow removal, or, if you have your gold Master Card with you we can offer type four, undiluted, the finest ice protection money can buy."

Owen loved the unexpected humor. He knew that lots of airline Captains would find the humor inappropriate, maybe even disrespectful. He could name several Alpha Captains who would write a report, want the poor kid disciplined, maybe even fired. Taking off in a blizzard was no laughing matter.

Owen was reminded of an old Captain he had flown with long ago. They were caught unexpectedly in a thunderstorm, the turbulence violent, the lightning close enough to reach out and grab, and Owen, young and inexperienced, was worried. The Captain had flown fighters in WWII, been shot up, and shot down, bailed out over the English channel and rescued by a submarine. "If you're not being shot at and hit, it's just flying," he'd said, sitting sideways in his seat, legs crossed, smoking a cigarette and watching Owen struggle with the airplane.

Owen looked out his side window. The kid had moved away from the nose of the airplane and was looking up at him. He was wearing an industrial strength snowmobile suit, complete with hood, gloves and goggles. He had every right to be cranky, spending his shift perched in the bucket of the spray truck in the middle of a blizzard, getting the occasional face-full of hot glycol when the wind gusted. They exchanged waves.

"Gold card," Owen laughed, "you see the name on the side of this airplane? You'll be lucky to see any money. Besides, our passengers don't pay enough to deserve type four, it's type two for them."

"Type two it is then Captain," the kid laughing along with him, happy to find another soul with a sense of humor on this miserable night. "I'll report the start and stop times when we've finished." He disconnected the headset and climbed into his bucket.

Owen made his announcement:

"Good evening ladies and gentlemen, this is Captain Swift and I would like to welcome you on board. We have shut down both engines because we're about to have the aircraft sprayed with glycol, a hot mixture, orange in color, that you will see the trucks dispensing in just a minute. This will take all the snow off the airplane, and keep it off long enough for us to get airborne. There will be a bit of odor, kinda like anti-freeze, and it will last until we've been flying for a few minutes. The first portion of our trip this evening, 10 or 15 minutes, is going to be a little bumpy and I've asked the flight attendants to remain seated until we climb above the rough air. The remainder of the flight should be smooth and fairly quick with a 60 knot tailwind; a little less than an hour and twenty minutes takeoff to touchdown in Clear River. Weather report shows cloudy skies, some light rain, a temperature of 38 degrees and a wind from the south at 5 miles an hour. We appreciate you coming with us this evening and will do everything we can to keep your flight safe, smooth and as close to on time as possible."

Larry had his manual open to the de-icing holdover charts and he asked a question: "Why are we using type two instead of type four? Is it really because type four is more expensive?"

"If you look at the chart you'll see that for the current tempera-ture, type two allows a 20 minute gap between the beginning of de-icing and take off. Type four allows 40 minutes and though it isn't shown on that chart it would cost about 200 dollars more. Look out the window. Nobody else out here. If I thought we would need the extra 20 minutes to get off the ground I'd spend the money, but we shouldn't, so I won't.

"Bear in mind that all these charts and holdover times are based on what the FAA calls the clean aircraft concept. Basically, you can't take off with any snow on the airplane. None. They don't tell you how to accomplish that, it's up to the airline to establish a procedure and put it the ops manual. This all came about 20 years ago when Air Florida crashed into a bridge in Washington DC trying to take off in a snowstorm.

"The pilots did a number of things wrong. They got de-iced, but then had to wait in line for an hour before they got cleared for takeoff. Some witnesses, other pilots, said they saw a large amount of snow on the wings just before they began the takeoff. Many thought they should have gone back to the gate and gotten de-iced again, and maybe they're right, but that wasn't the real killer of a mistake."

Owen reached up and pointed to two switches on the overhead panel.

"Engine heat," Larry identified them unhesitatingly.

"Right," Owen confirmed somewhat grimly. He had been Washington based when that crash occurred, had watched with fasci-nated horror the TV images of the aftermath. "Engine heat. Do you know what happens to a jet engine if you don't turn on the engine heat when it's flying through freezing precipitation?"

"Ice will form on the cowling and inlet guide vanes, disrupting air flow and causing compressor stalls," sure his answer was correct and proud of it.

"Excellent," Owen responded, although the answer sounded like it had been read from a text and not something Larry had given much thought to, "but that's the second thing that happens, what's the first?"

When Larry was silent Owen tried to work him through the problem: "The little hole in the engine inlet bullet is for what?"

"The air inlet for the PT2 probe," Larry had it now. "The bullet is heated so the inlet hole doesn't get iced over and mess up the EPR gauge (engine pressure ratio, a measure of thrust being produced).

"What happens if it does get blocked?"

Larry held up one hand, asking for more time to think it through. He knew this answer and stared at the two EPR gauges at the top of the instrument stack as if the answer was looking back at him. Both needles were pointing at the number one. "One EPR," he said, "the engines aren't running, so the inlet and outlet pressures are the same. At takeoff the EPR will read two point something, the number you get from the takeoff EPR chart." He looked at the chart, still thinking. Owen sat silently.

"If you blocked the inlet probe at takeoff, but the engine was running normally, the EPR system would think the engine was being more efficient, less inlet pressure than normal with the same outlet pressure. The gauge would read higher."

"Wow," Owen said, "very impressive, and if the gauge was reading high, where would the throttles be?"

"You wouldn't push them up far enough, you wouldn't have take off power set."

"Exactly, and that's what happened to Air Florida. They tried to take off using considerably less than takeoff power. At almost any point in the takeoff, right up until they hit the bridge, if they had fire-walled the throttles for maximum power they would have had a good chance of preventing the crash. In my opinion the snow on the wing had very little, if anything, to do with the crash. It was dry snow, the kind that blows off your car at fifty miles an hour. That crash was the beginning of the clean aircraft concept even though not turning on the engine heat was the real culprit.

"Rules like that, based on false theories, are what annoy me the most. A flight crew has to worry as much about legality now as they do safety. Penna, the guy who got this airport built with huge cost overruns was appointed head of the DOT by Clinton for his obvious qualities as a government official. He wanted to make crashing illegal, make it a felony, put the pilots in jail, if they survived. What an asshole." Owen shook his head ruefully. "Sometimes I'm glad that I only have six years to go before the age sixty mandatory retirement rule will force me to quit flying."

"Mon capitan," it was the de-icing lead on the inter-phone, "you're aircraft has been de-iced with type two fluid at a ratio of 50-50, start time 2040, finished at 2050, not a snowflake to be found anywhere, initials tango bravo, you gentleman have a safe flight home and come back when you can spend more time."

"Thanks for the help," Owen answered, "stay warm and dry."

"Warm and dry, what a concept, maybe I should be an airline pilot. You're cleared to start engines one and two, signalman will wave you out. Take care."

When they were taxiing toward runway 34, the aircraft configured for takeoff, Owen asked; "it's your turn, are you ready?"

"I'm not too sure about this," Larry answered nervously, "maybe you should make the takeoff. It's still snowing pretty hard."

"It's not like being shot at and hit, it's just flying," Owen joked, trying to ease Larry's fears. "The visibility is up to a mile, they're calling the ceiling 500 overcast, the wind has died considerably and I'm sitting right here. If we have a problem during the takeoff roll and I decide to reject the takeoff I'll announce REJECT, loud and clear. You take your hands off the controls and I'll stop the airplane. If you start to scare me too badly I'll say 'MY AIRPLANE'. Simple as that. I'm sure you'll do fine. You just need to relax a little."

In position on the runway and cleared for takeoff Larry pushed the throttles forward jerkily, apologized, then got them close to the takeoff setting before Owen said "I've got the throttles," per standard operating procedure. Larry concentrated on keeping them going straight down the runway centerline.

Owen's right hand was on the throttles, left hand resting on his left knee and inches from the yoke, toes resting lightly on the pedals which controlled not only the rudder but the nose wheel steering. He could feel Larry over reacting to the aircraft's side to side motion.

"Less rudder movement," he commanded, "don't step on the pedals so much as pressure them in the right direction. Don't fight the airplane, work with it."

As their speed increased Larry's little jabs at the pedals had Owen envisioning their passengers heads snapping back and forth in time to Larry's motions on the rudder. Owen increased the pressure of his toes on the pedals and commanded "Leave your feet on the pedals but don't push. Just feel what I do."

The side-to-side jerks stopped. "Pressure to zero the unwanted motion, then pressure in the right direction, then neutralize," Owen's voice calm, soothing, his eyes shifting constantly: engine instruments, runway, airspeed, tracking their continued acceleration.

"One hundred knots," Owen called, lightening his pressure on the pedals, once again letting Larry control their direction. "Much better with the rudder, much better."

"V1," Owen called, and then a moment later "Rotate."

Larry was far too engrossed to notice Owen's left hand move forward, the fingers curled lightly around the yoke, just in case. A moment later they were airborne and Larry started abusing the yoke the way he had the rudder pedals. The air was still quite turbulent near the surface and his overreaction to the bumps was doubling the effect they had on the airplane.

"Easy, easy," Owen soothing, "positive rate?" He waited for Larry's response but didn't demand it and answered his own question. "Gear up."

Owen let Larry flail a while longer while he called departure control who gave them a right turn to 090 to intercept the Plains Standard Instrument Departure. At a 1,000 feet he called for, then set climb thrust, knowing that Larry would not have noticed, and accomplished the after takeoff checklist. Then he went back to work on his student.

"Take your hands off the yoke." Larry did as commanded and started to apologize, "and stop apologizing."

"I can't," Larry pressed ahead, "I can't stand that I'm having so much trouble flying this thing. I always thought of myself as a good pilot, a smooth pilot, but I get in this seat and it's like I've never flown before."

"Nothing wrong with a little humility. Just don't overdo it."

Larry had his hands in his lap.

"Put your right hand on the yoke lightly, fingertips only, and feel what I'm doing." Larry did as requested.

The cockpit was illuminated by the eerie white glow of the instruments, outside only the rhythmic red burst of the two anti-collision lights could be seen, reflecting off and softened by the clouds surrounding them. The right wing started to drop and Owen let it go until it was down 10 degrees. He turned the yoke a few degrees to the left and held it there.

"Now watch," he instructed, and as the wing started to rise he held the pressure on the yoke until the wing was level then neutralized it. "See how long that takes? This is a much larger and more sluggish airplane than you are used to. It takes anticipation and patience to be successful. First thing I noticed is that you're moving your hands faster than your eyes. When you haven't flown instruments in a while that's a natural occurrence. Same thing happens if you use the autopilot all the time. Don't let your eyes linger on one instrument, keep them moving. You have to wait for this airplane to react to your inputs. Put some pressure on a control and wait for a reaction before you relax that pressure, and for fucks sake, try to relax. This is not that hard. You have to believe you can be successful or you never will be. If you're trying, if you're working at it, every check airman at Alpha will help you. Now put your hand on the yoke but don't squeeze so hard. Pretend it's your dick. Well, maybe not."

Larry was flying more smoothly and still smiling when the surrounding clouds began to lighten. Moments later they burst out of the cloud tops into a brilliantly moonlit night, the serenity in stark contrast to the turbulence below.

The seat belt sign had been off for about 20 minutes when there was a soft knock on the cockpit door. Cynthia stepped in and closed the door behind her.

"We've already finished in the back. Amy said I could come up here for a while if it was alright with you."

"Of course," Owen responded quickly, moving his seat forward. "There's a jump seat right behind me."

Cynthia squeezed into the space Owen had indicated. Instead of sitting she stood behind him, her hands on the seat back, fingers grazing his shoulders. She had to duck her head down to get a view out of the front windows which placed her lips next to his ear. He could feel the sweet warmth of her breath when she spoke.

"Wow," she said, with a hint of cinnamon, "how beautiful."

Owen nodded his agreement. He was still watching Larry's actions, but not with total attention. Their distance from the ground and the visible horizon allowed his mind to focus on issues other than whether they were right side up. Like, what was he doing with this girl? Their only night together had been entirely physical and had come as a complete surprise to him. He still wasn't sure how she had ended up in his apartment, his bed. He was accustomed to being in charge, in command, but with Cynthia that just wasn't the case. She had her own agenda and for the moment it included him. What could be bad about that?

12

C ynthia had dropped her hands from the seat back to his shoulders and was rubbing them gently. He leaned forward to give her better access while keeping one eye and a small portion of his attention on Larry's efforts with the airplane.

Cynthia had grown up in rural Missouri and come to Clear River to attend the state university. "You would have had a good farmer's daughter story, except my father owns three car dealerships." She had graduated a year ago with a degree in marketing. Her parents wanted her to return home, learn the car business, but she wasn't ready yet, maybe never.

"There is just so much more happening here," she said, "not just the social life, although that is certainly a part of it, but art and music and the museum, there's always something to do."

She had gone home after graduation but returned a week later. "It was great to see my high school friends, but I had drifted away from most of them. They were engaged, or about to be, ready to settle down, have a family, stay put. I'm just not ready for all that."

Two college girlfriends had called to tell her they were getting an apartment in Clear River for the summer and did she want to join them. "It was hard telling my folks but I think they understood. I still call them every couple of weeks and they came to visit last summer.

My mother loved it. I think she would move here in an instant. Maybe I could get her a job as a flight attendant." She laughed at the thought. "You would like her," Cynthia insisted.

"I'm sure I would, but she's probably too young for me."

They both laughed at that. Larry joined in the laughter although Owen doubted he knew what they were discussing. They had reached their assigned cruising altitude of flight level 330 and Larry, heeding Owen's caution about too much usage of the autopilot was still hand-flying the aircraft. The altimeter was drifting, up a 100 feet then down a 100 feet as he struggled to keep it pegged at exactly 330.

Cynthia began working her thumbs on either side of Owen's spine, more of an actual massage then a rub, and he was enjoying the sensations enormously.

"You are very tense here," she commented.

"That's probably from watching me trying to maintain altitude," Larry said.

"You're over controlling," Owen counseled, "remember what I told you about reversing a trend. Stop the negative trend first, then put in just enough pressure on the yoke to start a trend in the positive direction. Let me show you."

He sat up somewhat reluctantly, Cynthia moving her hands from his back to his shoulders where she left them.

"Leave your hand on the yoke and feel what I'm doing," Owen instructed.

The airplane had been a 100 feet low and Larry's pull on the yoke had started them in a 500 foot a minute climb. Way too much. Using just his thumbs, Owen pressed lightly on the yoke to slow their ascent, 400, 300, 200 feet per minute, and as the hundreds needle reached the top of the altimeter, an almost imperceptible forward pressure stopped them precisely at 33,000. The needle appeared frozen.

"Now it seems as though our vertical speed trend is zero," Owen continued the lesson, "but it's probably because we have vertical speed indicators instead of instantaneous vertical speed indicators like you would get in a new Cessna. As soon as the fat man in row ten, decides to come forward to use the lav, the nose will drop and we'll start down. The VSI will give the first indication. When it registers a climb or descent, check the altimeter to confirm, then apply pressure in the opposite direction, enough to stop the vertical trend. When the VSI registers zero, a tiny bit more pressure will head you back toward perfectly level. Repeat as necessary. You have the controls."

Larry improved quickly, the plus and minus deviation down to less than 50 feet with the needle occasionally stuck right on the mark. After several minutes of this performance Owen suggested he turn on the Autopilot. "Don't want to tire you out before we get to Clear River," Owen said, knowing how much concentration it was taking.

A few minutes later ATC called them: "Alpha 300, descend to and maintain flight level 290 for traffic, I need you level in 5 minutes."

Owen read back the clearance and stopped Larry as he reached for the Autopilot Controller. "I know you can do this with the autopilot on, why don't we let Cynthia try her hand?"

Larry sat back somewhat unwillingly. "Just for a couple of minutes," Owen appeased. He sat up, forcing Cynthia's hands back to the top of his shoulders, but she remained otherwise motionless.

"I've never flown an airplane, much less a 737."

"I'll show you how," Owen coaxed, "reach up here with your right hand and turn off the Altitude Hold." He pointed to the knob.

"Just turn it to the center?"

"Straight up, but don't dally, we've got 4,000 feet to lose." Owen had punched the start function on the clock when they had received the clearance. "In 4 minutes and 40 seconds or were liable to have a collision." Teasing her. He knew that he could lose 4,000 feet in less than a minute if it became necessary. Cynthia did as instructed, placing the knob straight up and down, and pulling her hand back with a jerk when it clicked into position.

"Excellent," Owen complimented, "now lean over my shoulder, put your right hand on the yoke, and press forward gently."

"My whole hand or just the thumb?" she said, having paid attention to the previous instructions, taking this very seriously.

"If you have enough strength left in your thumb after all that massaging, the thumb will do fine."

Steadying herself with her left hand on his shoulder, Cynthia put her right thumb on the control wheel and pressed. "Nothing's happening," she said, "the VSI's still at zero." She had been paying attention.

"Press a little harder, but gently, we don't want the fat man peeing on his shoe."

She tried again, watching the VSI. They started to descend, although barely. "Is that enough?" She answered her own question. "No, it can't be. If we have to lose 4,000 feet in 4 minutes we have to descend at 1,000 feet a minute."

Owen smiled at the comment. "You could be a math teacher," he said watching as she continued to press on the yoke until they were descending at 1,000 feet per minute. She took her hand away from the wheel. The rate of descent continued to increase.

"Oh shit," she said, puzzled. "Why's it doing that?"

Larry had been watching with some concern, afraid that he was going to be outperformed by a flight attendant who had never flown an airplane.

"It's ok," Owen soothed, "2,000 feet per minute is ok, but we have another issue," pointing at the airspeed indicator which had climbed from their 290 knot indicated cruise speed toward the redline of 340. "If you don't slow this baby down you'll burn the wings off."

"What do I do, what do I do," laughing excitedly, "tell me what to do." She had them all laughing now. The over speed warning began its machine gun staccato. "Shit, shit," Cynthia swore, "tell me what to do."

"Put your hand on the throttles and pull them slowly toward you," Owen said, pointing again, "more, more, good."

"That thing's still making noise," Cynthia pointed out.

"It'll stop." And it did. "Now, hand back on the wheel, and pull back gently, watching the VSI, looking for 500 feet a minute, 1,000 feet to go." Cynthia, serious now, giddiness gone, got back to business.

"Back to the throttles. Push them up, slowly, hold that, now hand back on the wheel, a little back pressure, see if you can stop us right on the mark." And she did. "Now throttles again, you want 3,000 pounds of fuel flow each side," pointing again, "and Altitude-Hold on." Cynthia remembered the location and reached for the knob before Owen pointed. She rotated it to alt hold and stood up.

"You've got the airplane," Cynthia said to Larry, a wide smile on her face. "Thank you, thank you," she said, "that was terrific." She bent to give Owen a kiss on the cheek then on impulse planted one on Larry's cheek as well.

"Wait till I tell..."

"That's not a story too many people should hear about," Owen interrupted, "it's not exactly legal."

"Oh, of course," she made a zipping motion across her lips, "not a soul. I better get back in the cabin before Amy comes looking. How long before we land?"... that last said almost as an afterthought.

It wouldn't matter whether she bragged or not, Amy would figure it out. Owen had let her do the same thing a number of times. "20 minutes." Owen said, "we're 100 miles out, and tell Amy we need a list of the seat cushions that are unusable and anything else she wants fixed."

When Cynthia opened the cockpit door to leave, Amy stepped in behind her. She handed a cocktail napkin to Owen. "You rang?" Looking suspiciously at both pilots. "Awful lot of smiling going on up here."

"You know my code," Owen said. "Have fun, make money."

She gave him an appraising look. "Indeed, I know your code all right. There's your logbook entry. Three seat cushions at least, if they have six that would be better, and somebody with a fire hose and some disinfectant. Last call. You boys want anything before I close the bar?"

A moment later she returned with the requested beverages; black coffee for Larry and a hot tea for Owen. "See you at the gate in Clear River," closing and locking the door as she left.

"Can I ask you a question," Larry began, then continued when Owen nodded. "Don't you worry about all these rules you break? I mean, the shoulder harness is one thing, but letting the flight attendants manipulate the controls? Aren't you worried someone will find out?"

"Is there a rule that flight attendants can't manipulate the controls?" Owen said in mock astonishment, "I guess I should reread that section."

Larry wasn't smiling. "You thinking of turning me in?" Owen's tone was light.

"No, of course not," he blurted embarrassedly.

"And neither is Cynthia or Amy or Judy, or anybody else that I know of. I'm banking on the theory that the people who say they like me actually do, and that the rules I break are of little consequence."

Larry shrugged his ok, but thought to himself that's a bit naive in this day and age. There were probably a lot of people who would like to be Chief Pilot.

Owen looked at Amy's neatly inked message on the napkin. Three seat cushions needed at row twenty, D, E, F, a bunch of reading lights out, the outboard coffee maker wouldn't perk, and the toilet seat in the aft left lav had fallen off. He entered the items in the logbook, thought about putting in the autopilot approach coupler and decided to wait. He'd have Larry try it on the approach into Clear River. If it had the same problems he would write it up when they got to the gate. He called Alpha dispatch on the number three radio, told them they would be at the gate in 20 minutes, then detailed Amy's requests for the cabin, including the fire hose.

"Roger 300, copy that, I'll let maintenance know, see you at gate 32 in 20 minutes. Are there any serious maintenance issues? We already have two aircraft down for maintenance and it looks like we're going to use your aircraft for the LA flight. They want to turn the aircraft as fast as possible."

Owen sighed. How could you run an airline if the airplanes kept breaking? It was frustrating for everyone. Maintenance wanted to fix things but there was never enough time, never the right parts available. Owen knew that most of the Captains would carry a broken airplane through several stops to get it back to Clear River where access to Alpha maintenance would mean lower cost and less time wasted waiting for a contract mechanic.

They would call maintenance on their cell phones, keeping the discussion off the radio waves and private, before they left on the last leg of a sequence into Clear River. They'd warn of the problem they were bringing in, only to have System Control request the airplane for a different flight that required a quick turn with no time to fix anything. System Control knew of the problems but they had little choice. They had to move the passengers.

Items that were not critical to the safety of flight suffered the greatest neglect. The inop coffee maker, toilet seat and reading lights would be entered in the continued items section at the back of the aircraft's logbook and languish there until a major bit broke, grounding the airplane. In the meantime coffee service would be slow, one of the three available lavs blocked off, and sleeping suggested instead of reading for the passengers with no lights.

The more experienced flight attendants would come up with imaginative solutions. Since the hot pad worked on the inop coffee maker they would keep a pot warm there while making a second on the working coffee maker, move the sleepers and readers around until the working reading lights were properly distributed, and the seatless lav, by virtue of a handwritten sign on its door, would become the men's number-one-only bathroom. Everyone coped with the mechanical irregularities that were the norm, rather than the exception.

"Alpha 300 you're cleared to flight level 240, pilot's discretion."

Larry looked at Owen, "Should we start down now?" he asked.

"Hang on just a second, let me get the ATIS." They both listened.

Clear River was reporting the ceiling as 400 feet overcast, visibility 1 mile in fog, with a temperature/dew point spread of only two degrees and calm winds, landing south on runways 19 Left and Right.

Bit of a worry, Owen thought. The forecast had predicted this wouldn't happen before midnight. A two degree or less temperature/dew-point spread and no wind? The 1 mile visibility wouldn't last long but the lowest forecast visibility was 1/2 mile. Shouldn't be a problem.

"Let me walk you through how I would plan this," Owen said. "We're 90 miles from the airport. Remember the ideal is to put the throttles at idle and leave them there until you need power to begin the approach. You want to stay as high as you can for as long as you can because the engines burn less fuel at higher altitudes. There are two possible landing runways, but we won't know which one we'll get until they change us to Approach control. To be conservative we'll plan on 19 Right since it's the closer of the two and the one we want because it's a shorter taxi to the gate. Approach control won't let us go below 11,000 feet until they turn us down wind, which will be about 10 miles west of the airport, 83 miles from our present position. We have about a 60 knot tailwind, figure a ground speed of 8 miles a minute, that will decrease as we descend but using 8 will give us a cushion. With the throttles in idle, the rate of descent will average 3,000 feet per minute at 320 knots, we have 18,000 feet to lose, when do we start down?"

Larry looked stunned. "You figure this all out each time you make a descent? It sounds like the three to one rule would be a lot easier."

Owen shrugged. "The easiest is not necessarily the best. Look, this isn't calculus, it's arithmetic. We have to lose 18,000 feet. At 3,000 feet per minute that's 6 minutes. With a ground speed of 8 miles a minute that's 48 miles. We want to be at 11,000 feet 10 west of the airport, add 5 miles to slow to 210 knots that's 63 miles which should be your descent point. Yes?"

"I guess," was all Larry could manage.

Owen relented. "Remember what I said before. The three to one rule works unless there is a strong wind. Of course, since we want

19 Right we'll get 19 Left, or approach will delay our descent for outbound traffic, which will create a whole new set of figures."

Approach control, when they were told to contact them did both, stopping them at 18,000 feet for crossing traffic and assigning runway 19 Left for landing. Owen put in a request for the right side but was told they would get on the ground faster on the left. "We've got three inbounds from the northwest, expect 19 Left."

"How are we doing on our descent?" Owen asked.

"We're 10 miles southwest of the airport and out of 13,000 for 11,000, so we should be alright."

"Fine," quietly patient, "what about the speed?"

"Well, we can do 320 knots till 10,000 feet; then I was going to slow to 250?"

Owen acknowledged the indecision. "That would be perfectly legal but we'd be in Iowa before we slowed enough to go below ten. At 320 knots indicated we're crossing the ground at nearly 6 miles a minute. Bring the throttles to idle now and stop the descent," he instructed. Larry brought the throttles to idle and gently raised the nose to stop the descent. The airplane slowed rapidly.

"Excellent," Owen complimented, although he could tell that Larry hadn't digested the lump of information he had just been fed. He was still at the stage where he could fly or think, but not both. Owen made a mental note to explain it when they got on the ground.

Owen glanced out the window. There were some sights in aviation he never tired of. They were skimming just above an overcast which stretched to the horizon in every direction. The moonlight had created a luminescent plain two miles above the invisible dark and rain soaked prairie below. Cloud tendrils, indistinct in the distance, flashed into focus then past in a blink, certifying their speed.

"Beautiful," Owen said softly, "this is certainly a privileged view. Take a look," he urged.

Larry broke his fixation on the instruments for a moment, glanced up, then went immediately back to the instruments.

"No, come on, look out the window," Owen urged but Larry remained locked in concentration. "Ok, I've got the airplane," Owen commanded, "release that death grip you've got on the yoke."

Larry glanced at him worriedly. "Relax," Owen said quietly, "you're doing fine, but you're way to tense. Let go of the wheel, I've got the controls," though his hands remained where they were, resting with fingers interlaced in his lap.

Larry relented. He took his hands off the wheel and placed them on the armrests. He took a deep breath and looked out. "You're right, it is beautiful," but his eyes were already back staring at the instruments.

"Larry, Larry, Larry." Owen said in mock frustration. "Look, the Autopilot is on. Now, I'll grant you it's not much of an Autopilot, state of the art fifties technology I'll agree, but it's holding the heading and pitch you left it with. I wouldn't recommend a nap at this point but there is certainly time to look out the window, relax for a few seconds and enjoy the view."

Larry looked at Owen who was more draped over his seat than sitting in it. "I don't think I can be that relaxed," he said.

"I have a few more hours of practice than you. Now, one more time." He curled his fingertips behind the control wheel and with a touch so light it was imperceptible raised the nose. The airspeed continued to drop until it was indicating 210 knots. With his thumbs, Owen applied forward pressure until the VSI indicated 1,500 feet per minute down. Owen let go of the wheel. "It's right here," he said, rubbing thumb and forefinger together gently, "right here. You've got the aircraft." They were descending through 11,500 feet when they crossed overhead the airport hidden from view by the cloud deck.

"Alpha 300, descend to and maintain 6,000 feet," approach instructed.

"Don't you ever get tired of being right?" Larry asked.

"Nope," Owen replied simply, watching as they slipped below the surface of their clouded sea. Then he continued the flying lesson.

"At 210 knots we'll descend at about 1,500 feet a minute. What part of the equation is missing?"

Larry had heard this question before. "How long a final is approach control going to give us?"

"Excellent," Owen said and called Approach. "How long a final can Alpha 300 expect this evening?"

"Alpha 300, you are currently number 2 on approach for the left side, looks like about a 10 mile turn to final."

Owen looked at Larry and waited silently.

"Well," Larry said, stalling to give himself more time to calculate, "10 miles out, 10 miles back so 20 miles plus 3 miles for the turn...23 miles, about 7 minutes. We should be in the ballpark."

Owen was impressed. "There's hope for you," he said, "very impressive."

"Alpha 300 turn left to 280, maintain 180 knots and descend to 4,000 feet."

"Flaps 5," Larry requested, raising the nose to reduce their speed and beginning the left turn.

Owen set 4,000 feet in the altitude alerter and with his left hand grasped the handle at the top of the Captain's forward window. With his right hand he released the fore and aft seat lock and slid the seat to his preferred landing position. Heels resting on the floor, toes lightly on the rudder pedals, he checked his eye height by glancing at the top of the glare shield then at the top of the instrument panel. Both were visible, although nothing outside the window was. They had descended through a mile of dense grey cloud and even the windshield wiper was hidden from view. "Visibility is less than two inches," he said.

"What," exclaimed a startled Larry, "I thought you said it was 1 mile."

"Joking, Larry, I'm only joking," Owen laughed, wondering how he was ever going to get this kid to ease up a little.

"Alpha 300, turn left to a heading of 230, on that heading you are cleared to intercept the 19 Left localizer, upon interception you are cleared for the 19 Left ILS approach."

Owen read back the clearance and watched as Larry began the left turn. "More bank," he instructed. "If we fly through this localizer we'll be into the approach path of the parallel runway with a collision a distinct possibility, or worse, an FAA violation. Then you'd never get that job with a major." Larry didn't laugh, but he did increase the bank angle which tightened the turn.

Ever more attentive, Owen watched as Larry switched the Autopilot and his Flight Director to VOR/LOC arming it to intercept the ILS localizer. Owen had already switched his over. "Localizer's alive," Larry called and moments later, "the Autopilot's not capturing, shouldn't we be capturing?"

"It's doing the same thing it did in Denver. Turn left now," Owen instructed, "start a turn to a heading of 190 degrees." The localizer bar was nearly centered and drifting left, indicating they were almost in the middle of the approach course but sliding through it to the right. "Turn the Autopilot to manual then back to auto, let's see if that will work."

Larry rotated the Autopilot mode selector to manual, waited for a few seconds, then placed it back to auto. The mode annunciator went from amber to green instantly. The control wheel gave a little shudder then jerked left, rolling them into a 20 degree bank before it sensed the error of its ways and started back to the right, leveling the wings on a 190 degree heading. The localizer course bar was dead center.

"I flew for a major carrier for more than 20 years," Owen said, "and mechanical failure was almost nonexistent. Never realized how good we had it."

Larry took his hand off the yoke, shaking the tension out. "Don't leave that disconnect button for long," Owen cautioned, "who knows what this thing will think up next."

The glide slope pointer wriggled once then bounced off the top of the scale. "Glide slope's alive," Owen called, then, when the indicator showed one dot above intercept Larry called, "Gear down, flaps 15." Owen eased the flap handle from 5 to 15 slowly, allowing the Autopilot to trim the stabilizer so the airplane wouldn't balloon upward. He placed the gear handle down, hearing the thunk as the nose-gear-up lock released, watching as the three gear lights went to red, then green. He gave Larry a few beats before inquiring; "gear down, flaps 15 and...?

"Oh, sorry, landing check."

"Get in the habit of saying it as one word; gear down, flaps 15, landing check," Owen said, always instructing.

"Flaps 25," Larry called.

Owen left the handle where it was. "I know they teach it that way in the simulator, but the simulator burns pretend fuel. Approach hasn't asked us to slow down yet so let's leave the flaps at 15 a little longer. When you get glide slope intercept, I should say IF you get glide slope intercept, set the throttles at about 60%. That should keep us at 180 knots down the glide slope. We'll get to the runway quicker this way and burn less fuel." He picked up the PA mike. "Ladies and gentleman, we are on our approach for the landing in Clear River. I would ask the flight attendants, please, to be seated."

They were 10 miles from the airport, 3,000 feet above the invisible farmland sliding silently beneath them. The airspeed was 180 knots and steady, approaching the glide slope from below. Owen nodded to himself; kid's doing a nice job, although he's only monitoring the autopilot. So far, so good. He flipped a switch by his left knee and a small spot light above his head came on, illuminating the check list he had placed in the clip on his control yoke. He began to read: "flight attendants have been notified, start switches are on, speed brake is armed, gear..."

Approach called: "Alpha 300, 6 miles in trail with a Delta 727, contact the tower on 128.2."

"Alpha 300 switching," Owen responded, tuning the new frequency while he continued with the check list. "Gear is down with three green lights...?" Waiting for Larry's response. It was mandatory that both pilots see and announce the three green lights.

"Flaps 25," Larry requested, oblivious to Owen's question, all his concentration focused on watching the Autopilot shoot the approach.

"It's still a little early for that," Owen said, "We're still 9 miles from the airport. You see three green lights?"

"Three greens," Larry responded, looking quickly at the gear lights then back to his instrument scan.

As the glide slope pointer centered on its scale, both flight mode annunciators clicked from amber to green. The Autopilot had captured the glide slope and they began to descend with it. Larry set the throttles to 60%. The airspeed stayed pinned at 180 knots.

Owen called the tower, "Evening Clear River tower, Alpha 300 on a 6 mile final for runway 19 Left."

"Good evening Alpha 300, you are cleared to land on 19 Left, wind is calm, ceiling was reported as 300 overcast by the preceding Delta 727, RVR (runway visual range) is 4,000 feet in fog and dropping.

"Copy the weather and understand Alpha 300 is cleared to land on 19 left,"

Both pilots watched in silence as the Autopilot continued to track the ILS flawlessly. There was no sensation of motion, only the DME (distance measuring equipment) counter showed their progress, 1 mile every 20 seconds. At 5 miles Larry called for flaps 25, and moments later flaps 30. This time Owen complied without comment, easing the handle to its landing setting which allowed the Autopilot to trim to the slower speed at a measured pace. Larry increased the power without any coaching from Owen, 70% and 135 knots occurring simultaneously with the blue lights blinking their pronouncement from both instrument panels, indicating passage of the Outer Marker.

"Final approach fix at 2,600 feet," Owen said, all business now, "instruments cross checked, flaps are 30, gear is down with three greens, we're cleared to land. Landing check is complete."

They were 3 miles and 90 seconds from the runway, 1,000 feet above the ground, when things started to go wrong. There was a loud THUMP and the right wing started to drop, rapidly.

"What the hell was that? What are you doing?" Owen demanded.

"I'm not doing anything," Larry insisted, the tension clearly audible in his voice. The right wing continued to drop, 15, 20, 25 degrees. The control wheel was turned to the left in a vain attempt by the Autopilot to maintain the correct heading. It wasn't nearly enough. The Autopilot didn't have enough flight control authority to prevent a turn, The nose, already 5 degrees to the right of the proper heading to remain centered on the localizer, and increasing.

"We can't go to the right, I told you that, there's other traffic over there for the parallel runway."

"It's not me," Larry said, pleading his case, "it must be the Autopilot."

"Well turn the fucking thing off then," Owen commanded.

The center of the localizer was now well off to their left, a full dot and increasing rapidly. Owen had a brief vision of the lake between the two runways. Wouldn't that be just great, he thought, 500 miles of prairie in all directions and we're going to crash into a fucking lake.

Larry hit the Autopilot disconnect button with his thumb, not remembering that in order to silence the warning siren you had to push the button a second time. Owen could barely hear his exclamation over the noise. Why are there so many warning noises in the cockpit of big airplanes that are guaranteed to induce panic, a tiny part of his brain was asking while the rest was frantically searching for a rational solution to their problem. "There is something VERY WRONG with this airplane," Larry shouted, "I think you better take the controls!"

Larry had both hands on the wheel and had turned it 90 degrees to the left, as far as it would go. The right wing had come up to nearly level but would go no further. They were flying in a slight right turn, but offset now and going further to the right.

There was no indication of a malfunction. No amber lights. No red lights. Every instrument looked normal, but after a quick scan Owen knew the first action had to be to regain control of the aircraft. "I've got the aircraft," he declared, putting both hands on the control wheel and hitting the Autopilot disconnect button a second time to stop its wailing.

Instinct took over. It felt like they were flying sideways, it felt like an engine had failed, but Owen had already checked the engine instruments and they were normal. An engine failure required rudder control to counter the adverse yaw produced by the imbalanced power output. Owen tried to feed in left rudder but it wouldn't move. He pushed harder. Still nothing. Larry, his concentration on the problem with heading control, had neglected the vertical component of the equation. As the rate of descent had decreased, the airspeed had decreased with it, down to 115 knots, well below the reference speed for a normal approach, and dangerously close to stall speed. Owen pushed the nose down and increased power on the right engine. They had drifted 2 dots high on the glide slope and would have to get down quickly to have any hope of landing from this approach. "Put your feet on the rudder pedals and push on the left one, I can't get it to move, and bring the flaps back up to 15 degrees. We're basically on one engine here and we need to lessen the drag."

Larry did as he was told but started shaking his head immediately. "That's as hard as I can push and the rudder won't budge."

Owen advanced the right throttle further, watching the engine exhaust gas temperature rise until it was at the redline. The left engine was at idle. Reluctantly the wings came up to level then into a left bank, turning them back toward the runway. As the flaps retracted their speed increased to a more comfortable 150 knots. "Call the tower," Owen said, "declare an emergency, tell em we have control problems and we want the equipment rolled."

2 miles from the runway. Owen's brain was jumping around like a numbered ball in a lotto machine. There were two sets of problems. If they had sight of the runway, getting the aircraft on it might be possible, though they were already at the edge of the recommended parameters for a visual maneuver and having to steer left and right by using the throttles was not something Owen had ever attempted.

But they couldn't see the runway. It wouldn't be visible until they were below the bottom cloud layer at 400 feet above the ground. If they were locked on a normal ILS, 400 feet would occur when they were a little more than a mile from the end of the runway. Once outside the boundary for the localizer, determining your position relative to the runway was guess work. The closer to the runway you got the narrower the localizer beam became, making minute heading adjustments essential. A nearly impossible task with only the throttles for heading control.

The second part of the problem would become evident if they abandoned this approach. If that was the plan, now was the time, while they still had adequate ground clearance. Trying to salvage this approach was fraught with risk, but what was the risk with continued flight?

Owen had no idea what was wrong with the airplane, or if the malfunctioning piece was as broken as it was going to get. Abandoning the approach would require raising the gear and flaps while simultaneously adding power. What effect would that have on his ability to maintain control? One of the maneuvers practiced during a check ride in the simulator was a single engine missed approach, but not with the rudder frozen and unusable.

Owen thought of the litany he'd leave his young Captains with before giving them their first command: Flying is simple. Takeoff from runway A, the point of intended departure. Land on runway B, the point of intended landing. Don't bump into anything in between, moving or fixed. If a crash becomes inevitable, make a long shallow hole, not a short deep one, and always try to return to earth right side up. Let's see if I can practice what I preach, he thought.

"Ok Larry, here's what I'm thinking." Owen stopped the left turn at a 140 degree heading to try and re-intercept the localizer. He pitched the nose down and increased the descent rate to 1,500 feet per minute, the airspeed increasing with it to 160 knots.

"I'm going to try to put us in a position to land out of this approach. If it doesn't work then we'll miss and hope there is enough control to keep us right side up."

"Should we tell the flight attendants," Larry asked.

"There wouldn't be enough time for them to accomplish anything. We'll be on the ground before you could explain what's going on. If we miss then we'll tell them, but for now I need your eyes. Call out what you see. This is as non- precision an approach as I've ever attempted." Owen gave a brief thought to having Larry make a PA announcement about assuming the brace position for a crash landing, but decided against it. It would just create panic and wouldn't save anyone.

"You're one dot high on the glide slope," Larry cautioned.

Owen raised the nose to shallow the descent rate to 900 feet per minute. "I'm going to start a right turn now," Owen said, "try not to fly right through the localizer." Thinking, I do not want to miss this approach.

"Here it comes," Larry warned as the localizer course deviation bar started moving rapidly from left to right.

THUMP, the rudder released, the left pedal, with both pilots pushing, went to the floor, the airplane lurching into a left turn.

"Take you feet off the pedals," Owen commanded, while pushing up the left throttle and retarding the right, simultaneously stomping on the right rudder pedal to get them into a right turn to try to catch the localizer

"The course bar is almost centered," Larry said, "I'm going outside, "I don't see anything."

Owen pushed hard on the left rudder. The heading was now 180 degrees. He had to get the wings level, stop the turn, and had only 10 degrees to do it in. He cranked the wheel to the left with both hands, using every control surface available.

They were descending through 400 feet. "What do you see Larry,? It should be right in front of us." Thinking: I do not want to miss this approach.

"We're still solid, no ground contact."

350 feet. "No contact, I can't see shit. This is no 400 foot ceiling."

"300 feet, still nothing."

"Fuck," Owen swore through clenched teeth. His mind was still racing, examining all the possibilities; I do not want to miss this approach, not after that enormously fortunate turn onto final. We have enough fuel for another hour of flight, an airplane crippled by some unknown malady, and now the weather is going to shit? This was not forecast, which means that if Clear River is going on its ass, who knows what the nearby airports will have for weather. We've declared an emergency so I could, in theory, go below the normal minimum altitude of 200 feet. I could in fact try to land blind, but doing that in the simulator is not the same as in real life. Fuck it up in the simulator and nobody dies.

"Minimums," Owen called.

"Still nothing," Larry's voice pinched up an octave.

"I'm going to a 100 feet," Owen said, determined now. The ILS deviation bars were dead center. Owen hoping the rudder didn't freeze again before they got on the ground. Thinking, I really, really don't want to miss this approach.

"Ground contact", and a second later,"runway straight ahead,"Larry sounding relieved.

"Wipers on, landing lights on," Owen said urgently. He could see the spinning red lights of the emergency vehicles on both sides of the runway. Raising the nose only slightly to reduce the descent rate he let the aircraft fly itself onto the runway, the touchdown smooth, the runway surface greased by the rain. As the main wheels touched he lowered the nose and pulled the spoiler handle, destroying the wings ability to fly. Owen didn't want to risk reversing the engines so he used the brakes to bring them to a stop on the runway. The emergency vehicles swarmed around them.

"Tell the tower we're ok. Emergency's over. We'll taxi to the gate."

13

1-9-98

The cockpit door popped open and Amy stuck her head in. "Something wrong I should know about," she asked, "you've got a lot of worried passengers back here."

"Sorry," Owen said, suddenly feeling very tired. "Everything's ok now. I'll make an announcement."

"Ladies and gentleman, sorry for all the red lights and excitement. We had a bit of a problem on the approach and we asked the equipment to meet us as a precaution. The problem's solved now. We'll be at the gate in five minutes." He didn't elaborate but Amy wanted more information. She stepped into the cockpit and closed the door.

"A bit of a problem?" She punched Larry lightly on the shoulder, assuming it had been his doing. "The landing was great, but there were times on the approach when I thought you were trying to throw us out the side doors."

Larry looked at her over his shoulder. "I wish I could take the credit for the landing but if it had been me flying the airplane, we'd probably all be dead now."

"Dead now?" She looked at Owen for more information. "What does he mean we'd all be dead now? Why didn't you tell us something was wrong?"

"The whole thing happened in the last 90 seconds of the flight and we were pretty busy. I don't know what was wrong," he admitted, "but something definitely was. We'll know more when we get to the gate."

Larry reached for the flap handle but Owen stopped him. "Let's leave everything the way it is. Just start the APU (auxiliary power unit that provides electrical power and air conditioning on the ground) and tell dispatch we need maintenance to meet us at the gate."

The outbound flight crew was standing on the jetway when the agent snugged it up against the side of the aircraft. The captain, John Green, tapped on Owen's sliding window and he opened it. "Not just some puke on the seats anymore?" the captain inquired.

Owen shook his head. "I don't think this airplane will be going anywhere for a while."

Larry had the aircraft logbook in his lap. "How do you want me to write this up?"

"Good question. Any ideas?"

Larry just shook his head. "This is not something that was discussed in ground school,"

"How about this? At 1,000 feet on final approach aircraft experienced..." Owen paused giving it some thought. Control problems were serious and could ground the aircraft for some time, something Alpha could ill afford. The FAA and the NTSB would have to be notified. It couldn't be helped, Owen thought, I didn't create this problem and someone else is going to have to solve it.

"Experienced rapid roll to the right. Autopilot unable to control it. Rudder was frozen at full right stop. Both pilots applying pressure on the left rudder pedal did not unfreeze it. Required application of max power on the right engine and idle on the left plus full left aileron to counter rolling tendency. Situation lasted for about one minute then rudder control returned to normal."

When Larry had finished writing he handed Owen the logbook to sign. "I meant what I said before," he said, "I don't think I could have gotten this aircraft on the ground, certainly not having to fly the approach to almost 100 feet."

"Don't beat yourself up about it," Owen counseled. "This environment is still new to you, when you get more familiar it will get easier, and to be perfectly frank, this little incident scared the shit out of me." He stuck out his hand and Larry shook it firmly. "It certainly has been an interesting evening."

Owen packed his charts into his flight bag and stepped into the cabin. The girls had finished cleaning up and were gathering their things. Cynthia was speaking into her cell phone, her back turned towards them. Amy looked at her watch. "We're going to catch the 9:30 crew bus," she said, "you going to stop at the Final Approach for a drink? We're buying, since you apparently saved everyone's life."

"Not tonight, but thank you. You can owe me one."

Amy started to protest. "Hey," Owen laughed, "you know I can't keep up with you, number one, and number two, I have to work tomorrow. I can't sleep till noon like some people."

Amy and Judy, with a last look at Cynthia, who was still talking on her phone, grabbed their bags and headed for the door. "Tell Cynthia we'll see her on the bus, unless you have other plans for her," Amy said, before she disappeared up the jetway.

When Owen turned, Cynthia was looking up at him, the cell phone no longer in view. "Do you?" she asked, " have plans for me?" She walked toward him, pulling her bag up the isle until she was standing a foot away. She tilted her chin up and examined his face. "You look like you could use some quiet company."

"What I could really use is a vodka, a large iced vodka, then another one, then some shrimp and scallops in lobster sauce with a glass of Chardonnay, then a good nights sleep and someone to attend tomorrow's eight o'clock meeting in my place."

"That's it? That's all you want?" She smiled, teasing, "nothing else?" Owen just nodded.

"Well, I could stop at the Gung Ho for the shrimp and scallops, meet you at your apartment. If you don't want company after the second vodka I'll go home. Is that fair?"

"Sure," Owen agreed, knowing that he was being not so much manipulated as maneuvered, but not really minding it. He reached for his wallet but Cynthia stopped him.

"My treat. It's the least I can do for having my life saved."

Owen smiled. "I didn't do anything that another highly skilled, gifted, experienced and occasionally lucky airline pilot wouldn't have done. I may be here awhile. There is a key on the ledge above the door."

"Do this often, do you? Let a young woman into your apartment?"

"I do have fond memories of the last time," he admitted.

Owen took a seat in the front row of the airplane and waited. The gate agent appeared, and with a glance at Owen got the information he was seeking.

"Bad?" he asked.

Owen nodded. "Very bad."

The agent walked off the airplane and up the jetway, disappointed, but not surprised. Next came two mechanics. Owen knew one.

"Must have been pretty exciting," Dave said while reading the logbook entry, "for you to have declared an emergency". Dave and Owen looked at each other. "Fuck," Dave swore quietly, "system control is not going to like this one bit." He pulled a cellphone out of his pocket and hit a speed dial number then handed the phone to Owen. Harvey in maintenance control answered on the first ring.

"Harvey? It's Owen." It took him 10 minutes to explain what had happened in the last 90 seconds of the flight. When Harvey asked, he admitted that he had no idea what the malfunction was and although they discussed some possibilities, neither could come up with a rational reason why the airplane had acted the way it did. Finally Owen apologized.

"Extend my sympathies to System Control, but I've had enough fun for one day. I'm going home."

Forty minutes later he was turning the knob on his apartment door. It was unlocked, and as he entered he could hear the crystalline voice of Joan Baez bemoaning her stay at "the house of the rising sun". Cynthia was reclining on the couch, wearing the same sweat-shirt he had loaned her last week, a towel wrapped around her wet hair. She rose to greet him.

"I hope you don't mind," she said, "my uniform smells like puke.

"Mind? Let me think. Coming home after a hard day at the office to discover a freshly laundered, long-legged blond reclining on my couch? No, I don't think so. The only thing that's missing is that first iced vodka."

She stepped around him into the tiny kitchen, reached into the freezer and pulled out a crystal wine glass. It was filled with a clear liquid, two olives and a lemon twist visible, the edges of the glass frosted with ice.

"Lemon twist? I didn't think I had any lemons left?"

"I guessed that and got Lee Chin to give me some. He said to say hello."

"I'll bet he did, and grinned when he said it," Owen wondering what comments Lee would have the next time he went to the restaurant.

Cynthia had poured herself a glass of wine and they clinked glasses. Owen fished out an olive and popped it into his mouth. He chewed slowly, savoring the flavor. "Like one of Pavlov's dogs," he admitted. "I'm lucky there's no drool on my chin. There are few delights that compare to the first sip of iced vodka."

He was taking that first sip when the phone rang. "Shit," he muttered under his breath, "I was afraid it would follow me home."

"You want me to answer it?"

"No, it won't help, there's no escape." He picked up the phone on the third ring.

"Owen? It's Harvey, maintenance control."

Harvey and Dave had been in the original group of six mechanics that Alpha had hired. Their relationship with Owen was based on a shared fascination with the diverse set of mechanical problems a fleet of thirty-year-old aircraft presented, the desire to understand and resolve those problems, and the occasional round of golf and social cocktail. They each respected the other's abilities.

"The problem now is the VP's are getting into the act. This is the only aircraft available for the LA flight. They've got a hundred passengers booked and there is no other way to get them there tonight. That's five grand worth of hotel rooms if the flight doesn't operate. My boss wants us to swap yaw dampers with aircraft 402 which is stuck here with other problems, then either me or Dave to sign it off. He says if we won't sign he'll come to the airport and sign the logbook himself."

Harvey and Dave's boss was the VP of maintenance, Donald Frost. It was the maintenance department that got most of the blame for the destruction of the schedule although it was the age and decrepit condition of the aircraft themselves that was the real culprit. Owen had pointed that out on more than one occasion. He got along with Frost pretty well and didn't think he would push the issue if he knew what was at stake.

"Did the page mention that I declared an emergency?"

Owen could hear the shouted question and the no answer.

"Have you paged Rossi?" Owen asked, knowing that his boss would be unlikely to get in the middle of a pissing contest but would understand the inherent problems in signing off a control malfunction and emergency declaration without any attempt to resolve the issue.

"He hasn't checked in yet,' Harvey confirmed.

"How about Boeing, has anybody spoken with them yet?"

"Yeah. They told Frost that the control problems the 737 have experienced have all been due to a yaw damper actuator malfunction. They're the ones who recommended changing it"

"And they probably called their lawyers right after they hung up. The yaw damper has what? Maybe 3 degrees of rudder travel to work with. That much displacement from center should have been easily handled by the ailerons and we used all the aileron travel available and it wasn't enough. Differential power was the thing that saved us. This airplane can't go anywhere until we figure out what's wrong, whether it's intermittent or not. Are we in agreement there?"

"You and I are. I can't speak for the rest of them."

"I'll see if I can find Rossi. I think once he hears what happened he'll help us with Frost. Have you talked to the Captain yet?"

"John Green, he's standing right here. He wants to talk to you when we're finished. I appreciate your help."

"Hey, we're all in this together. Keep me posted."

John Green had been a Captain for 6 months. Owen had hired him 2 years ago and given him his first Captain's line check. Now he explained the mechanical issues, ignoring the political ones.

"So you don't think I should accept this aircraft?" Captain Green asked.

"You're the Captain John," teaching even now, "but I wouldn't fly it."

"You'll back me up if I refuse the aircraft?" They both knew that was a given.

Cynthia had lost interest. She had taken her wine, found a book in her suitcase, and was back on the couch reading. Owen had the feeling that if he ignored her much longer she would be gone. He couldn't really blame her. He had promised himself when he accepted the position as Chief Pilot that it wouldn't rule his life. How's it going so far, he thought, and called Andrew Rossi's home number.

"Owen?" Andrew answered on the first ring, "what the hell have you started now? You have the whole airline in an uproar."

"Let me give you a quick summary of the evening's events so far." unable to keep the anger out of his voice. "I nearly killed 30 people, myself included, and destroyed an airplane, but I didn't. The cause of the problem has been diagnosed by Boeing as a yaw damper malfunction and your fellow VP wants to get that changed and send it to LA in the hands of a 6 month Captain."

Owen and his boss had disagreed many times but Andrew had never heard him raise his voice. "Frost has called me twice already. Said you told the Captain to refuse the airplane."

"I told Captain Green that I would refuse the airplane under these circumstances, and so would you. Let's leave Captain Green out of it for the moment. There was something very wrong with that airplane. That's a fact. Sending it back out without at least making some attempt to discover what malfunctioned would be negligent, and I'll share that opinion with anyone who asks."

"Take it easy, take it easy, the airplane's not going anywhere to-night. Even if we changed the yaw damper actuator, which is what Boeing is recommending, we'd still have to do a test flight and our policy prohibits that at night." Andrew was not happy with Owen's threat, but let it slide for the moment. "They're already trying to find enough hotel rooms, though I would guess that policy will get changed when Spencer sees the bill. Are you going to be at the eight o'clock meeting?"

"Do I have a choice?"

Rossi actually laughed, though it sounded like an angry bark. "Not really." Owen knew that if he didn't go, Spencer would require his boss to be there. One thing they did agree on, the meetings were a complete waste of time. "If they get the yaw damper changed in time you can do the test flight before you go to Dallas for the sim evaluations tomorrow."

"We've talked about the two crashes, right? You do remember those?" Owen said, "United in C Springs and US Air in Pittsburgh. Boeing claims that the United crash was caused by a mountain wave, and US Air by pilot error. You comfortable taking Boeing's word on this? I don't think what happened tonight could have been caused by the yaw damper, it only has 3 degrees of authority and we should have been able to counter the roll with the ailerons. I mean, could a malfunction of the yaw damper freeze the rudder? Doesn't make sense. The NTSB still hasn't come up with a probable cause for either accident. They are number 1 and 2 on the list of the longest investigations by the NTSB, ever."

"Well, you tell me whose word the NTSB, the FAA, and Boeing are going to take. Yours?" Andrew hung up without further comment.

That man is always one step ahead of me, Owen thought draining his vodka. Cynthia was asleep on the couch. Her wine glass, half empty, sat on the cocktail table. Owen's sweatshirt fit her like a miniskirt with the hem riding high on her slender thighs. She lay with her bare feet toward him, crossed primly at the ankle.

Owen opened the freezer door as quietly as he could, trying to fix another vodka without waking her, but at the sound of ice on crystal her eyes opened and she smiled. She stretched languorously, shook out her hair, carried her wine to the two-seat table and sat. "Solve all the airline's problems?"

"Yes, yes I did. We should be profitable by next week, new airplanes have been ordered, the whole management group has been terminated, including Spencer, I got a big raise and have been named CEO."

"That's great, now you can give the flight attendants a raise."

"I'm afraid that I agree with my predecessor that flight attendants are too easily replaced to waste scarce financial resources on a pay raise for them," Quoting one of the more famous Spencer-isms.

She dipped a finger in her wine and flicked it in his direction. "I'm starving," she said, "can we eat yet?" making it sound like half pout, half demand.

She uncoiled from the chair, and taking a sniff as she walked past him into the kitchen said: "May I suggest a quick shower while I prepare dinner?"

7 minutes later, when Owen returned to the table in sweats and a Tee shirt, there were two plates of steaming shrimp and scallops with rice, two paper towels folded to look like cloth napkins, a candle flickering and the glass of wine she had poured for him.

Later, Owen left Cynthia snoring lightly, tiptoed into the kitchen and poured himself another glass of wine. He had been unable to sleep and had left the warmth of his companion in the bedroom to contemplate his fears.

He hadn't been afraid on the approach. Just like everyone before him that had been in similar situations where the outcome had gone from certain to unknown, there had been no time for fear.

In the tranquility of his living room he replayed the images in his head. Should he have abandoned the approach? They had certainly been at the limits, both horizontal and vertical, that the rules allow. The FAA, by comparing the tape of the tower radar with the flight data recorder, could determine if he was in violation. It would take hours of investigation, not the seconds he had to make his decision, but it was not unknown for the FAA to proceed in that manor, issue a letter of investigation, and 6 months later suspend his license. Owen knew from previous experience that a safe landing would not prohibit the FAA from conducting an investigation.

If he had abandoned the approach, then what? There had been no indication in the cockpit of any particular problem, but the real question was could he have missed the approach and then kept control of the aircraft while they tried to figured out what was wrong?

There was a procedure for uncommanded roll, a recent addition to the 737 manual of every airline that operated the type. Added after the NTSB's assertion that while the crash of the USAir 737 in Pittsburgh was probably the result of pilot error, it might have been caused by a yaw damper malfunction, despite the fact that the investigation was ongoing, no probable cause had been identified and many operators of the type disagreed with the findings.

There was even a boxed section in the procedure, indicating that the wording should be memorized verbatim by the pilots. "Maintain control of the aircraft using all available flight controls. If roll is uncontrollable, immediately reduce angle of attack and increase airspeed. Do not attempt to maintain altitude until control is recovered."

"Why don't they put, don't crash if you can possibly avoid it?" Owen had laughed when Chuck Bert showed him the directive from the FAA several months ago, "and what happens if reducing the angle of attack results in unintended ground contact because you're not intending to maintain altitude?"

"Doesn't take direction well," Chuck had said with a smirk as he exited Owen's office. "That's what it says on your psych profile."

Owen felt the slightest pang of guilt for abandoning Cynthia, but there were too many troubling ideas swirling around in his brain for him to pay attention to her. She had wanted to cuddle, and so he had, wrapping his arms around her until she drifted off to sleep moments later, then unwrapping without awakening her. She had rolled over, taking most of the comforter with her, mumbled something unintelligible, and begun to snore gently. No dark fears to interfere with her beauty rest. Surely his leaving while she was asleep wouldn't be considered unacceptable, he hoped, while knowing perfectly well that in matters of this sort there were no certainties.

So what, he thought now, wrapped in his spare comforter and laying on the couch alone. This relationship, if that was what it was, would be great while it lasted and a relief when it was over. Owen defined relationship as anything monogamous that lasted more than 30 days and had been in many. Two had lasted for 6 years before they disintegrated. He knew that perfection was offered in tiny slices, a few hours, a few days. He accepted the occasional loneliness the single life dictated, willing to trade for the independence it allowed. While not at all sure what he was searching for in a partner, Owen was quite sure he wouldn't find it with Cynthia.

Owen checked the small alarm clock on the table next to the couch he reclined on. He knew it was set for 7 am, left that way because he often fell asleep on his couch. He also knew that Cynthia would sleep better if he stayed where he was.

It had been an eventful day. An airline pilot could go months without having to shoot an instrument approach to minimums. The older airplanes that Alpha flew had unreliable Autopilots. Hand-flying approaches in marginal weather was a lot more work than the visual approaches that were more the norm. And the control malfunction? Whole careers were completed without anything that exciting happening. He was tired, no doubt about that.

It would be a fitful night for him, at best, and his snoring was legendary. He finished the wine, set the glass on the table, and tried to turn off his mind.

14

1-10-98

Owen had never had a 9-to-5 job until he accepted the position as Chief Pilot, hadn't worked five days a week since some between semester construction jobs in his teens. He had been hired by a major airline at the age of 23 and had worked 12 to 15 days a month for the 23 years the job lasted, his career interrupted by deregulation, management ineptitude, or employee intransigence, depending on whose story you believed.

Owen valued his private time. He had no idea when he accepted the position as Chief Pilot at Alpha just how much of it he would be required to give up. It wasn't just the 9 to 5 responsibilities. Alpha aircraft flew night and day, 365 days a year. While it was gratifying to have his advice sought after, his aviation wisdom respected, it was less so at 11 o'clock on a Saturday night, half in the bag, full of Chinese food, and recumbent in front of the movie of the week.

Life as a pilot for a major airline had been simple. He took no part in the running of the airline, the daily decisions, the long-term plans. He showed for his trip, flew where he was supposed to in a safe and economical fashion, wore his hat when necessary, shined his shoes on occasion, then went on with his life.

Those were the days, he thought, while tiptoeing around his apartment to avoid waking the still sleeping Cynthia. Having shaved and showered he left her a note.

"Off to work then Dallas overnight. Will call when I return. Please lock up and leave the key over the door."

The conference room used for the Tuesday meeting was already half full. B was in a corner talking earnestly with Carl Jackson, the director of reservations. They both looked up as Owen approached, reached in his briefcase and pulled out a handful of papers. He handed each a copy.

B looked at the paper and groaned. "Not this again, isn't this the same thing you gave Spencer at your first meeting?"

Owen admitted that it was. "What makes you think he will be any more interested now than he was then?" she asked.

"It's what we should be discussing at these meetings Owen stated flatly, letting his mood show, "not whether the baggage handlers should or should not be given radios."

B was the only person that had seen this paper other than the CEO. Carl, reading it for the first time was nodding his head in assent. "He's right, this is great stuff."

"It's not on today's agenda," B countered. "You know Spencer won't allow discussion of anything that is not on the agenda."

Owen's cellphone started ringing. He handed the stack of papers to Carl. "Give a copy to everyone and leave one at the head of the table for Spencer," he requested, ignoring B's warning stare, pushing the talk button on his cell phone and walking toward the door. "I'll be back in a minute."

It was Tim Granger, Alpha's principal operations inspector from the FAA.

"Owen, must have been pretty thrilling for you to have declared an emergency last night."

Owen was immediately on guard, wondering how the POI had found out so quickly. It was not yet 8:00am, only 11 hours since his "event". They were sort of friends but Tim did work for the FAA and Alpha was his primary responsibility. It would be like having your buddy the traffic cop riding in the car with you when you were in a rush. Owen knew he had to be careful.

"I haven't filled out the form yet, but I can have it for you before I leave for Dallas this afternoon."

"I'm not worried about the declaration of emergency form at the moment," Tim said, "just tell me what happened."

Owen had stepped outside the conference room and turned toward the wall to take the call. Now he felt a presence behind him. It was Spencer, the normal inpatient glare on his face.

"I can't talk with you now," Owen said into the phone, nodding to Spencer as he spoke. "Keeping the CEO waiting is probably more job threatening then making the FAA wait." Spencer frowned at him, walked through the door, and closed it behind him, leaving Owen standing there like an errant schoolboy.

Owen went back to the phone call. "Jesus the guy is arrogant. I may have more time on my hands when he sees the agenda I'm proposing for the next meeting. I'll give you the short version of last night's events. At about 1000 feet on final, aircraft configured for landing, we heard a thump, felt it really, and the airplane started to roll to the right fairly rapidly. We couldn't move the rudder pedals initially, used differential power and all the aileron travel there was to stay right side up, then the rudder broke loose and operated normally until we got on the ground. Boeing says we should change the yaw damper actuator because that's been the problem in other instances when this happened. Maintenance is supposed to be robbing a replacement part and changing it out with the theoretically faulty one. They'll need a test flight. Want to go along?

"Not my job," Tim answered immediately, "that's what they keep you young guys around for. How long is this meeting going to last?"

"An hour, maybe an hour and a half."

"I'll be there when you get done," Tim said, "meet you at Maintenance Control."

"Great," Owen said and pressed the end button. Great, he thought. He knew the FAA would be interested in his little episode and had given some thought to the story he would tell; deciding to stick to the truth. It would be easier that way.

It would not have been out of character for Spencer to lock him out of the conference room, but the knob turned when he tried it. Everyone was already seated. Spencer stopped in mid sentence and glared him to his seat next to B, who pretended to be reading. The room was silent.

" That phone call more important than what we are discussing here?" Spencer's voice always seemed to have a sarcastic undertone.

" Possibly" Owen answered in an identical tone, staring back at the CEO. Owen smiled at the room. Most looked away, but he got a few smiles of sympathy. He was not the first to be dressed down in public.

Spencer changed tacks. "That was the FAA on the phone?"

"Yes, the POI, Tim Granger."

"What does he want."

Owen shrugged. "To know what happened last night. Hear my side of the story."

"And what, exactly, did happen?"

"Honestly, I'm not really sure. Boeing says it was the yaw damper, but I'm having difficulty believing that. The rudder pedals wouldn't move. There have been a number of incidents like this one, rudder problems, including two fatal crashes, but I've never heard of the rudder freezing."

"You declared an emergency?" making it sound like an accusation.

When Owen nodded Spencer continued. "You know you were on the morning news?"

This surprised Owen, although he realized immediatcly that it shouldn't. WKCR was always looking for dirt on Alpha, something about the two owners not liking each other very much. "They want to do an interview."

"With me?" Owen protested, "that's not a good idea. There is the potential for all sorts of possible legal problems. Better have Eric do it."

Eric Wright was the VP legal Owen was always kidding about having to shave only once a week. He was seated at the end of the conference table next to the CEO. "Eric doesn't know which end of the airplane goes first," Spencer stated bluntly.

"He's right," Eric agreed readily, "I'm a lawyer not a pilot."

"I'll write a statement for him to read, tell them we're conferring with Boeing and the FAA and we will keep them appraised of the situation. I would be real careful what we told the press."

There was a moment's silence then Eric spoke, "Andrew said at this morning's VP meeting that we were lucky you were the pilot. It could have been much worse."

That surprised Owen even more. He was not accustomed to compliments from his boss. B had been doodling on her yellow pad. Now she spoke up. "We really don't want to be telling the public that only our most experienced Captain could have solved last night's problem without crashing, or that Alpha's aircraft have rare and dangerous mechanical issues. I think Owen's right. We should keep this as quiet as we can. At least until we have more concrete information." There were nods of agreement around the room.

"All right, I'll excuse you from this meeting," Spencer said. "You probably don't really care if the baggage handlers get radios anyway. Get the blurb, or whatever the press calls it, written then give it to Eric."

"I do, actually, care if the baggage handlers get radios because it will allow them to do their jobs better. I think all the employees should be given the tools to do their jobs. You know that."

"That what this is about," Spencer said, waving the sheet of paper that Owen had distributed earlier. He put on his glasses and began to read:

"Alpha's problems: One, we have no stated goal or plan making it impossible for any department to be properly prepared or for any employee to see their future with the company. Two: The Alpha product does not compare favorably with our competition, canceled flights, late flights, worn interiors, no legroom etc. etc. Our only weapon is price, and cheapest does not always equate to perceived value. Three: Alpha has never been properly capitalized. Four: Alpha does not own one piece of quality equipment. Not aircraft, tugs, trucks, computers. Everything that has been purchased or leased has been the cheapest available. Five: Alpha has been unable to keep quality employees. Historic and current turnover rates will prevent us from ever having a skilled, motivated, and experienced work force. Six: The solution to the above problems will require money. Our short term costs will go up. With price our only weapon, we will be at an increased competitive disadvantage."

Spencer paused and looked up. Nearly every head was nodding in the affirmative, though no one was looking at him. He continued reading: "Alpha's solutions.

One: Define our goals, i.e. number and types of aircraft in a specific amount of time, target cities, route structure, base or hub cities, etc. Two: Ask the employee groups to define their needs then address them in a meaningful way. Include the employees in the planning and success of the company; share the vision." Spencer paused again, looking at Owen who met his gaze. "Three: Create a plan that will transport Alpha from its present state to the airline we all want it to become. Four: Take the vision and the plan to the investors and secure sufficient financing. Five: Upgrade all of Alpha's equipment so that it works on a daily basis instead of causing daily problems. Six: Empower the employees to help create a product that is value-based not price-based. Give the employees the tools to do their jobs and we will develop a satisfied and loyal customer base which is the cornerstone of any successful business."

The silence was now palpable. It lay over the room like a shroud. Owen had made his case. He knew that most of the people in the room, with the possible exception of Spencer, agreed with him. In fact, most everyone who had ever had contact with the airline would agree with this assessment, but there was only one person in the room who had the power to institute change. Spencer removed his glasses, put the sheet of paper on the table and looked around the room. "Any comments?" he asked quietly.

There was a shuffling of papers and numerous clearing of throats, but it seemed no one was willing to risk speaking first until B raised her hand and without waiting to be acknowledged said with a shrug of her small shoulders: "It's all true, anyone who has worked here knows that."

Carl Jackson agreed with her. "My employee group has the highest turnover rate of any in this airline. In the exit interviews the same things get repeated again and again." He held up his sheet of paper: " All the complaints are right here. A res agent has to deal with the sum total of everything that's wrong with this airline; all the delays, the cancellations, the lost baggage, we hear about all of it and it gets old in a hurry and good people get tired of it and quit and go elsewhere."

Suddenly the room was flooded with conversations, the hopelessness dispersed by excited voices awakened to a new possibility.

Owen looked at B. She offered a tiny smile and repeated the shrug. "Maybe this time something will change," she said quietly," maybe."

Spencer had to stand to get everyones attention, waving first one arm, then both, finally rapping his knuckles on the table until the room fell into an anxious silence. He looked directly at Owen who again returned his gaze. "Apparently you've exposed a nerve here."

"I just put on paper what most of the people who work here think," Owen said. "I don't claim to have all the answers but it's depressing to come here every week and talk at length about all these problems that are of little consequence and never speak of the larger issues, the ones that at least have some chance of changing the way Alpha does business."

Again silence in the room. This time almost complete. No shuffling of papers or clearing of throats, just breathless anticipation. It suddenly occurred to Owen what B had been warning him about all along; before Alpha he had spent the previous 20 years as an airline Captain with unquestioned authority over his airplane, crew and passengers, authority granted and backed by the federal government. In this room he had none.

Like a first officer taking control of the aircraft without the Captain's permission, and against all known convention, he had challenged every executive decision made in Alpha's name and done it in front of 20 witnesses. Spencer was the Captain of this ship, and after 20 years on Wall Street was equally accustomed to the exercise of power over those of lessor rank. If Owen wanted to promote his agenda he would have to demonstrate the benefits Spencer would accrue. He would have to play at the corporate power game, no matter his disdain. Drawing his sword, as he had on many other occasions, would only hasten his speedy demise.

This morning he was lucky. Owen watched Spencer's face as he mulled the potential positive and negative aspects of his next move, eyes focused somewhere in the distance on things only he could see. When he next met Owen's gaze a flicker of a smile crossed his lips, then he returned to his public persona.

"OK," he said, " since there seems to be a great deal of interest in discussing the contents of this sheet," holding Owen's paper aloft, "here's what we'll do. I want each of you to post a copy of this paper on your workroom bulletin boards, talk with your workers this week, see what the employee group thinks of these ideas, and solicit their opinion on how to make this a functional airline. Put the suggestions on paper and bring them with you to next week's meeting.

Under the table B gave Owen's thigh a quick squeeze, causing a smile.

"I think everyone agrees the ramp leads should have radios. I'll have the VP of ground ops get a few bids out, see what that will cost, and bring the information to the next meeting. I'm sure you all have work to do so we will adjourn this meeting until next Tuesday. Before you leave," Spencer looked at Owen, "I would like a word."

There was an excited buzz in the room as people stood and gathered their papers to leave. Nods and smiles of appreciation were sent in Owen's direction. Carl Jackson walked around the table and shook his hand. He was smiling broadly. "At least we'll get to talk about some things that matter," he said," this is great. Maybe we can turn this place into an airline."

Owen waited until the room had cleared then walked to the end of the table where Spencer was seated. "Have a seat," Spencer said, indicating the chair across from him.

Spencer studied Owen's face for a moment, then said, "you don't think very highly of me do you? Don't think I'm qualified for this job?"

The question was so out of character that it took Owen completely by surprise. He had no idea where this discussion would lead and was ill prepared to answer any way but truthfully, knowing full well the problem that could create. "Well..." he started, then quit with a shake of his head.

Spencer was studying his face. "You have the reputation of being totally honest, which I can attest to from personal observation, so lets cut the bullshit...just tell me what you're thinking."

The remark flipped a switch in Owen's brain. "OK, I'll be honest. It concerns me a great deal that you are the CEO of an airline without ever having worked in the industry. Your bio indicates that you spent years on Wall Street as a "turnaround" expert, working for a firm that bought failing corporations for pennies on the dollar, then breaking them apart and selling the pieces. I'm not sure that experience will translate well in the aviation world, unless you've been sent here to do the same thing to Alpha.

"I was a Captain with Eastern Airlines when Frank Borman dropped out of space into the CEO's office and the results were a disaster. I wasn't close enough to the management to tell how much of that was his fault or Lorenzo's, but he was in charge when we went into Chapter Eleven." Owen paused. Spencer remained silent. Owen plunged ahead.

"You haven't been here very long," Owen admitted, "but this is what I've seen so far. When we first met, and I gave you the paper you're holding now, you dismissed it out of hand, gave me a lecture on the responsibilities of the Chief Pilot position, which sounded like you were reading from a book, and basically told me to stick to my own job."

Owen stopped. He felt deflated suddenly, like he was wasting his time. This, he thought, was never going to work. "I'm sorry," he apologized. "I get carried away sometimes. Four years of frustration I guess."

Spencer dismissed the apology with a shake of his head. "I've only been here three months and I've been frustrated for two and a half of those. Let me take this point by point.

"First, I agree it would have helped me a great deal if I'd had 20 years in the airline business. Mr. Bentworth was in my class at Harvard. I've known him more than 30 years. His family has had a seat on the exchange going back 3 generations. He's a billionaire and I'm not, though I'm comfortable enough. TL called me when this enterprise was starting and offered a position on the board of directors, but I had other interests at the time. We spoke occasionally during the years Alpha was failing; he was growing tired of losing money and the succession of CEOs who did little to reverse the negative numbers, but I told him I wasn't qualified." Spencer smiled slightly: "See, we agree on something,"

Owen was so taken aback by the smile that out of politeness he smiled in return.

"I started doing some research, read books, talked to friends from the Street who had ended up in the airline industry. I'm still no expert but at least now I can speak the language. Four months ago when TL asked again I said yes. I was very much ready for a change."

Spencer reached into his battered blue-black briefcase and pulled out two pieces of paper that were stapled together, glanced at them, and tossed them across the table to Owen. It was the paper Owen had given him three months ago at their first meeting, now covered with scribbled notes, arrows and underlines.

"The first thing I did when I arrived was hold a series of meetings with senior management as a group, then individually. I asked them to evaluate the people who reported to them. Rossi said you did your job well enough, but he felt that you were a little too soft on the pilots. I distinctly remember he used the word soft."

Owen began to protest but Spencer silenced him with a glance. "Let me finish please. The conversation with Rossi took place the day before you gave me this report. One of the most difficult tasks when you are the latest addition to a management group is determining where the truth lies, who to believe.

"When you change CEOs, the next level gets worried about their jobs so I have to assume they are telling me what they think I want to hear. In order to get at some semblance of the truth at Alpha I spoke with a number of the employees, including mechanics, pilots and flight attendants. They were pretty much universal in their approval of you and dislike and distrust of Rossi. Why do you think that is?"

Owen was not a big fan of self-promotion, but he sensed an opportunity here and a willing audience. There was a possibility for real change. "First let me say this about Andrew Rossi," Owen began, "there are a lot of issues we disagree on but he knows aviation. He has been around this business as long as I. It's just that he spent most of his career in the office behind a desk so he is more fluent in office speak: the rules, the meetings, the memos. I have spent most of my career in the cockpit. It's one reason I have more sympathy for the flight crews than he does. I'm more connected to them then I am to my office. However, the biggest difference between us is a philosophical one. He's a stick man, whereas I'm more likely to use a carrot to get results."

Owen paused. Spencer waited, sensing he wasn't finished. "I'll give you an example. About a year ago, Andrew rewrote a portion of the crew scheduling policy without asking either Barbara Morgan or myself. It now states that if a pilot or flight attendant is on a day off when crew scheduling calls, and they answer the phone, they have to accept the assignment or it will show as a missed trip and they will be punished accordingly. Andrew thought it would give scheduling more flexibility to cover trips when we were short crews. I said it was enormously unfair and would accomplish just the opposite, which it has. Now no one on a day off answers the phone."

"And how would you get people to work on an assigned day off?"

"Make it advantageous for them to do so. Pay them more or give them some other benefit. In theory, the employee covering a trip in this manner keeps the airline from having to hire another employee. If you paid a 50% bonus for flying on a day off, the airline would still be saving 50% over the cost of an extra employee. It's a policy that helps both parties. I've talked with pilots and flight attendants and they love the idea so long as they have some say in the matter."

Spencer had been jotting something on a yellow pad and he continued writing after Owen stopped speaking then looked up. "Interesting idea," he said, "I assume you have others?"

"I have tons of ideas but it's the basic philosophy that has to be addressed first. It's not just Alpha, most corporations have this broad line drawn between management and the employees. Management at the top of the page in capital letters, then the line, then everybody else below the line in small print. It doesn't work well.

"Neither group can function without the other. You don't need a Harvard degree in business to understand that simple fact, it's just common sense. You can't demand extra effort any more than you can demand respect."

Spencer glanced at his watch. "We don't have enough time to get deeper into this discussion now, but I'm interested in what you have to say. I apologize if I was a bit short with you the first time we met. After two days of being told what I should do by a bunch of VPs who were only trying to keep their jobs, the last thing I needed was another lesson in airline economics from a middle manager I had never met. I should caution you, however, that my management style has always been considered somewhat brusque."

Spencer retrieved the paper he had shown to Owen and stowed it in his briefcase then stood. "I would like to continue this conversation off the airport. Would you consider joining me for dinner sometime in the next few days?"

The offer surprised Owen as much as the smile had, but he readily agreed.

" I would also like to keep the contents of this meeting confidential for the time being," Spencer said extending his hand, "let me know what happens with the FAA."

When Owen was alone in the conference room he called B on her cell. "I need a favor," he said, and explained what he thought should go in the press release and asked if she could write it up and get it to Eric.

Andrew Rossi was standing in his office doorway when Owen walked by on his way to System Control. Andrew waved him inside and closed the door. "Have you seen Granger?"

"Not yet, is he here already?"

"I just talked to him. He stopped on his way to Maintenance Control. Have you got your story ready?"

"Story? I was just going to tell him what happened."

Owen could never tell what his boss was thinking. Andrew had a yellow pad on his desk and he flipped though the pages until he found a blank one. "Tell me the whole story from beginning to end," he said, pen poised and ready. He took notes as Owen related the incident, interrupting a few times to ask a question. When Owen had finished he asked one last question. "Did you go outside the boundary of the ILS localizer?" It was THE question, the one Owen was most concerned with.

"Simple answer, I don't know. The tower never said anything and we didn't get a TCAS warning (a cockpit system that warns of impending collision with another airplane) about the traffic inbound for the parallel runway. We were nearly off scale to the right, more than two dots on the instrument but there is no way to translate that into horizontal distance without looking at the radar tapes. You know that. Plus, we had declared an emergency. In theory I could have gone anywhere."

Andrew was silent for a moment, tapping his pen on the pad. "Eric has asked me to make the statement to the press which I can now do."

Like the delay was my fault, Owen thought, but said nothing.

" I already talked to Barbara so that's squared away. I'll tell the press that Boeing has recommended that we make a precautionary change of the yaw damper actuator."

"Do you think the yaw damper could freeze the rudder at its limit of travel?" Owen said. "You never answered that question last night."

"We can't very well ignore a suggestion from Boeing. Unfortunately it will keep the airplane out of service until tomorrow. Maintenance can't get the parts before tonight, so the test flight won't happen before tomorrow morning. If you catch the early departure back from Dallas you should be here in time to fly it. I'm sure the FAA will examine those radar tapes very closely." Owen got the distinct impression that Andrew was more worried about how this incident would affect him and his career than he was about his Chief Pilot's reputation.

Edward was seated at the Maintenance Control desk when Owen walked into the room. Tim Granger stood behind him reading over his shoulder. As Owen walked past the System Control desk Quincy waved a sheet of paper at him. "You got some good shit in here," he said, grinning at him, "good luck getting any of it implemented." Owen recognized the list from the morning meeting. Quincy had been a small town banker for years, retired, got bored and took the job in System Control as a lark. He was always ready for a drink or a laugh.

The pages Edward and Tim were pouring over were covered with schematic diagrams of the rudder and its power control unit. "I see what you're saying about the slide," Edward said,"but it seems like you would need multiple malfunctions for that to happen."

Tim looked at Owen and gave him a thin smile. "Let's grab a smoke," he said, and led the way out of the room.

"Here's what's going on," Tim started to explain when they were alone. "Your little incident was reported to the FAA last night, as it should have been, because of a suspected inflight control malfunction. The report was forwarded to the NTSB this morning, also standard procedure. What everyone is excited about is the similarity to the US Air 737 crash in Pittsburgh which still has no probable cause two-plus years into the investigation. The most popular theory until last night was a rudder malfunction, step on the right rudder pedal and it moves in the opposite direction. The fact that your rudder wouldn't move seems to point to the PCU (power control unit), that it froze for some unknown reason. Despite the evidence to the contrary there are still those who are convinced that the yaw damper is the problem and there are some heavy hitters in that group including some operators with large 737 fleets. Also, the Boeing aircraft company."

"Boeing?"

"Sure. They have already spent lots of time and money on this theoretical rudder problem. I get the feeling that the board was about to announce a probable cause. It's not to anyone's advantage to take off in another direction. There are more than twenty-seven-hundred 737s in operation around the world. No one wants the responsibility of grounding a fleet that large unless there is a definitive problem and solution."

"I'll tell you why I have a problem with the rudder malfunction theory," Owen said, "and I felt this way before last night. Most pilots use the rudder during takeoff, for directional control on the runway, and to guard against the possibility of an engine failure at low altitude. They use it again on landing, especially in a crosswind, but I don't think I've ever used more than fifty percent of available travel and that was in the sim with an engine failure at rotation. The USAir aircraft was on approach. From what I've seen of the findings of the investigation so far both engines were operating normally when they had their problem. Even in rough air or wake turbulence most pilots use the ailerons and spoilers for lateral control, not the rudder. In fact I have to yell at guys to at least keep their toes on the pedals or they would leave their feet flat on the floor. The USAir pilots didn't have any reason to use the rudder. According to the NTSB there would have to be an input to the rudder before the pilots even knew there was a problem. Their theory doesn't make any sense to me."

"Me either," Tim agreed, "but be careful who you say that to. There are a lot of important people who just want this problem to go away."

15

"Tracy wants to come with us," Josh Logan said as he walked into Owen's office on the upper level of the terminal. "She's at the gate filling out her pass form."

"Do we have any say in the matter?" Owen kidded him, already knowing the answer.

"You may have but I certainly don't," Josh admitted lightly. "She's going to end up with more simulator time than some of our pilots,"

Josh had been running the simulator for the new pilot evaluations. Tracy came along whenever she wasn't working. She tried to schedule her flights around the days she knew there was going to be an eval in the hope that there would be a few no-shows, leaving some time at the end of the 4 hour periods for her to get a chance to play in the box. The only way Alpha could get sim time was rent it in 4 hour blocks. There wasn't a refund if you didn't use all the allotted time. Owen didn't mind. He found the pair a very entertaining diversion and took his laughs where he could get them.

Though she had never flown an actual airplane Tracy was already proficient at visual approaches in the simulator, more than half of them ending with the aircraft on the runway. "Damn," she'd say when the airplane ended up in the grass, mad at herself.

"THAT was PERFECT," when she stopped on the runway. "I keep this up and you're going to HAVE to give me a job. Suppose the pilot gets shot, like in that movie with Doris Day. I could land the airplane and be the hero. Maybe get on some talk shows." Then she'd laugh, "Let me try just one more." She found most things in life worth laughing at.

Now she stood with Barbara Morgan and Anna Long, their own little sorority, away from the other passengers waiting in the gate area for Alpha's flight to Dallas. Tracy was telling a story, using her hands to emphasize her points and had the other two laughing along with her until she spotted Josh and Owen approaching, a hurried whisper, more laughter, then silence as they came within earshot. The tale not meant for men's ears.

"I just talked to Amy," Tracy said holding up her cell phone. "She said you had quite a time last night." Owen wondering if she was talking about the rudder malfunction, or later, with Cynthia. "Said if it hadn't been you, they would probably all be dead," this last in a stage whisper, not for the passengers consumption.

"Amy's prone to occasional exaggeration," Owen replied and smiled a greeting at Anna. "I see you've met Alpha's resident wit and gossip."

Anna was still smiling and now she extended her hand, very professional looking in her black slacks and simple white blouse, no jewelry. A woman on a mission she was a head taller than the other two. "Very funny lady," she agreed, "and an encyclopedia of information about the airline," raising her eyebrows and making Owen more curious about their secret conversation.

Major Crown walked up to their little group and introduced himself to the ladies shaking their hands, then Josh, then Owen. A politician hunting for votes, pompous without realizing it. When he walked away Tracy faced the others and made a gagging motion, pretending to stick her finger down her throat. "Please tell me you're not thinking about hiring that guy," she said to Owen who showed her his bemused smile and remained mute.

When the others started for the jetway door, B held him back. "What happened with Spencer after I left?"

Owen thought of his pledge of secrecy but this was B. "This is for your ears only, absolutely no exceptions." B crossed her heart with a quick motion.

"We actually had a nice chat, imagine my surprise, and he still had the original list of Alpha's problems that I had given him months ago. I told him some more of my ideas and he seemed interested. He wants me to have dinner with him when I get back."

"Dinner? Really?" B was impressed. "That's a start. You think he's actually going to listen?"

"Who knows? But he did say that he wasn't qualified to be the CEO of an airline, a remarkable statement, which gives me some hope, and he smiled at me. Can you believe it?"

"That is amazing…actually smiled?…so Spencer has possibilities. What about Tim Granger?"

"He told me to be careful what I said and to whom, which I find interesting. I can't change what already happened. He thinks there was about to be a probable cause announced for the USAir crash and a lot of interested parties don't want this incident to interfere." Owen shrugged. "Maybe we'll all pretend it never happened." The gate area was empty and the agent was standing by the jetway door looking at her watch. "I have to go," Owen said, "I'll see you tomorrow morning."

Anna Long had followed Josh and Tracy down the jetway and onto the aircraft. Tracy introduced her to the two flight attendants standing in the forward galley area as one of Alpha's new pilots. They were very friendly, enthusiastic about Alpha getting it's first female pilot, even after she explained that congratulations were a little premature. She still had to pass the sim eval.

"With Josh and Owen?" one of them remarked and they both laughed. "there's no way you can fail."

Anna thanked them for their confidence. In truth she felt as well prepared as she could be. One of the pilots she had flown with at Red Hawk Aviation, her current employer, had gotten hired by Alpha 3 months earlier. " Don't worry about the sim," he had told her. "I've seen you fly. You'll do fine; but he did agree to lend her his 737 manual.

She had been studying it every spare moment since, especially the cockpit photographs and the flight profiles. Last weekend, on her day off, she had come to the airport, and using the jump seat privilege her Red Hawk ID allowed, had ridden on an Alpha flight to Denver and back, sitting on the cockpit jump seat, observing the crew and asking questions. She was as ready as she could be.

Now, as she walked toward the back of the airplane she recognized and smiled at the other two pilots she had interviewed with. Major Crown, a few rows further back, tried to wave her into the seat next to his, but she declined politely, and chose an isle seat even further back in an empty row. Once seated she could look up the aisle at the little knot of people standing at the front of the aircraft. All three of the flight attendants working the trip were there now with Tracy and Josh. The Captain had gotten out of his seat and was laughing along with the others at some story Tracy was telling. Then Captain Swift stepped aboard, greeted with obvious affection by the crew, the same tired smile still on his face.

Anna wondered if he ever stopped smiling, wondered what he would be like in private. She watched as he made his way down the aircraft isle, acknowledging the other pilot candidates with a nod but continuing purposefully rearward, stopping next to Tracy and Josh for a brief conversation then sliding into a window seat across from them. He was wearing the same shirt as he had the day of her interview, white with blue vertical stripes that accentuated his height, not that it needed any help. He was tall, six two or so Anna guessed, broad shouldered and narrow waisted, all legs and long arms, big hands, smiling to herself at that last observation. But it was his eyes that had first caught her attention during the interview. Wide set, in a face that looked like it had lost a few of life's battles, but still had plenty of fight left, and blue, very blue.

It had been 5 years since Anna's divorce. She had dabbled with men, that's how she thought of it, a few times, but had found little satisfaction. One man had awakened her to her sexual potential but his was a mechanical skill with no emotional involvement allowed, and she was relieved to see him depart after a month, saying he wasn't ready for a long term commitment. Her married sex life had been rather straightforward, Jim's idea of experimentation was for her to be on top, his orgasm the signal that they were done, her relief found later after he'd gone to sleep. It was one of the things they had fought about at the end, when she had started demanding more, and hating herself for it.

"I'm starting to think that men aren't worth the effort," she complained to a friend who was having marital problems of her own. This was said during the course of a long lunch and after her second glass of wine. "It must be possible to find someone who cares who I am, what I want, what I feel. Who wants to share their dreams with me." That sentiment had been uttered more than a year earlier. Now the friend was divorced and hunting again, wanting Anna to accompany her on her Saturday night safaris. Even her daughter urged her on. "You've got to get out there Mom, or you'll end up the prettiest divorcee in Clear River. She tried, but without much enthusiasm.

Anna's schedule, if that's what you wanted to call it, did not allow for much of a social life anyway. Since moving to the Citation Captain position 2 years ago she, had been on call or flying 22 days a month. Her days off were rarely granted in advance, based more on the aircraft's utilization than her social needs. This had been discussed with her daughter, the need for her to accumulate jet time, and they had worked out a system where they could spend time together, just not as much as before. As a freight pilot, Anna had reported to the airport at 8 pm, flew her 4 legs, and was back by 6 am, in time to have breakfast with her daughter before she went off to school. They shared their evenings, talking, laughing, gossiping through dinner before Anna was off to the airport.

The Citation had been purchased by a medical group and then leased back to Red Hawk for charter use. It was used a lot and Anna flew as often as possible, the 1,000 hour mark and an interview with Alpha her targets, the rest of her life on hold. She had a new target now, a pilot job with Alpha airlines, and all she had to do was perform in the simulator.

Looking forward she could see that Chief Pilot Swift had leaned his seat back, placed a pillow against the sidewall, and appeared to be sleeping.

He can sleep, she thought, he's got nothing to worry about. Reclining her seat and closing her eyes she envisioned herself in the right seat of the simulator, felt the nervous energy building, and shook it off. No nerves, she admonished, right hand on the wheel, left gripping the throttles, she silently mouthed the words: set takeoff thrust, and went through the drill one more time.

Owen had asked one of the flight attendants to make an announcement when they arrived instructing the pilot applicants to please remain onboard until all the passengers had deplaned. Now he had Josh take roll. 8 of the 12 left standing were scheduled for the 2 pm session. Those he instructed to meet him where the hotel vans picked up their passengers and get on the Hilton's bus to go the simulator building. The bus, he said, would be outside in about 20 minutes.

"If you think food is important, get it here. No food is available where we're going. The rest of you are on your own for the next three and a half hours. You can go to your hotel if you have one, hang around the airport, or you are welcome to go to Flight Safety with us and wait in their lounge."

The group exited the airplane and broke up, wandering off in different directions. Tracy was going to the hotel to wait and she took Anna with her.

"They have a great salad bar in the hotel restaurant. We should be able to get there before they shut it down. That will give us time to rest up for our sim period later." She smiled at Owen and Josh. "You boys enjoy your McChickens."

Two more applicants were waiting at Flight Safety when the group arrived from the terminal. Ten out of twelve, Owen thought, not too bad. Three hours later he wasn't so sure. He and Josh compared notes after they had finished testing the first group. Three they had both really liked, four were acceptable, the rest would get a job offer if none outshone them in the next group. "We will let you know within 24 hours," Owen promised. He went outside for a smoke and Josh joined him.

"There are only three guys waiting in the lounge," Josh told him as the hotel van pulled up and four more got off, including Anna. "Plus four on the van, and we need five more plus two alternates. These guys don't realize it, but if they don't pass out from fear they are going to be Alpha Airline pilots."

Josh led the new group toward the lounge area. Tracy stayed outside. "Anna's great," she said, "not to try and influence your opinion or anything, but you'd both be idiots not to hire her."

"I thank you for your humble opinion," Owen laughed at her," but don't you think we should wait and see if she can fly?"

"I'd be willing to bet she's as good as any guy you've seen so far." Tracy was always ready to take the distaff side of any argument about a woman's traditional role versus her entry into the man's world. "In fact, I'm so sure I'll bet you the first round tonight."

"Since we only have seven showing for this session, and it looks like you are going to get your free simulator time thanks to Josh and me, you'd be buying anyway. I don't think I would ever want to bet against you, too risky."

They joined the others in the pilot lounge. Josh asked the pilots to call out their names as he checked them off the attendance sheet. Then he collected the hundred dollar fee saying: "checks made out to Captain Logan or Captain Swift will measurably increase your chances of success." When that business had been concluded, amidst some nervous laughter, Owen bade them be seated and standing in front of the group gave his little pep talk.

"Ok, listen up. What I'm going to share with you will help you succeed in this endeavor and is based on my experience watching more than 300 wannabe pilots struggle with this simulator." The room went completely silent.

"This is not an airplane. You may have thought that was obvious but would be surprised at how many lose sight of that fact in the heat of the moment. This simulator is much more difficult to fly than the aircraft it purports to represent. When you walk into the simulator bay you will notice the four hydraulic legs the sim is supported by. Once you start trying to maneuver it you will swear it is balanced on the head of a pin. The two best ways to overcome this instability are to be smooth with the controls and to maintain your instrument scan. Your eyes should be moving twice as fast as your hands.

"The basic flight instruments in this simulator are in the same position as any instrument aircraft you have flown and you should be familiar with their layout. Use them. Most important is pitch, found on the artificial horizon and marked in five degree increments above and below the horizon line.

"During the takeoff roll, when I call Vr, rotate the nose to 10 degrees above the horizon line and keep it there. When the aircraft lifts off, and you have a positive rate of climb, call for gear up and simultaneously bring the nose to 15 degrees nose up. As your speed increases to V2 plus 20, call for flaps up. At 3,000 feet AGL (above ground level), which in Dallas is 3,600 feet, call for climb power. I will set that for you."

"You will be cleared to 8,000 feet and will be given some turns while you climb. 30 degrees of bank angle will give you a standard rate turn and will be your target for all turns except, obviously, the steep turns which I will address in a moment."

"Notice the location of the fuel flow gauges at the bottom of the engine instrument stack on the center instrument panel. At climb thrust they will indicate approximately 6,000 pounds a side. When you leave 7,000 feet, pull the throttles back to about 3,500 pounds a side. Lower the nose to about 8 degrees nose up, which should translate to a climb of about 500 feet per minute. If you don't change anything leaving 7,000, you will be charging toward your assigned altitude at 2,000 feet per minute and have great difficulty stopping the climb.

"In level flight, fuel flow approximates airspeed. Want to go 250 knots, set 2,500 pounds of fuel flow. Notice that the 3,000 pound mark on the gauge is at the 6 o'clock position. That way you won't have to concentrate on the gauge, which, by the way, is very difficult to read." A few groans followed that statement causing Owen to smile. "You wouldn't want this to be too easy would you? Then anybody could do it.

"Once you are level at 8,000 feet with the speed at 250 knots you will do two steep turns of 180 degrees duration, one to the right, one left. I recommend using muscle rather than stabilizer trim to maintain altitude. I have seen more success that way, but I've seen it done both ways. It's your choice. Roll into and out of the turns SLOWLY, adding back pressure on the yoke as the angle of bank increases. When you go through about 30 degrees of bank angle bump the throttles a couple of 100 pounds each. 45 degrees of bank is your target, plus or minus 5 degrees. Maintain 250 knots, plus or minus 10 knots, and 8,000 feet plus or minus 100 feet. These are ATP (airline transport pilot) standards accepted the world over and I expect nothing less.

"You should ALWAYS be at your targets or working back toward them. If your airspeed is increasing, check the vertical speed as well as the power setting. Like any aircraft this simulator will show an increase in airspeed when it descends. Stop the descent first. DO NOT try to reverse a trend. Don't attempt to go from a 500 foot a minute rate of descent to a 500 foot rate of climb. The difference in pitch between level flight and 500 up or down is less than 2 degrees and nearly impossible to read on the artificial horizon. USE ALL THE INSTRUMENTS. That's why they're there.

"On the completion of the steep turns, you will be vectored to the Dallas airport for an ILS (instrument landing system) approach to runway 18 Left. I will coach you through the descent, made with the power at idle, speed of 250 knots, and show you how to slow to approach speed. You will call for the descent checklist at this time and the landing check list when the gear goes down. The ceiling will be set at 250 feet with a visibility of 3/4 of a mile, wind calm, altimeter of 29.92. Now," Owen paused for a five count. No one spoke as he looked over his audience.

"Now, here is where most people have problems and where it is most important to remember that this box you will be in is a simulator and not an airplane, more like an expensive video game. If you have done everything correctly, are centered on the localizer and glide slope, at 250 feet above the simulated ground I will see the simulated runway, and I will say: Runway in sight. Glance quickly at the runway visual, then right back on the gauges. Whatever pitch, heading, and power it took to stay on the ILS will take you, with perhaps some minor corrections, to the runway.

"It is MOST important to reference the glide slope. DO NOT point the nose of the aircraft at the end of the runway and dive for it or you will crash in the grey simulated grass, short of the grey simulated runway.

"To stay on the glide slope will take a descent rate of 750 feet per minute. Let the airplane continue to descend at that rate. I will call 100 feet, then 50 feet. When you hear the 50 foot call raise the nose SLIGHTLY, bring the throttles to idle, and let the aircraft touch down. DO NOT try to grease it on or you will most likely overshoot. Keep the aircraft on the centerline with the rudder pedals and stop it with the toe brakes. DO NOT try to use reverse. That is for the more advanced class.

"All of this may sound complicated, but remember this is just another airplane and you are all pilots. We do not expect perfection. Do not get down on yourself if you have trouble at rotation or at any time during your ride. I will coach you. There are those who would tell you that I know what I'm talking about, and they would suggest that you listen to what I have to say. We are looking for a learning curve so DON'T GIVE UP. Keep trying till it's over. I know how important this is to you and that some of you are nervous. All I can say is try not to be, it won't help. If you want to fly big airplanes you will be going to a simulator all your professional lives. Attitude is VERY important. Try to enjoy yourselves. Good luck to all."

Owen turned to Josh. "And the first 3 winners are?"

Josh read off 3 names including Major Crown's.

"I'm going to grab a smoke. I'll see you in the box in 10 minutes."

As he was leaving the room, Owen looked over Josh's shoulder at the pilot list. Anna's name had been circled with an arrow pointing to the third group, now a group of one. "Tracy's idea," Josh explained, "she's already asked Anna if it would be ok with her. This way Anna can do her ride with Tracy in the sim. Then they can swap seats and Tracy can get to play for awhile. Then the 4 of us are going out for cocktails and dinner."

"Quite the little organizer, that girlfriend of yours. I'm smelling something suspiciously like matchmaking going on here."

"You gonna complain about being set up with Anna"? Josh asked, giving him a look.

"It hasn't occurred to either of you that I'm likely to be her boss and that having dinner with one candidate and not inviting the others, especially when the one being invited is a mighty fine looking woman, might get me in a little trouble?"

"I brought up that very topic with Tracy and she said you don't pay attention to the rules anyway so why should this be any different. Her exact words. She also said that if you are interested in this particular lady, you better not dick around like you normally do, waiting for women to come to you. This one won't show up at your door. I don't know what she meant by that last statement."

"I do," Captain Swift said with a rueful smile, "I know exactly what she's referring to," and let it go at that. Thinking once again, as he walked to the door for some fresh Dallas air and nicotine, that there were no secrets at Alpha airlines.

16

The simulator bay had always reminded Owen of an airplane hanger with its cavernous space, high ceilings and no windows. It had the temperature of a meat locker, the lighting dim, the constant hum of electricity, even when the 3 sims were not in use. There was a 727, a DC-9, and their 737. The other 2 were in motion as Owen entered the room, lurching in all directions, mounted on their skinny legs and putting out a nearly constant hiss of hydraulic function. They didn't look anything like airplanes, more like boxy insects with a giant bundle of wires running from underneath to the computers at the back of the 3 story space. As he walked past the DC-9, it suddenly pointed its nose skyward, slewing to one side then down. They'll be having some fun now, he thought, knowing full well that what the pilots inside the box were seeing and feeling bore no resemblance to the exterior appearance, the hydraulics meant to convey a sense of the G forces in flight.

He walked across the grated metal bridge of the 737 sim and closed the safety gate, then flipped the switch that would raise the bridge, watching until it rose to the vertical position that would be necessary before the sim could be put in motion. Stepping inside the box he closed and latched the aft door, pausing to let his eyes adjust to the dim glow of the instrument lights, then squeezed past

Josh, who was in the instructors spot facing the control panel behind the Captain's seat, slid into the Captain's position and looked over at Major Crown who was thrashing around in the First Officer's seat trying to adjust it. He was jerking his body fore and aft and fumbling with the levers at the seat's bottom that were used to adjust hight and distance from the controls. Owen put a hand on his arm.

"Easy, easy," he said, "you break the seat, you fail the ride," a sudden and unexpected anger in his tone. Owen quickly realized that he wasn't so much mad at the Major, but at the circumstances that caused him to be invited in the first place. He softened his tone but spoke loudly enough so the other two pilots, who were crowded in behind Josh at the back of the sim, could hear him.

"These seats are machines, part of the aircraft, and are to be treated with the same respect I expect you to treat the whole airplane with. There are 3 levers on the side of the seat at the bottom of the cushion. The most forward is the vertical adjustment. Lift up on the lever while taking your weight off the seat and it will rise." He demonstrated and indicated to the Major that he should try. "Sometimes you have to jiggle the seat at the same time you raise the lever," Owen instructed, then watched as the Major struggled until the seat suddenly shot to its highest setting. He turned to his left and pretended to be fiddling with some papers to avoid letting the Major see his laugh.

When Owen had first proposed the sim evals to his boss he had joked that if they would just bolt a seat in his office, squeezed in against the wall so it was as difficult to get into as the real one, he could tell by the way the applicants mounted the seat and adjusted it whether they would be good pilot candidates. He wouldn't have to see them fly.

Josh had put the evaluation forms they would both fill out in a clipboard against the left side of Owen's seat. While Major Crown continued to struggle with his seat, he entered in the space labeled comments:

"ham-fisted." Finally, the Major was ready.

Owen and Josh had left the sim on and set for departure when they had finished with the previous group, but Owen, out of habit, scanned the overhead and forward panels, confirmed the flaps were set for takeoff, the trim and the brakes set. In the dim light of the cockpit Owen could see the Major working his jaw, and for a brief moment almost felt sorry for him, a premonition that this was not going to go well.

"Ok," Owen told him, "You are at the departure end of runway 18 Left in Dallas, the taxi and before takeoff check lists are complete, the brakes are set and you are cleared for takeoff to maintain runway heading and 8,000 feet."

"Well, we'll have to start the engines before we can takeoff," the Major stated, sounding like he thought he was being tricked.

While the cockpit portion of this simulator, from the circuit breaker panel forward, was an exact duplicate of a real airplane, there were important differences. It was always night time. The visual presentation at the front of the simulator was on a mono-color set of screens, shades of grey, light to dark, to differentiate between the pavement and what was supposed to represent grass at the runway edge. There was no view out the sides, only blackness. No peripheral vision cues. No noise. The sound level was the same whether the engines were at takeoff power or shut down.

Again Owen had to stifle his laugh with a cough and heard Josh doing the same thing behind him. "The engines are running," he said, "I know you can't hear them in this box and that's a little confusing, but we're all set. Just push the throttles forward."

The Major did as instructed grudgingly, shoving them to the midpoint of the quadrant. Nothing happened. "I think you're wrong about the engines," he said, not knowing it took 5 seconds for the engines to produce thrust from idle. The simulator lurched as both spooled simultaneously, but they remained glued in place. "Something's wrong with the sim," he stated flatly.

How nice, Owen thought, the Major is going to make my decision easy. "I don't know about an F-18, but you will have trouble getting a 737 rolling with the brakes set," trying, but failing, to keep the sarcasm out of his voice.

When the Major did release the brakes, he released the left one first, causing the sim, when it started to roll, to head for the right side of the runway. The Major countered this transgression by slamming in full left rudder, slewing the sim across the runway centerline and heading for the left edge. They went back and forth 3 times in this manner, full left rudder followed immediately by full right, before Owen commanded "take your feet off the pedals," guided the sim to the middle of the runway with his toes on the pedals then said, "Now, put just your toes on the pedals and feel what I'm doing."

The Major did as instructed. "They're not moving at all,"

"Exactly," Owen said, then, "one hundred knots...V1...rotate."

The Major, an all or nothing kind of guy, pulled the yoke back into his lap, creating such an extreme nose up angle, that the sim thumped once, then they were airborne. "Wow," Josh said behind them, "I don't think we've ever had a tail strike in the sim. I didn't think it was possible."

Owen was trying to coach while thinking that he might as well let the Major flail around for his 20 minutes then cross his name off the list. "Ok, ok," Owen said, "you're using way too much control movement, just let the wheel go for a moment." When the Major complied with this instruction Owen put his own hand on the wheel saying, "Now...put your right hand on the wheel but hold it with only three fingers. Much better," he complimented, "you've got the airplane."

When Owen let go he reminded the Major "You're out of 7 for 8." He didn't take the hint, missing the altitude by 500 feet and forcing the nose down like it was the simulator's fault. His steep turns were rough, though he stayed within the required parameters. The approach was more of the same; back and forth across the localizer, above and below the glide slope, over controlling all the way down until he thumped onto the runway in what could best be described as a carrier landing or a lucky accident, no attempt at smooth.

"Your aircraft," Major Crown said in a tone that would lead you to believe he excelled at everything he tried, and was not surprised by this recent result. As he climbed out of the seat he gave the next man a few pointers, already an instructor.

Owen jotted a few notes at the bottom of the Major's score sheet. He liked to fill out these sheets immediately after a ride was finished, otherwise the pilots tended to blend together, difficult to differentiate Jim from Joe and John, but not this pilot. He knew he would not have any trouble remembering the Major. Owen had never seen anyone, including the 30 fighter pilots he had observed in the simulator, fly with such a lack of grace; almost as if the Major was numb to the G forces he was inflicting on the sim. It would be interesting to hear Josh's opinion.

The next two rides went well. If it were not for the Major's lurking presence at the rear of the sim he would have promised them jobs on the spot. They left the sim and Owen went outside for another smoke. The Major followed him. "I'll need to know pretty quickly if you want me in this next class," he said, "I'd have a lot of loose ends to clean up," letting him know what an important guy he was.

Owen wondered briefly if maybe the Major didn't know how obnoxious he was, and what his response would be if Owen pointed it out, then dismissed the idea. The Major probably wouldn't listen.

"You, like everyone else that is attending this sim session, will be advised within 24 hours if you have a seat in the next class," Owen said, somewhat testily. "We will need your answer within another 24, so you should start considering now whether you can arrange your busy schedule to be in class in 2 weeks. It is unimportant to me what modifications you have to make to your life in order to be available." Owen took a deep breath, not sure that he wanted to continue his train of thought or let it be. The Major started to speak and Owen shook him off.

"If you are offered a job it will be as First Officer Robert Crown, not Major anything, You can be Major when you go to your Guard meetings," Owen said, "but not here," and walked into the parking lot before the Major could reply. When he returned to the door the Major was nowhere to be seen.

The next hour's session was a complete waste of time. Not one of the three candidates could manipulate the simulator in even an acceptable fashion. Two crashed short of the runway trying to land. The third hit the runway but lost control quickly, spun the sim 180 degrees and ended up in the grass. All three were embarrassed by their performance and Owen felt badly for them. They seemed like nice guys so he offered a little encouragement. "In six months you can reapply and we'll probably still be hiring," he told the trio. "I know it's expensive but it might be worth the money to rent a sim somewhere for an hour of practice. It should be enough to get you the job next time."

When the three pilots had left the sim, Owen and Josh compared notes. They had both liked five candidates, four were acceptable, leaving the Major and Anna, and one position open. "This should be an easy decision, even if she can't fly," Josh stated. "The Major is a serious asshole...but we need two alternates anyway."

"Let's hold off on the decision," Owen suggested, "until we see how she does. Then we can figure out who's in and who's an alternate."

The competition was over before it even got started. Owen and Josh returned to the sim with Anna and Tracy in tow, Owen sliding into the Captain's seat as Anna watched carefully. He noticed. "The trick," he said, "to getting into the right seat is to slide your left foot far enough forward between the seat and the center console to allow space for your right foot to go up and over the seat and into the footwell."

Anna nodded her head once and followed his instruction to the letter, making it look like a ballet move, fluid and graceful.

"Ok," Josh said, "now if you can adjust the seat without breaking it, you pass and we can go straight to the bar."

Owen showed her the use of the seat adjustment handles and showed her the eye alignment device on the center windshield post. In just a few moments she was set, resting her right hand on the wheel, left on the throttles, eyes checking the instrument panel, her lips compressed in a purposeful line, her posture erect, sitting on the seat, not in it. "If you don't mind waiting just a bit for the drinks I'd like to give this a try," she said with a quick smile.

"He's joking with me," Owen said, and explained his theory on seat adjustment and how it was a predictor of pilot skills. "You seem a little tense. Roll your shoulders around a little and try to loosen up. We won't start until you're ready."

Owen realized that if it had been a male pilot he would have reached over and given him a light punch on the arm, but decided that in this case it would be a bad idea. At the moment Anna viewed him as just another man she had to prove herself to; she wouldn't ask for help, but she did take her hands off the wheel and throttles and rolled her head and shoulders for a moment before placing them back on the controls. "I'm ready," she said.

"Ok...you're on the departure end of runway 18 Left in Dallas, the brakes are set..."

When Owen called "rotate" Anna pulled the wheel back gingerly, bringing the nose up to 10 degrees and holding it there until they lifted off then adding back pressure until the attitude indicator showed 15 degrees. "Gear up," she said, her voice sounding hoarse. Owen could see the muscles bunched in her forearms.

"Try these," he instructed, reaching over and pulling down the left armrest. Anna reached behind her and pulled the right one into place. "Now let your arms rest, that way you will be flying with just your hands, it'll be easier." He called "V two plus 20," and Anna immediately recognized the cue and called for flaps up, climb power, and the climb check list. She had been paying attention during his briefing.

"Right turn to 250, " Owen said, and she complied with the instruction, rolling into a 20 degree bank at first then correcting it to 30, "Out of 7 for 8,000," Owen cautioned, and she reached for the throttles, pulling them back till the fuel flow was at 3,500 pounds and lowering the nose to slow the rate of climb. They were still in a turn, Owen having timed the maneuver that way to add a little difficulty. She would have to level the wings, stop the climb and reduce the power almost simultaneously. Nearly perfect, she missed the altitude by 100 feet and the heading by 10 degrees but started immediate corrections for both. The airspeed she nailed right at 250 knots. He could see her talking to herself, mad, wanting to be perfect.

"Nobody's perfect the first time," he soothed, "you're doing great. You want to take a break for a minute?"

"However you do it with the other guys," she said, wanting no favors.

"Ok, when you're ready, one steep turn to the left then roll immediately into one to the right, 180 degrees each."

The first turn was almost perfect, the little mistakes made corrected before she was done with the second. She paid careful attention to everything Owen said, incorporating his suggestions into her technique, getting smoother, more sure handed. At one point she even smiled at a joke he made, though her eyes never left the instruments. It wasn't until she had completed the approach and landing, brought the airplane to a stop, and asked that he set the brakes before she finally relaxed, letting her hands fall into her lap.

"Whew," she sighed, "that's almost like work."

"It does take a lot of concentration at first," Owen admitted, "but it will get easier when you get used to it."

"When would I find out," she asked quietly, " If I'm going to get a chance to get used to it?"

Owen held his hand over his shoulder. "Are you done with the grading sheer?" he asked Josh, who placed the paper in his hand without a word. Under the comment section he had written: fast learner, smooth, be careful what you tell her because she will remember it, definitely hire.

"Looks like we're in agreement," Owen said, smiling and extended his hand toward Anna who shook it warmly. "The job is yours if you want it, ground school starts in 15 days."

"If I want it? Oh I want it all right. Where do I sign?" laughing giddily and giving his hand one exaggerated shake before reaching back and shaking Josh's hand as well. Tracy leaned over Josh's shoulder and gave Anna a high five. Both women were laughing now, leading Owen to think there was some kind of sisterhood thing going on. He didn't care. He was happy to have Anna going to class instead of Major Crown.

"My turn now," Owen said, instructing Josh to put them back at the departure end of the runway and clear the overcast while he set up the sim for takeoff. He showed Anna how to work the timing function of the clock on her instrument panel. "My personal best for the world's shortest flight in a 737 is 50 seconds. Start the clock when I release the brakes," he instructed Anna, pushing the throttles forward to their stops and saying: "now," as they surged forward.

As soon as the wheels left the ground Owen began a left turn, rolling into a 75 degree bank, more than twice the normal limit, pushing the nose over to keep them 300 feet above the ground, retarding the throttles and leveling the wings momentarily until they were abeam the end of the runway they had just departed then back to the 75 degree left bank, pointing the nose at the end of the runway which was just swinging into view, using so much left rudder to hurry the turn that the sensations the simulator was giving off were more like a ride on a roller coaster than an airplane. He did not flare, letting the sim thump onto the runway and setting the brakes while they were still indicating 130 knots; an action that in an airplane would have blown all four tires, but in the simulator was the quickest way to stop. "Time," he said, as they lurched violently to a halt.

"I can't tell for sure, the clocks not digital, but it looks like 48 seconds to me, a new personal best," Anna was shaking her head and laughing. "How did you ever think up that maneuver?"

"It gets pretty boring spending hours in this box teaching the same thing over and over. Everyone has their own little game they play. Let's swap seats and let Tracy and Josh have a turn."

He let her get out of her seat first, admiring again the graceful way she moved, then realized that Tracy was watching him, gave her a quick smile and mouthed the word "nice".

"Bad boy," Tracy mouthed back, shaking her head at him, then punching him lightly on the shoulder when he squeezed past her as they were trading places.

Tracy did really well, getting the airplane stopped on the runway three times in a row, Anna applauding her efforts. Josh managed a perfect single engine approach with the sim set to zero ceiling and visibility, the nose gear resting on the centerline when Owen "improved" the weather and they could see.

"Enough fun for one day," Owen said, "it's cocktail time."

Tracy wanted to go to the Two Step, a country and western bar in their hotel. It featured long neck Lone Star beer, spicy chicken wings, fries in a basket, and a raucous atmosphere with live music and dancing, none of which Owen was interested in. "I need a little peace and quiet, some vodka, and a nice steak. It's the Cattle Baron for me."

Josh probably would have preferred that over loud music and dancing, but he had little choice in the matter. "It's long necks and chicken wings for me," he said with an apologetic shrug.

Owen looked at Anna. "I don't mind eating alone," he explained, "there will be more excitement at the Two Step. There are two crews laying over here and they will almost certainly be in the bar"

"If you don't mind the company," Anna said without hesitation, "the steak dinner sounds good to me. I'm not that big a fan of line dancing."

It was a short walk across the hotel parking lot to the restaurant where they were seated immediately, opposite each other in a red leather banquet, the soft light cast by the flickering coach lamp on the wall like firelight. The drinks came quickly, Owen's in a heavy cut glass tumbler, the olives swimming, the lemon twist floating on the clear liquid's surface, Anna's Merlot in a long stemmed over sized crystal goblet. "To achieving the first step in your dream," Owen said, reaching across the table and touching his glass to hers with a faint clink, then taking a sip.

"And yours?" Anna asked, "what are your dreams?"

Owen was taken aback by the question. "My dreams? I haven't given dreams that much thought lately, too busy with reality," realizing as he spoke how sad it sounded.

They were both silent for a moment, then started to speak simultaneously and laughed nervously at the momentary confusion. Anna started again. "I'm sorry, that's kind of a personal question I guess. I don't mean to pry."

"That's ok," Owen took a long pull on his drink. Anna another sip. "My life lately is pretty much day to day, try to manage problems as they come along, not get too angry or frustrated, put a smile on someone's face, maybe teach something that will be of use. I have six years before I have to stop flying for an airline. I haven't really thought much about what comes after that."

"You're fifty-four?" It was Anna's turn to be surprised. "Tracy would only tell me that you acted younger than you are."

So she had asked Tracy about him. "What else did she tell you?"

"Oh, Tracy's a pretty big fan. If you ever need a little PR she's your girl." She paused…"You could just walk away from aviation?"

"I've been flying big airplanes for thirty years. That's a long time to be doing anything. I might look at some other areas, be a bush pilot in Alaska, fly floats, that sort of thing. I had a United Captain on my jump seat a while back and he summed it up pretty well, "When I retire," he said, "I'm never going back to a big airport unless I have to cross a body of water that takes more than a week by boat.""

"I thought you loved to fly?"

"I do. I just don't like what flying has become. They've taken all of the joy out of it, whoever "they" are, all the bullshit now, all the rules, all the people watching, second guessing every decision." Owen shook his head, "It's just not the same. I had an old Captain I flew with years ago say that I had been born twenty-five years too late, that I should have been a fighter pilot in WWII, I had the perfect mindset for it. I think he was right. I've been struggling with the rules since I first soloed," He drained his drink and signaled the waiter for another. Anna had barely touched hers. "Maybe I belong in Alaska where the rules are few and far between, flying the bush, living in a cabin in the woods, on a river bank even. There, that's my dream."

Anna was studying his face, her head tilted slightly to one side. "Can't you still be the chief pilot when you're over sixty?"

"Turning sixty wouldn't keep me from being the Chief Pilot, but my boss probably will. We're not getting along that well lately."

She asked the obvious question with her eyes.

Owen shrugged. "He thinks I care more about the pilots than the airline, which is not the case, it's just that I believe in telling the truth, I think it's the best way to manage people. Some of the more senior pilots are talking about starting a union." He smiled, "I mean an association," he corrected himself, "and they came to me with the idea. I told them I could appreciate what they're trying to accomplish but I went through the whole ALPA (Airline Pilots Association) thing at Eastern, and in my opinion all it did was cost the pilots their jobs."

"I told them the simple truth: Alpha has no money, there is none to give, all the employees are paid less than their counterparts at the major carriers. It's one of the reasons our turnover is so high, but there are some things I thought we could do that wouldn't cost very much, and would make the pilot's jobs a little easier. I told them I would talk with Rossi.

"When I told Andrew about my conversation with these pilots he got angry, told me that discussing compensation was not in my job description. If the pilots wanted to form a union they would have to talk to him. He didn't want to hear about my ideas to avert this confrontation, in fact I think he likes confrontation, it's how he manages people."

"Have you talked with the new CEO? Maybe he would be interested in listening to your ideas."

"He's a hard one to read," Owen said, realizing that he wanted to tell Anna all about his conversation that morning and knowing that he couldn't, or shouldn't. Of course, he had already told her far more than prudence would dictate. It didn't really matter. Pretty much everyone knew what he thought. It was why he always lost at poker.

The waiter's arrival saved him from having to explain further. Owen ordered a New York, rare, with ancho chili butter. Anna asked for the petite fillet, also rare, and at Owen's suggestion the ancho chili butter, "on the side, please."

Owen had finished his second drink and ordered a glass of Merlot while Anna had only sipped her wine, the glass still half full. This was truly a strange situation, Owen thought. Either she doesn't drink much or she's being careful because she's with her future boss and doesn't want to make a bad impression. Like a first date, only much more complicated.

They had finished their meal with little else being said and were sipping their wine. Owen, having first asked if it would bother her, had lit a cigarette. Both appeared lost in thought. Cigarette finished, he stubbed it out in the ash tray and signaled the waiter for the check.

"I have a problem," he admitted to her, "If this situation were different, if I wasn't likely to become your boss and have to make the decision whether you pass or fail, continue to be employed at Alpha or not, I'd tell you that you intrigue me, that I'm attracted to you, that I'd like to see more of you. I realize that we barely know each other, and a whole lot of things in your life are about to change.

"I know this is inappropriate, there's a whole chapter in the employee handbook that cautions against it, but I don't really care. You could probably get me into some trouble if you wanted to, but I'll take that risk. Forgive me if this seems too blunt or too fast, but I'm a pretty straightforward guy. Believe me when I say that your opinion of me, or what you say now, will not change your chances of success at Alpha."

The waiter approached and Owen reached for the check. Anna remained lost in thought for a minute then looked directly at him. "Here's what I think," she started, then paused, collecting her thoughts some more. "Sorry, don't mean to draw this out, but while I've been thinking along the same line since my interview, it was a surprise to hear you say it out loud.

"I have no desire to get you into trouble. I like the idea of us together. I probably know more about you than you think, I mean, you do have a reputation, and people talk. I would like to get to know you better though I don't know how we can manage it without our jobs getting in the way. I don't want people to think that I got this job as a favor, I'm likely to be pretty fierce about that, but I don't want to lose this..."she paused, "connection? because of what other people think. Does that make any sense?"

Owen hesitated, intrigued by the reflection of the flickering lamplight in her green eyes, by the suggestion of warmth in her gaze.

"I'm a big fan of independent women," he said, "but could I ask you for a favor? Would it be possible to do this, you know, the getting to know you better thing, without too much drama? I've got all the drama in my life I can handle right now and I think what I really need is to have a few laughs occasionally."

"I think I could manage that, though I should warn you, I'll probably be slightly more demanding than your twenty something flight attendant."

17

The next morning Owen called maintenance control from the hotel before leaving for the airport and the flight back to Clear River. The yaw damper actuator had arrived and been installed. The rudder and yaw damper had been ground tested thoroughly with no abnormalities found. Aircraft 412 would be put back together, the paperwork finished, and ready for a test flight as soon as he got back. He told Harvey that he would get Josh to ride in the right seat, but he would like a mechanic to ride along and observe. If things went well it shouldn't take more than thirty minutes. If they didn't...

It turned out to be a non-event. They climbed to 15,000 feet to conduct the tests, did some steep turns in each direction with Owen using far more rudder than normal; first with the flaps up, then slowed, extended the gear and flaps, and did two more.

"Maybe I'm missing something," Owen said, "you try It," and had Josh take the controls and repeat the series of maneuvers.

"Seems completely normal," he confirmed.

When they were approaching the airport Owen asked the tower for morc than standard separation between them and a following airplane, did some steep turns, then turned on the autopilot as they approached the runway. Everything worked. When they were back at the gate Owen signed off the writeup as flight checked ok and Harvey co-signed it. The three men were puzzled, but agreed that unless it happened again, there was nothing more they could do. It made Owen uneasy, but you couldn't ground an airplane on suspicion.

One of the items listed on the before engine start check list was a review of the aircraft log book. Fifty pages of that individual aircraft's most recent mechanical irregularities, and illegal to depart without assuring it was in it's assigned spot in the cockpit, it would provide both a warning and Owen's solution if the rudder froze again. To make sure the next crew would notice he left the log propped on the radar screen, open to the page about the rudder malfunction. Ten o'clock in the morning. Owen went up to his office, his day just beginning.

During the morning phone call with maintenance control they had mentioned a departure from Chicago's Midway airport the previous evening that had rejected the takeoff at about fifty knots because of some loud banging noises from the area of the nose gear. The Captain had taxied back to the gate. The ground crew had transferred the passengers and bags to another Alpha airplane that had been scheduled to overnight, and they headed for Buffalo without further incident. When Southwest maintenance, who worked with Alpha in Chicago on a contract basis, got to Alpha's airplane about 6:00am, it was discovered that both nose wheel tires were flat and had pieces of glass imbedded in the tread. When the departure runway was checked, tire tracks were found in the grass off the right side and three runway edge lights were crushed.

A lot of people had now gotten involved. Midway facilities maintenance had looked at the nose tires and were stating that the crushed runway lights and tire tracks had obviously come from Alpha's airplane. Southwest maintenance agreed. Someone had contacted the FAA district office in Chicago, who had called their counterpart in Clear River, who had called Alpha maintenance, who had notified the Chief Pilot.

Owen reached the Captain on his cell phone. From the sound of his voice he had been asleep. "Tell me what happened with your rejected takeoff last night," he requested.

'Wasn't much" the Captain started, "short taxi and a new First Officer so things were a little rushed. We had just finished the taxi and before takeoff check lists, lined up on the centerline lights on runway 31 Center, and started the takeoff roll when we heard a couple of loud bangs..." Owen stopped him there.

"Don't say anything else," he said, I'm going to have to replace you with another Captain and you will deadhead back to Clear River. Crew schedule will call you with the details."

There was a moment's silence on the line before the Captain responded angrily; " what the hell are you talking about, replace me, what the hell for?"

"For starters," Owen said quietly, "there are no centerline lights on runway 31 Center, there are tire tracks in the grass, and it looks like glass from three busted edge lights in the nose tires of the aircraft you were the Captain of. It appears as though you lined up to take off with the nose wheels on the right edge of the runway and the right main tires on the grass. I can't imagine another way to explain the physical evidence.

"You should think about finding an aviation lawyer, something Eric Green in our legal department can help you with. I'll talk to our POI, but I'm guessing the FAA will want you to take some time off or maybe spend some time in the right seat. You fucked up and the FAA is going to want its pound of flesh. Talk to a lawyer and call me after you have. I can't put you back on the flight schedule until this is resolved."

"So now you're judge, jury and executioner? I'm guilty without a presumption of innocence? Maybe you'd like me to quit?"

"Do what you think is right. I'll try to be fair, but there is only so much I can do. This is the way the system works now. A lawyer could probably get you before an NTSB law judge if you want to try that, but I'm no expert. My hands are essentially tied. My advice would be to admit the mistake, take the punishment, and get it over with, but that's my thought. Talk to a lawyer then tell me what you want to do."

Owen called Andrew next, told him what he had done: "I know it's really dark and can be kind of confusing at the departure end of 31 but..." "You had no choice," the VP interrupted him. Owen could picture him shaking his head when he said it. They agreed on some things, including the phrase borrowed from late night TV; "stupid pilot tricks".

Owen pulled out the performance sheets for the sim rides from the day before. He and Josh had compared notes on the trip home from Dallas. There was no question that Anna was a better choice than the Major. The two alternate class spots went to a couple of guys who, while not flying the sim as well as she had, managed to get it on the ground without crashing, and seemed to be nice guys who would be far easier to manage than Major Crown. There had to be some benefits to sitting in this office.

Benefits. He spun his chair around and thought about Anna while staring out the window at the airport's seemingly endless expanse of blacktop and grass; airplanes landing and departing, the hum of the offices surrounding his, everything peaceful for the moment.

They had walked back to the hotel together and managed to get up to their floor without being spotted by any Alpha flight crew members laying over in the same hotel. He'd walked her to her door, which seemed like a completely natural thing to do, then leaned down and kissed her lightly on the lips. When they separated she looked at him for a moment then stood on tiptoe and kissed him back. Lightly, almost tentative, but when she stepped back she was smiling. "This is going to be fun," she said, and disappeared into her room.

"Fun," he thought, what a concept, but before he could get any further there was a rap on his open door and B stuck her head in. "Sorry, time to stop daydreaming. Captain Charles has created another problem."

Another problem, 10:30 and already two issues, three if you counted the test flight. "What did he do now, I hesitate to ask."

B stepped into his office and took a seat. "Put your phone on speaker and punch in line one. There are some flight attendants who want to speak to you."

"Flight attendants? Aren't the flight attendants your responsibility?"

"Not this time Babe. We're in this one together."

Owen put the phone on speaker and selected line one. "This is Owen Swift and Barbara Morgan on a speaker phone. Who are we talking with?"

"Owen, it's Lynda, Cathy and Mary, we're in Denver with Captain Charles and we have a problem. It's snowing, and on the before landing announcement he very clearly told the passengers that it was snowing, and that could be pretty exciting because he had never landed in snow before. I shit you not, that's what he said. We're supposed to go to Salt Lake next and he already told us it was snowing there. We want your word that he is not going to kill us. The guy is scary. It's a good thing this is not a through flight because we were getting a lot of comments from the departing passengers about the Captain's sense of humor."

B had a grim smile on her face and a "told you so" look in her eye. Lynda, Cathy and Mary didn't need last names. They had been with Alpha since the beginning and they always bid to fly together. "Where is Captain Charles at the moment?" Owen asked.

"He said he was going outside to smoke. We know he's different, we've flown with him before, but this is a little over the top, even for him."

Owen readily agreed. "I'll talk to him and call you back. It won't take five minutes. He's not dangerous or I wouldn't let him fly, but he is sometimes incredibly stupid. Give me your cell number."

Owen had a Captain's cell phone number directory on his desktop and he consulted it now, then punched up the number, still on speaker. B could see the anger rising and gave a gentle warning look which was ignored. Captain Charles answered on the third ring in his Louisiana drawl. "Hay-low."

Owen gave it a two count but couldn't restrain himself any longer. Too many things had gone wrong in the last couple of days. "Captain

Charles, this is Captain Swift. Would you dispute my opinion that you are a dumb fucking cracker and I ought to fire your ass right now. Leave you in Denver to find your own way back to the bayou. Do you have any possible excuse for making an announcement about the exciting possibilities of landing in snow, which you have certainly done before without a problem, that will change my mind about firing your fucking ass? If you do you better spit it out. You have thirty seconds."

There was a pause then lamely; "I just thought it would be something different, you know, a little more exciting for the passengers instead of the same old, same old... Not a good idea, I guess."

Without a moment's hesitation Owen fired back; " this is another on a long list of bad ideas, next time you're done. I want you to find the flight attendants right now, get down on one knee and beg their forgiveness. When you get to the layover in Salt Lake you will buy them all cocktails and dinner at the restaurant of their choice, whether they invite you to go along or not. One more fuck up and you're gone."

He punched the end button and grinned at B. "Call the girls, tell them he's safe but ignorant, and they should order the most expensive menu items they can find. I feel better already." B was laughing as she walked out the door. "you are a piece of work," she said as she left.

Piece of work indeed, he thought, reaching into a desk drawer and pulling out the manilla folder that had the not too cryptic title "fuck ups" across the top, then rummaged through the loose leaf pages until he found the sheet devoted to Captain Brenton Charles. The file had become necessary when the legal and HR departments had advised that in order to fire someone he would need a written list of mistakes or attitude problems.

Captain Charles had some odd habits. While taxing for takeoff several years ago he had demonstrated the rejected takeoff procedure to a new first officer by pulling the spoiler handle, putting both engines into maximum reverse and jamming on the brakes. All without warning the flight attendants, who were, fortunately, done with the emergency demo and strapped in their seats awaiting takeoff. He did make a PA announcement advising that he liked to practice rejected takeoffs in case they had an emergency during departure. That got the passengers attention. Owen got a few angry passenger letters from that stunt.

Then there was his habit of removing his shoes on longer flights, especially night flights, then walking back into the cabin in his stocking feet, grabbing a few pillows and a blanket, and heading back to the cockpit with only a smile for an explanation to the worried passengers who wondered what their Captain was up to. Owen had gotten some letters about that as well.

Captain Charles had a wife and three kids at home and a steady companion, Randi, who was a twenty-one year old Alpha flight attendant. They flew together as often as they could arrange it. The relationship was no secret at the airline. There was no shortage of this sort of pairing up going on, and it was not something that Owen would normally bother mentioning until his crew, two flight attendants and the First Officer, had come into Owen's office to tell of the pair's inability to make it to the hotel before beginning their foreplay in the back of the hotel van.

Apparently, there were three passengers from the inbound flight on the van, going to the same hotel, and the Captain's actions were an embarrassment to the rest of the crew.

Owen got B to help him with that one. They got Captain Charles and Randi together in Owen's office, but when Owen tried to point out how their actions put the airline in a bad light Randi started to cry. "But, I love him," she sobbed, then turned away and looked at the wall, refusing to talk about it anymore. B had taken her arm and walked her out of there. "What are you all going to do to her," Captain Charles demanded.

Owen shrugged. "If I were you I would be more concerned with what I'm going to do to you," he stated flatly, "or what your wife is going to say when she hears this story."

"You going to tell my wife?" suddenly sounding contrite, "I mean, what's a guy supposed to do, gorgeous young thing drapes herself all over you. Push her away? Not like there's not a lot of other married pilots doing the same thing."

"Not on the crew bus with passengers going to the same hotel. You couldn't wait till you got to your room? I must admit that you sometimes amaze me with how fucking stupid you can be. It's like there's a disconnect somewhere in your brain. I really don't give a shit who you diddle. Don't do it in uniform while in public. And no, I'm not going to tell your wife, but you can rest assured she will find out. I saw you pass riding with your family last week. You don't think one of the flight attendants will slip her a note?"

That incident was dated six months ago and Owen knew they were still an item, if now a more discreet one. He made a new entry with today's date and the latest embarrassment. Maybe somebody else will hire him, Owen thought. He wasn't a bad pilot, but he was a nearly constant pain in the ass. He knew the Captain had resumes out. I'd write the letter of recommendation myself, he thought, if it would get rid of him.

He put the fuck up file away and dug out the FAA forms folder, took out the sheet for a declaration of emergency and began to fill it out. Name, date, time of incident, aircraft type and number, flight number, other crew members names, then the important part; stage of flight and a description of the event. Then even more important; FAR's (federal aviation regulations) deviated from. He thought about that before writing: "descended below minimum descent altitude (MDA)without sufficient visual contact to identify and land on the runway." There was no hiding from the facts. He knew the FAA had already pulled the cockpit voice recorder and the conversation between Larry and himself on final would confirm his actions as illegal. He added: "runway visual confirmed at approx.100 feet."

He considered calling Andrew to get his opinion, but decided against it. Andrew wouldn't care; he wasn't the one being threatened.

Maybe Tim Granger? Tim had been a 737 Captain with USAir before taking early retirement to try to save his pension. They had met for cocktails on several occasions, discovered they were both products of grass strip aviation and felt the same about rules and regulations. Tim seemed to chafe at the FAA's dogmatic approach but he needed the income. "I have two ex wives and two kids in college," he had admitted one night when they were halfway through their third drink. He didn't think Tim would risk his own career to protect him, but he might give an honest answer about where the process was heading. No, Owen decided, unwilling to put Tim in that spot, just fill out the form truthfully and see what happens. He took the form out to Miranda and asked her to type three copies and give them back. He would sign and deliver them to the FAA office on his way to lunch.

The FAA complex was in an office park three miles from the airport. Owen drove, parked, entered the lobby, and stopped at the receptionist's desk. "Hi Louise," he said with a smile, and handed over the envelope addressed to Tim Granger. "He's in his office if you would like to deliver this in person, Captain Swift," she said, smiling back at him; "I'll ring him if you like?" "Why not," Owen said with a shrug. Tim appeared and escorted him back to his office, then closed the door quietly.

"Before I open this," holding up the envelope, "let's talk about it first," Tim said, sitting behind his desk and motioning Owen to take a seat also. "I've heard some things that I think you should know about, but you can't tell anyone where you heard it, and I will deny that I told you if you decide to pursue it." He paused, then continued; "There are a lot of whispers about the investigation into the Pittsburgh crash. I'm still pretty close to a few of the USAir pilots who have been attending the hearings. Boeing started out claiming that pilot error was the cause. The airplane had flown through the wake of a preceding 727 and the bumps had caused the F/O to apply full left rudder in an attempt to remain in control, but instead put the aircraft into an uncontrollable nose down attitude from which recovery was not possible.

"The NTSB, from what I hear, is going to say that the rudder had deflected rapidly to the left and reached its aerodynamic blowdown limit shortly thereafter. They will also say that examination of the system revealed that it is possible, let me repeat that, possible, that the rudder power control unit had jammed due to a number of factors. Also, and this is the good part though still rumor and not confirmable, they are going to state that if the rudder PCU design was submitted for certification today it would be turned down. Here's the puzzle though, they are going to give Boeing and the airlines that operate the 737 five years to redesign and replace the controllers. Five years. They're claiming that chances of this reoccurring are so remote that there is no rush.

"Some of the USAir team contacted the company that makes the hydraulic filters used on most 737s. They claim that contaminates found in the accident aircraft's hydraulic fluid could cause a valve to quit functioning and jam, then start to function again, explaining the intermittent problem you had with the rudder. I think we need to make sure the hydraulic fluid, filter and PCU in the airplane you were flying get at least tested, and preferably changed. The sooner the better."

"Why not let the PMI (principal maintenance inspector) pursue it?" Owen had never met the man, but knew of his existence because all the mechanics complained about him always looking over their shoulder.

"This is seriously sensitive material that was brought to me in confidence. He is unaware of it and I can't afford to let the powers that be find out that this information came from me. They would want to know my source and not cooperating might cost me my job. I need this job. You know how rapidly your pension disappeared at Eastern when they went broke? I'm likely to have the same problem with USAir."

"I do have another possible way we could work this," Tim continued, "Remember the Eastwind control problems over Richmond about seven months ago? On paper it sounds exactly like what happened to you except it started at 4,000 feet. That pilot submitted a long report but it was dismissed by the FAA and the NTSB and shelved. I have that Captain's name and phone number. Maybe you could call him, one Captain to another, and that would give you the ammo to get the rudder valve changed and the hydraulic fluid checked. If it looked like you had brought the information to me, I could cover my ass, and maybe help you a little bit.

"I know you and Rossi don't get along all that well, but he's still a pilot. Maybe he could be convinced that a preemptive change would be worth the expense. Then the two of you could work on Spencer to get the switch approved. It has also recently been leaked that in the week before the United crash at C Springs there were two reports of rudder malfunction. After the second report the yaw damper was changed. Six days later the airplane did the same thing yours did, rolled to the right and nosed down. The only difference; they crashed, you didn't.

"One more thing; I knew the Captain and First Officer on flight 427, knew them well. I had flown with both before I retired and they were both good pilots. Besides, no experienced pilot would push a rudder pedal to the floor without good cause, even with an engine failure. Boeing is trying to railroad those guys."

"Let me have the Eastwind Captain's name and number," Owen said, "I'll call him when I get back to my office."

"People call me Tony," Captain Anthony Paige said, when he returned Owen's call early in the afternoon, "my wife said you were a 737 Captain and the Chief Pilot with Alpha?"

After Owen told him his story Captain Paige said; "I hope your management will be easier to convince than mine was. I had to go public, wrote a ten thousand word dissertation and sent it to the FAA and the NTSB. They denied the possibility that my story was true and did nothing. Then I gave it to the Richmond paper. They did a full piece in the Sunday edition. Richmond's a small market, like Clear River, and people noticed. Only then did they ground the airplane and get the PCU and the hydraulic filter changed. They told me the parts were fifty grand, plus labor, blah, blah, blah. I pointed out that the airline wouldn't last a week if we had a fatal crash. A little airline is not like United or US Scare that can shake off an incident like this. Management's not very fond of me still, but I'm ok with that. I'll help you if I can,"

"I might ask you to talk to my VP or maybe the CEO."

"Like I said, happy to help if I can. Boeing says the odds against this happening are a million to one, but there have been two crashes in the US, two more internationally, plus a bunch of incidents that sound like the rudder was the cause of the problem. Now we have two near misses, yours and mine. And these are just the ones we know about."

"Also, I had a lawyer call me. Name's Lance Thompson, I'll give you his number but I'd guess he'll call you first. I think he's got someone on the inside, either with the government or Boeing, who is feeding him information. He's representing the wife of a guy that died in the Pittsburgh crash, and was looking for information. I told him my story and sent him the report I sent to the NTSB and the FAA. He claims there has to be collusion between Boeing and the government. He's suing everybody on the wife's behalf, and talking some pretty big numbers. My management knows about this guy and I think it was the reason they agreed to change the rudder PCU. Might come in handy if your management needs a push in the right direction."

Owen sat and doodled on his yellow pad when the phone call was done. Do this, then an arrow to the possible result, then another arrow. There were lots of different scenarios. He scratched out what he'd written, started again. It took him thirty minutes but when he was satisfied he picked up the pad and walked next door to B's office. She was doodling as well but looked up when he walked in. "Nobody else has done anything stupid," she said, "can we leave and go to a bar. I'm in the mood for a drink."

"I need to talk to Andrew first, but let me run this idea by you. That "event" I had the other night, I just talked with the

Eastwind Captain who had the same thing happen to him about seven months ago. He thinks that the NTSB and the FAA are just parroting what Boeing is telling them to say. Eastwind finally changed the rudder PCU on the problem airplane, but only after all the adverse publicity the Captain generated with letters to the FAA, NTSB and local paper. He's already had a lawyer call him who's suing pretty much everybody on behalf of a USAir passenger that died in the Pittsburg crash."

B had the ability to sit absolutely motionless when she was thinking. She had sat perfectly still during his explanation, but her whole face slowly scrunched into a pained expression.

"Let me make sure I understand where you're headed," she said. "You want to convince not only Andrew, but Spencer and T.L. that they should ground an airplane and do about $50,000 worth of work that the FAA, NTSB, and Boeing say isn't necessary, to remedy a problem that they all claim has a one in a million chance of reoccurring? Have I got it right so far?"

"Not quite. What I want them to do is swap out the PCU in 412 for a new or rebuilt one, then get the problem one bench tested to see if they can figure out what went wrong. Maybe they could compare it to the PCU from the United and USAir crashes, see if there are similarities."

She shook her head slowly, disbelieving. "You are a glutton for punishment, no question about that."

"Do I have another choice? What if I do nothing and the airplane crashes, then what? If I do something stupid and kill myself...well ok...I mean it's my fault. But, If I do nothing and other people die...?"

B was silent for a moment then stood and leaned over her desk resting on both palms, putting her face closer to his. "How about this? If you tell this story to the powers here, point out the fact that the United crash was preceded by the same mechanical problem you just had, and the consequences a fatal crash would have on Alpha? " She stopped, deep in thought.

"It doesn't make sense though," she continued, "what about our other eight airplanes? Who's to say they don't have the same faulty part biding its time, waiting to break at the least opportune moment. Where do the odds go if you include all nine airplanes? For that matter how about Southwest? Their entire fleet is 737s, and they have money. Why aren't they changing the PCU on all of them? Why aren't the rest of the airlines that operate the type?" She answered her own question: "They don't think the risk is worth the cost to eliminate it, at least not till some authority says it is, which means their lawyers don't think they're liable, which probably means we wouldn't be either."

She stopped talking and sat back down, the tight frown relaxing into a neutral gaze. Owen realized he had been hunching over the desk and he sat straighter now, lost in thought. "You're probably right," he admitted, quietly.

There was another moment's silence. "I can see you doing this, jumping off the cliff," B said, "it's in your nature and you see it as the right thing to do. Maybe it is, but suppose you're wrong, you go public with your theory and scare away what little business Alpha has and the company goes broke. How is that going to make you feel?"

"You're making me feel like now I'm the one who needs a drink.". There was a knock on the door and Miranda poked her head in. "There you are," she said, looking at Owen. "A lawyer named Lance Thompson would like to talk to you. He's on line one." She ducked out and closed the door.

They both stared at the blinking light on the phone. "That was quick," B said, "you might want to give this some thought before you talk to him."

Owen nodded, "You talk to him. Tell him I'm unavailable, but I will call him tomorrow morning if he gives you a number he can be reached at."

Owen called the VP of flight ops next and explained his idea about changing out the PSU and the call from the lawyer. "Good luck with that," Andrew grunted, "you're just going to create more trouble," then hung up, leaving Owen to swing in the wind.

Ten seconds after Owen had replaced the handset Miranda knocked again, gave him a knowing smile and said: "now Christine Saunders is on line one for you. You remember her? Spencer Elliot's executive assistant?"

Owen was unaware of any man who had met Ms. Saunders and forgotten her. She was a tall, willowy brunette who managed to combine a professional appearance with a come-hither look.

"Thank you Miranda," Owen said, as she pulled back and closed the door behind her. "Mind if I take it here again?" B handed him the phone without comment and punched in line one.

"Owen Swift," he spoke into the phone in his best rumbling Captain's PA voice.

"Captain Swift," Christine's voice was buttery smooth and precise. She was a New Yorker, Owen knew, but didn't sound it. What inducement Spencer had used to get her to leave her Wall Street employer and move west with him was a constant topic of speculation within the company.

"Mr. Elliott asked me to apologize for the lateness of the invitation, but wondered if it would be possible for you to meet him this evening, around 7:30?

Owen took a quick glimpse at his watch. 5:00, plenty of time. "Fine," he said, "where would he like to meet?"

"Are you familiar with the Clear River Club? If you arrive before Spencer he asks that you go to the casual bar. He will join you there."

18

6-16-97

Owen had access to inside information. He knew all the Alpha VPs, and would pester them until he got the information he wanted, take it home, and at night, or on weekends, try to make sense of it all. It wasn't a pretty picture. Alpha's cost per available seat mile (CASM) was high. At ten cents a seat mile they were as high or higher than the major competition they faced, while their revenue per seat mile (RASM) was considerably lower.

"If you are buying apples for a dollar and selling them for fifty cents you shouldn't waste money on advertising," he told Jeffrey Tanner the VP of finance.

"No shit," was the terse reply, "you think we don't know that? When you figure out some way to reverse the numbers let me know."

Stabbing in the dark, Owen called the office of the US Department of Transportation. "The top 1000 City Pair report is what you need," he was told by the woman who answered the phone, "they are issued quarterly." He ordered the last four reports.

Going through the 150 pages of documents he was sent allowed Owen to find and compare all of Alpha's city-pairs. Then he compiled a list of other airlines that were close to Alpha's size. The one that stuck out was Midwest Express.

Alpha had to charge 40% less than its major competitors on a given route to get it's 20% share of passengers.

Midwest Express was an entirely different story. They were the only small airline Owen could find that charged more than their major competition. All of their seats were business-class, there was no middle seat, and they were making money. Owen found this out by sending for, and pouring over, their Form 40 report filed with the FAA.

Midwest Express' cost was two cents a seat mile higher than Alpha's.

"but that's for a business-class seat," he had told B, excited by his discovery. "That means it would only cost us $20 more to take a passenger to San Fran in a business-class seat than it does now in coach."

"It can't be that simple," she replied, "more people would do it."

Bruce Franklin, the VP of marketing, had been an airline analyst with an investment banking firm. He would neither confirm nor deny that he had been hired to look out for the interests of Alpha's owner, Mr. T L Bentworth. Slender, immaculately groomed, and deceptively soft spoken, Franklin was not easily separated from his convictions.

"It's not that simple," he said when Owen cornered him later that afternoon. "There has never been a successful first class airline."

"Not first class, business class," Owen persisted. "There is a big difference. Midwest Express uses DC9s. They start with five across seating, three and two, so when you take out the middle seat you only lose twenty percent of your capacity. The others have used Boeing equipment, six across seating requires the removal of two seats per row. You'd lose one third of your seats, plus they increased the between row spacing so you lose another two whole rows. Midwest uses the same spacing as we do and you'd have to admit that since they have been in business for over a decade and they're making money, the idea has some validity."

"Not here it doesn't," Bruce replied with an exasperated sigh. He waved Owen to a chair. "Look, Midwest Express was started as the corporate aviation arm of Kimberly Clarke; they had a built in clientele and no expectation or need to make a profit. There was interest from other corporations so they started selling seats. They didn't make a profit for the first three years."

"Alpha has been in business for four years and we've lost something like fifty million dollars," Owen interrupted.

"But it's not because we're an all-coach airline. If maintenance could keep our aircraft flying we would be doing fine." Bruce finished his thought.

There was a momentary silence. Owen gave a small shake of his head. "I don't know how you can say that. We get run out of every new route we try. Des Moines to Chicago, United was charging $250 dollars one way until we put in a morning flight, then they switched their 727 for a 757 and sold seats for $59 dollars, same as us. They kept at it until they ran us out of the market then went back to a 727 and the $250 fare.

"Clear River to Dallas, American did the same thing. Clear River to Minneapolis, Northwest put the screws to us. Even if we had new airplanes, or at least airplanes that worked, how could we defend against that tactic? And lest we forget Southwest, the dominant carrier in Clear River. Not one airline has successfully competed against them at the low cost game. How do you intend to manage that?"

Owen realized that his voice had been rising almost to a shout. He was perched on the front edge of his chair and now he sat back and mumbled: "Sorry".

Bruce dismissed his apology with a wave of his manicured hand. "We don't compete with Southwest, at least not for now. We stay away from them, and we try not to get into any major's honey jar until we find a few routes we can dominate. Then we can use the cash-flow from those routes to sustain us while we try more new routes."

Owen realized that Bruce hadn't heard a word he had said, or if he had, was ignoring the gist of his argument. "Stay away from

Southwest, that's a good long term plan," he said as he stood, assuming the irony would be missed.

Bruce stood at the same time. "You've really been doing your homework. Very impressive. Maybe you should think about becoming a consultant," but he was smiling when he said it. "If you don't mind, let me make a copy of those figures you've compiled. I'll try to take a look at them later."

19

The Clear River club had been formed by ten newly minted Wall Street millionaires at the height of the Roaring Twenties extravagance to exhibit their new found wealth. It had suffered the indignity of foreclosure shortly after the 1929 crash took the members on a dizzying ride from riches to ruin, then sat in increasing disrepair for decades until a new group of investors, buoyed by Reagan's election and some tax loophole possibilities, had bought it for pennies on the dollar and restored it to its original glory. A millionaire could still join, though most of the current membership had a considerably higher net worth. There were 700 acres of pristine forest and grassland, 18 holes of a Donald Ross golf course with a pro shop, a tennis pavilion with a dozen clay courts, barns with stables for 50 horses, a dressage ring and miles of trails. The clubhouse was a stone, glass and wood beam prairie design overlooking the river, with a restaurant for those more formal members who thought dressing for dinner meant suit and tie, and the casual bar and grill whose dress code allowed the younger- minded sports among the membership to eat and drink in their playing attire; golf slacks, tennis whites, jodhpurs, and even jeans allowed.

A hostess at the front door told Owen that Mr. Elliot had not yet arrived and directed him to the bar, a polished muted space, his

Absolut rocks with a spear of blue cheese stuffed olives arriving within minutes of being ordered, accompanied by a small bowl of still-warm roasted macadamia nuts. Owen had puzzled over Spencer's request to meet at the club instead of his office. Scanning the bar area he realized that there would be little chance of meeting another Alpha employee here, little chance of this meeting being observed, the contents leaked.

He took a sip of the vodka and popped an olive in his mouth. First class, he thought, reminded of his conversation with Bruce Franklin: first class versus business class.

Spencer arrived and the hostess showed them to a table in the back of the smoking section. Owen, trailing along behind, noticed the deference with which she treated the CEO. A regular customer and good tipper, he thought. The man did look like New York executive material; accomplished, reserved, a distinct presence, slightly aloof, above the crowd in his pressed black jeans and open necked starched white shirt, 60's Ivy League frat boy success story.

"We don't have to sit in the smoking area. I can get through a meal without smoking," Owen offered.

"I was thinking I might bum one from you. I quit, in theory, but if my wife's not around to yell at me I sneak a few when I'm drinking."

Owen put his pack on the table and Spencer picked it up, shook out one cigarette, held it to his nose and sniffed. "I didn't know you could still buy Chesterfields," he said as he lit up.

After the drinks had arrived, A Macallan single malt, "one ice cube please," for Spencer and another Absolut for Owen, the conversation got serious.

"What's happening with the FAA?" Spencer asked.

Owen told the story, including his conversation with the Eastwind Captain, but omitted how he had discovered that link. He underlined the chain of events leading to the Colorado Springs crash with specific emphasis on the fact that United had changed the yaw damper actuator before the fatal crash six days later, but had done nothing with the PCU. "I think we need to change out the rudder power control unit and check the hydraulic fluid for contamination, even if it's not required."

"What is Rossi's take on this?"

"He said I should bring it to you. I would guess he'll wait and see which way the tide is running before deciding how to vote. I'm on a thin limb here and Andrew doesn't volunteer to go out on limbs."

"Do you feel the same way as the Eastwind Captain? If Alpha management doesn't go along with your assertion that this is a life threatening, end of operation issue you will go public with the information?"

"I don't think it will matter what I say or to whom. The press already knows that I declared an emergency and someone will figure out what happened. I think it would be better if you decided to be proactive, rather than reactive. Spend the money to address the problem because it's the right thing to do to protect the investment in Alpha, social as well as financial. This airline would not survive a fatal crash. Look what happened to ValuJet, and they were a lot bigger than we are."

"Are you looking out for TL's investment or spreading the blame? Telling me relieves you of sole responsibility if there is a crash." Spencer was staring at him intently.

Owen shrugged. "I'm not a soapbox kind of guy, I'm a numbers guy, though I would not want to be in the position of feeling that I didn't do everything I could to prevent a fatal accident. There are several potential outcomes here. We do nothing, the airplane crashes, the press gets the story, which they will whether I talk or not, and every airline that operates the 737 is fucked, including Alpha. Or, you could roll the dice.

"There are 2700 first-generation 737 aircraft that have been operating world wide for more than 20 years and you are statistically twice as likely to die riding in one of those than you would be in the newer series. It now has been leaked that the NTSB report will say the rudder PCU was responsible for the C Springs and Pittsburgh crashes. There have been 4 fatal crashes that appear to have been caused by a problem with the rudder plus at least 2 near misses that I know about, but no one, not Boeing, the FAA, or the NTSB and certainly not the airlines that operate the type are requiring a change. I will tell you that a lawyer representing the wife of a passenger on the USAir crash in Pittsburgh called my office earlier."

"And you told him?"

"I said I would call him tomorrow, but I'm told that he is already suing everyone even remotely connected with the accident. The older 737/200model that we operate may be twice as dangerous to fly on, but what gambler wouldn't jump on million to one odds. No other airline that operates the type has done anything about potential PCU problems. That probably means their legal departments don't think they would be liable if a PCU caused a crash so, in theory, Alpha wouldn't be either.

"It can't be known for sure what the results of a fatal crash would be for Alpha and I'm not sure I'm right about the correct course of action. If you look at the outcome from the steps Boeing is recommending, and United took before the C Springs crash," Owen shrugged, "if we change the yaw damper, but not the PCU, then end up with a fatal crash... 50 grand seems like a pittance though I freely admit, it's not my money. I also admit that this is not a black and white decision, there is a lot of grey."

Spencer continued to stare, picked up his glass and without looking took a long pull, then picked up his cell phone and called Donald Frost, the maintenance VP, asked him to find out how long it would take to get a new PCU for aircraft 412, change it, and to figure out what it would cost. "Call me back, I'll be waiting," he said, then sipped his whiskey while they waited for an answer. It took 5 minutes. He listened briefly then, "I'll call you right back," ended that call and hit speed dial. He turned away from Owen for this conversation, the words private, the speech clipped and short. He ended that call, hit the speed dial once more, and again looking directly at Owen said into his phone; "Schedule the change as soon as possible," then put the phone back in his jacket pocket.

"You are one persuasive son of a bitch," he said with grudging admiration. "Hopefully that will cover our ass on the rudder problem.

"Now," Spencer continued, "have you ever given any thought to moving up the corporate ladder?

The question gave Owen pause. "Well..," concerned about the direction this conversation had taken and stalling for time to think.

"Sure, I mean anyone with half a brain has the occasional thought that they could make better decisions than the person in charge. Only natural. And yes, I've had those thoughts."

"How about Andrew's job? VP of Flight Operations, have you considered that?"

When Owen sat in stunned silence Spencer continued. "I'm serious. You seem completely unaffected by titles, mine included, and while I know you like being the Chief Pilot, and I could recruit someone from outside with more management experience than you have to be the VP, executing the changes TL and I have been discussing would be easiest if we brought the whole pilot group along. There appears to be no one in this company, myself included, who has more respect or whose word is more trusted than yours."

"What happens to Andrew?" Owen had occasionally had to fire people and it was the part of his job he liked least.

"Andrew goes away." Spencer said simply. "There would be no place for him here. He gets to keep the vested portion of his stock options and if Alpha is successful he'll make some money. If it's not... it will be his loss and not your concern. This is the way corporate management works. He's not protected by a seniority list. You won't be either.

"You were right about my previous career," Spencer continued, "I did take companies apart and sell the pieces and while that does create a profit it is not particularly satisfying. I want to try something different with Alpha and TL is interested. He wants to own an airline he's proud of and could make financing available, a substantial amount of it, if I... we...could come up with an idea we could sell him on. You told me you had lots of ideas. We both know without serious change Alpha's days are numbered. Tell me what you would change to make this a viable airline."

Owen took a deep breath and exhaled slowly. Returning Spencer's gaze he said; "You're serious? This is a bit of a stretch and totally unexpected so you'll understand my reluctance to voice my opinion."

"Absolutely serious, and I haven't seen much reluctance from you in the last three months. I know you don't care about titles but you would need one. I have been thinking for a while of replacing Andrew. That, by the way, is obviously in strictest confidence, though it will be common knowledge within a week at the latest. You understand that I'm crawling out on my own limb here, trusting you. I've already interviewed several other candidates for the position and the change will happen with or without you. It is my understanding that you have the flight and management experience the FAA requires to be the VP of flight operations. You would get the same stock options the other VP's have and the same pay. More importantly for you, if I'm reading you correctly, you would get to have input on the direction this company goes. Get the chance to create something new, to set a new tone. Don't, however, get the idea I'm doing this solely for your benefit. This is business and there is risk as well as reward. I do have some questions about your...let's call it your management philosophy... we will have to discuss before this goes any further."

Their waiter paused at the table and Spencer, with a glance at Owen, ordered another round, took the pack, shook out and lit another cigarette, his impatience hidden behind the cloud of smoke for the moment but then said, "I'm not joking, and I know this a leap for you, but this is a small window we're looking at and I will need your answer fairly quickly. Tell me how you would manage flight operations, what would your tone be? What about slowing down the employee turnover rate, especially in the pilot group? Andrew said about a month ago that the pilots were talking to ALPA, and looking at the possibility of joining. How would you handle that?"

"The pilots came to me 3 months ago. I took their complaints to Andrew and he got angry and started threatening to hire the nastiest labor lawyer out there. He likes a fight. The truth is we pay our pilots one third what they would make at a major carrier, any major. It's not just the pilots, starting flight attendant pay qualifies them for food stamps. Ground positions are equally under compensated. We'll never keep anybody unless we raise the compensation level."

"Just how high do you think it has to be raised?

"There's no specific answer to that question. For pilots it depends on who else continues to hire and how many pilots are available. Less than 20% of the pilots we hire move to Clear River. The others share commuter apartments, put in their 18 months, get some heavy jet time and maybe a type rating, then move on. It's a risk for them to stay here any longer than they must because the pay and benefits of the next job are based on their seniority there. If we want to keep them here a couple of things have to happen.

"You already admitted that without serious change Alpha's days are numbered. The pilots are well aware of that. It's one of the big reasons they leave. If they saw serious investment and the plans to acquire a functional fleet, that would freeze a lot of them in place, for a while anyway. If it was my decision to make I would draw up an agreement, one that extended out maybe...5 years and covered pay raises over that period. Link it to the financial performance of the company. Alpha makes X profit the employee gets X bonus. We now pay a Captain less than he would make if he leaves and gets a job as a First Officer with a major. That has to change if you want to keep him here, but I would also look at an employee stock option plan; maybe give a Captain 15,000 options, a F/O 7,500, and have them start to vest in 5 years. The stock's at a buck now. If in 5 years the airline is profitable and the stock's at 50, no pilot will be leaving. In fact, I think you should give every employee stock options based on their salary, make everyone an owner, at least until the new Alpha is established and we can afford to raise the pay scale closer to industry standard. It's easier to motivate owners than employees.

"This is a public service business," Owen continued, "the big carriers seem to have forgotten that. We need employees who recognize that doing an excellent job is in their own best interest as well as the company's. It's as important as having airplanes that work, if not more so."

"I'm not sure that TL will accept an employee stock option plan," Spencer said.

"Really?" Owen paused thinking this might be a bad road to head down, then went ahead anyway. "Correct me if I'm wrong, but didn't I read somewhere that as part of your employment agreement you received one million stock options? VPs got 250,000 options each when they signed on? The rest of the employees got none."

Spencer sat silently for a moment, his face creasing into a frown.

"You sure you know where you're going with this?"

"You said a short while ago that this was business. Besides, It's public knowledge," Owen said quietly, "though it may not be the best way for me to secure a VP slot. I can guarantee you the employees know, and they can do the math. It's not whether TL will approve an employee stock option plan, he already has. It's a question of who gets to reap the benefits. The employees are worth more than they are getting, they know it, and if we don't address that fact, in the long run Alpha is, as you said, doomed.

"We have 9 aircraft now," Owen continued, "that's 45 Captains, 45 First Officers; to expand to even 25 aircraft we'll need 125 Captains. We would have to upgrade every First Officer plus hire and train 35 more. That's if no one else quits. I've been Chief Pilot for three years and done all the pilot hiring and I have not seen one qualified airline Captain walk in the door. It's nearly impossible to hire Captain-qualified pilots off the street, certainly not at our current wage scale and with all the majors hiring. If you know of some other way to get and keep pilots on the property so we'll have enough experienced pilots to expand the fleet, I'm happy to listen."

"How about more guys like you," a trace of sarcasm in his tone, "from failed carriers but with enough experience to go straight into the Captain's seat?"

Owen showed a tight smile then; "I came here when Alpha was just getting started four years ago," a little heat in his voice, "nobody else was hiring. I saw the initial pre-startup ad Alpha ran looking for Captains while I was trying to decide if it was worth the money to try and get on with Southwest as a First Officer. I had been a Captain at Eastern for 15 years before they went broke. I liked being the Captain and I didn't want to go backward so I spent the money, got the type rating, and came here where I could start as a Captain. I figured if the company lasted four months I'd have the training costs back and could apply with Southwest if Alpha went belly up.

"Now all the majors are hiring," Owen continued, "and I don't think you'll find many fifty-something Captain-qualified pilots available who would be willing to relocate or commute to a cramped apartment and be at the bottom of our seniority list. Not at the wages we offer. If they are still flying, they're in someone's corporate jet making a lot more than we pay. Also, I can pretty much guarantee a lot of outrage if we bypass the pilots already on the seniority list and promote new hires to Captain before the 45 F/Os who are here now. We don't have much of an agreement with the pilots, but there is a published seniority list. I don't think we could get away with ignoring it without the bottom half of the pilots suing or leaving."

They were both silent for a moment then Owen said, "I'm sorry if you are unhappy with what I'm telling you or my manner. I have spent a lot of time looking at Alpha's problems and what I'm giving you is my honest opinion. I'm not trained in VP speech, not a politician, wouldn't know how to make something up that you might like better, and have no interest in operating that way. If it's a yes-man you're looking for and you want to retract the VP offer, we'll just forget that this conversation took place."

"I can see why Andrew would think you are more concerned with the employees' well being than the corporation's. You sound more like a union organizer than a Chief Pilot."

"Oh please" Owen said with even more heat, "Their fortunes are directly linked. One doesn't succeed without the other. Not for long anyway. You should know that, and I certainly do. If you know some other way to have a stable workforce, I'm happy to listen."

Owen shook out and lit a cigarette for himself, inhaled, exhaled, took a gulp of his vodka, not looking at Spencer now, but thinking, hard. Did he even want to be a VP reporting to Spencer? Sit in an office, go to meetings, write memos, not fly? The idea had crossed his mind before but it had never seemed like an achievable goal and so far didn't sound like a lot of fun.

He loved being in command. This move would put him in command of not just one airplane, but the whole flight department; pilots, flight attendants, crew scheduling, training. He might be able to institute change though it seemed he would have to fight for it. Would the $50,000 pay raise and stock options be worth the aggravation?

If Alpha succeeded, he could afford to retire. He hadn't thought that would be possible after his pension had lost 90% of its value when Eastern went broke and dumped him on the street, jobless and 45 years old.

If this scheme worked he might still have a job in aviation after age 60, unless he screwed up. Of course he could screw up as Chief Pilot and Andrew or his replacement could demote him, or fire him for that matter. Interesting, Owen thought, there is a "him or me piece" to this equation. Andrew is gone no matter my decision. It's not like, if the roles were reversed, he would make much of an effort to help me. Why not take the chance?

Owen had seriously studied Alpha's economic dilemma, was fascinated by the possibilities, had even approached the VP of marketing,

Bruce Franklin with his ideas. He had, he thought, been dismissed. This might be a chance to change that.

Owen gave it another moment's thought then decided to try another tack. " Let me tell you what I've been looking at, then you tell me if it works for you and if you think we could work together. Are you familiar with Midwest Express? The no middle seat, all business class airline based in Milwaukee?"

Spencer showed a small smile. "Continue," he said

"Really?" Owen wondered if he was stepping into quicksand but pressed on.

"The problem is that they use Douglas equipment, DC-9 aircraft which have coach class seating of 5 across. The 737s we fly are 6 across. If you eliminate the middle seats on a 737 you lose a third of the capacity. In the DC-9 you lose 20%. It's the difference between profit and loss. To make this work we would have to change airplanes, that won't be inexpensive."

Spencer nodded agreement. "I know who TL got to write the aircraft leases and they will be difficult to get out of. The aircraft are owned by GE Capital and they are as hard-assed as anyone in this business. The only idea we have come up with so far is a pre-planned Chapter Eleven bankruptcy, which is one of the reasons I want you in management; to help get the employees through the initial scary phase, have someone on my side that they're more likely to believe. It is your connection with the employees I'm hiring." Spencer had a moment's hesitation. "You do realize the sensitivity of this information? I told TL that you had the reputation of being completely trustworthy."

"I appreciate your confidence and I stand by my reputation, but there might be another way to approach this. Are you familiar with the Boeing 717?"

"I've heard of it of course. It's a modern version of the original Douglas DC-9, but I thought they were having trouble selling them."

"That's the good news, they are, which makes them all the more willing to deal. A couple of months before you got here, I called

Boeing, told them Alpha might be looking at acquiring a new fleet and asked for some general numbers on what it would take to get 25 717s on the property with options for 25 more."

"You called Boeing? Just picked up the phone and called the 800 number?" the amazement in his voice clearly audible, "you told them you were the Chief Pilot and they took you seriously?"

"It surprised me as well, but I have enough of an aircraft background and had looked at Alpha's numbers so I could ask the right questions, though I've never been involved in the purchase of an airplane. They told me that we could put 717s on the property for around a million each. That would include 3 month's lease payments, a simulator for training the 5 crews we'd need for each airplane, access to spare parts inventory and full time maintenance assistance. They also said they might be able to help getting rid of our 737s. Ship them off to the third world. That offer was from a phone call with the Chief Pilot. You could probably do better if you had a title and a checkbook with some serious money behind it. The way I've looked at the numbers I think we could operate new 717s for a seat cost 2 cents per mile higher in an all business layout than the coach seats we have now."

"You've looked at the numbers for an all business class version?"

It was stated more as a fact than a question and it gave Owen a moment's pause. "You've talked to Bruce," he said, also stated as fact.

"Bruce talked to TL, they've been friends for a long time, and TL talked to me about the idea. I should mention that Bruce gave you full credit for bringing the idea to his attention. He has a Wall Street analyst background in aviation and was dead set against the idea of all first class because it had been tried before and failed quickly. He hadn't looked at the numbers for an all business class setup on Douglas aircraft. He thinks it just might work."

"I don't see any other way for a startup carrier to compete with the majors," Owen said. "Our current seat mile costs are nearly the same as theirs, but we have to charge 40% less or nobody rides with us. There's no profit margin. I think that would change if we could offer new equipment and a business class seat at a cost increase of only 2 or 3 cents a mile more than a major's coach fare, $20 or $30 bucks more to ride in business class from Clear River to San Francisco...that...that would be a product we could sell and make money with."

They were both silent for a moment then Owen said, "I firmly believe that to have a successful corporation you need satisfied employees and their compensation is part of the equation. If you disagree, like I said earlier, retract the VP offer and we'll call it a night."

Spencer paused, seemed to consider the idea for a moment then discard it. He glanced at his watch then said, "Give me a moment," pulled out his cell phone and pushed a button, waiting while the connection was made then, looking at Owen, said, "TL...no, all we've done so far is drink and disagree a bit...nothing serious and I think there are some valid ideas...worth discussing, just the 4 of us...I'll let Bruce know...tomorrow at 6:30?" As he asked the question Spencer was looking at Owen asking the same thing with his eyes. Owen nodded, thinking that at least he would have a day to consider the ramifications of taking this path. His mind was already swirling with possibilities.

Spencer put the phone away. "Good," he said, we're set for tomorrow. Meet at TL's office at 6:30. Building should be empty by then, but there is a guard station in the lobby, just tell them who you're there to see." Spencer chuckled, "TL signs the checks. We'll see what he thinks of your ESOP idea."

"Now, what about the FAA?" Spencer asked, "Is your rudder problem going to create difficulties.?"

"I don't think so. From what my...source... tells me they just want the rudder issue to go away. If they pursue me they'll just stir up more questions. Apparently that's the last thing the government or Boeing want. I would, however, still change the rudder servo on aircraft 412, and I would make sure it was the first airplane that we got rid of."

"We're in agreement there," Spencer said, then, "Source?"

"Confidential source," Owen smiled, "It's one of the benefits of being trustworthy."

20

1-11-98

Back in his apartment, sweats and a tee shirt, sitting on the sofa, staring through the slider at the clear winter night and sipping diet Coke, Owen contemplated his past and future. He had been living in this one bedroom, one bath furnished rental since accepting the Chief Pilot position had required his move to Clear River, renewing his lease every 3 months, his reluctance toward permanence dictated by the financial cliff the airline had been clinging to since its first flight. Clear River was alright, as small mid-West cities went, but if the job went away, so would Owen. He liked living in the mountains or by either coast, just not the plains.

Eastern Airline's demise had caught him off guard. When he had been hired, a job with a major carrier was promoted as a lifetime of earnings, like a government job, only more money. The government's airline deregulation act of 1978 changed that. Now a pilot was in the same precarious position as every other corporate middle manager, back to dog eat dog jungle law.

As Chief Pilot he was paid six grand a month, enough to afford a more upscale lifestyle, but Owen was reluctant to indulge when his employment future was so uncertain.

The only thing left in his life now that was fancy or expensive was his stereo: state of the art MacIntosh amp and Sony CD player with a set of Sennheiser head phones that allowed deafening sound levels without disturbing the neighbors. Female folk from the sixties, anything Beethoven, opera(the arias, not the three hour drama in a foreign language), country rock with a pedal steel twang; Joan Baez, Maria Callas, EmmyLou Harris. Lost in the music. His version of mental therapy. Maybe not as good as 100 miles an hour on a motorcycle, but close.

No music now, his mind didn't need more stimulation, was already sizzling. So many possibilities.

His last year at Eastern he'd made a hundred grand; never thought twice about buying stuff. He owned a house on the water, a 42' Grand Banks trawler he named 'Stall Speed' for cruising, a Honda CBR1000f-130 horsepower-150 mph motorcycle, or his black Porsche 911s for mind cleansing warp speed. And a retirement plan, the corporate promise of a seventy-five grand a year lifestyle forever, retired at fifty-five, south in the winter on his boat, parties with friends on the deck of the waterfront cottage he had designed and built in Annapolis when his financial future seemed secure. All of it gone. Lorenzo, Borman, corporate lies and liars. Chapter 11, followed by chapter 7. Sorry about the promises we made and please excuse us for taking your money and disappearing.

What would he do if he was permitted to join the corporate executive fraternity he held in such low esteem? Would he have to abandon his grass strip pilot soul? Would he be willing to? How much was his soul worth?

Did you have to be a prick to be successful as a Vice President? Would Mr. TL Bentworth expect it? Demand it? Did the good guys have to finish last? Could he work with Spencer? Would he be willing to swap a cockpit seat for an office chair?

Owen knew he couldn't answer these questions without accepting the offer, if he even got one. Work five more years, put enough money in the bank to quit, skip the house, buy another Grand Banks, live aboard, heading south when it got cold, north in the summer. Not bad.

Money might not be the key, but life was certainly more pleasant if you had it. And redesigning an airline...how much fun would that be? I need some talking points, he decided, got a yellow pad and pen from his desk and began sketching out a plan.

The next day was a blur. In the office early but mainly sitting with the door closed working out his ideas, writing and rewriting and revising some more. He'd only get one chance.

B was curious first, then suspicious, sure something was going on. Owen couldn't lie to her so he told her the truth. "I don't know for sure what's going to happen but there will be changes made, that I do know. Can't say anything now," but promised he would tell her first.

Owen was pretty sure he had on paper all the questions a new VP of operations would face and the answers he believed correct when he realized he was hungry. In the excitement he had completely forgotten about breakfast. Forgotten? What else was he missing? He was rereading his notes about Boeing helping swap out the old fleet for 717s when it hit him; old airplanes, 412, where was 412?

Dreading the answer he would get he called System Control. Quincey picked up, sounding cranky, and said before Owen could speak; "Now what?"

Uh oh, Owen thought, though he knew if something catastrophic had already happened to 412 he would have heard.

"I need to know where 412 is," Owen asked without preamble. He knew Quincey would recognize his voice.

"412, 412," Owen could hear Quincey clacking away on the computer keyboard that he hammered as if it was his old typewriter. "On the way to Dallas, off Wichita at 10:30, estimated arrival 11:45, 45 minutes from now"

"Dallas? What the fuck?" Unable to keep a sudden surge of anger out of his voice. "Did maintenance already change the PCU?"

"No, they didn't change the PCU, the part won't get here until tomorrow morning. And don't yell at me, Mr Chief Pilot," his voice hardening into stern banker mode. "The instruction I got was the work should be done as soon as possible and that can't happen without the new part. Nothing was said about grounding the airplane before then. Harvey asked Frost first thing this morning. Harvey told me you both agreed there was nothing wrong after the test flight yesterday. We've got two airplanes grounded that we'll be lucky to get flying before tomorrow morning. What do you want me to do? Call the bus company?

"SHIT," Owen swore into the phone, then louder, "Shit..Shit..Shit. Has anyone told Spencer?"

"No, no one told Spencer. He gets a report at the morning's VP meeting from maintenance about what broke in the previous twenty-four hours. You know that. What are you so worried about?"

"It would take too long to explain," thinking he needed to call Spencer immediately, get this stopped. "What other flights have you got 412 on the schedule for?"

"Dallas, back to Wichita, to Denver, Salt Lake, Denver, Clear River then San Fran and return. Be back tomorrow morning by seven. The PCU should be here by then and it will get changed."

"Who's the Captain on it now?"

"Dick Brown has it all day, then Josh goes to San Fran tonight. He's the only Check Airman available and the First Officer's still on IOE, Dan Stern."

Dick Brown had been a Captain for several years which made him relatively experienced, at least for an Alpha Captain. He had never had a problem with a check ride, not that that indicated more than a base level of competency. He was thorough, and was certain to have looked at the logbook writeup. Owen thought briefly about calling Brown on his cell phone when they landed in Dallas. And tell him what? Please try not to crash. You're flying an airplane with a potentially deadly flaw and there is nothing I can do about it. Did he want a phone call on record warning the Captain of possible life-threatening mechanical problems? Or was he already starting to think like a VP?

And Josh? Josh should know what to expect if the airplane made it through the next 5 legs and back to Clear River without a disaster.

This could be so much easier, Owen thought, if I was a VP. I could order the airplane grounded until the PCU arrived and was installed. Argue with Spencer and Frost if necessary. Tell them the risk wasn't worth the potential cost. Better safe than sorry. That platitude would go over well. Be unemployed the next day. For the moment it seemed that the decisions he had made as pilot in command for 20 years were a lot simpler than this whole VP thing.

"You still thinking?" Quincey asked, his voice returning to it's more normal amused tone. "I get off at 3:00 and you owe me a fucking drink," laughing as he said it. "Yelling at a man 15 years your senior. You ought to be ashamed."

"You're right," Owen apologized, "I owe you a fucking drink, but I can't make it tonight. Something going on."

"Doesn't have anything to do with Alpha's new female pilot candidate, by any chance?"

"Don't be starting any rumors, talk to you later," Owen said, suddenly remembering Anna's smile, her kiss. Quincey was still laughing.

Now what? Call Spencer? Spencer had already agreed to ground the airplane. Owen had no hard evidence that would lead to an immediate grounding. Just a bad feeling. A suspicion. A hunch. The United airplane had flown for 6 days before it had crashed. 412 was only in its second day, but you couldn't rely on the statistical evidence from a sample of one.

Call the FAA? They wouldn't care unless the airplane crashed, then they would be looking for someone to blame. Him?

Do nothing and hope for the best? That really was thinking like a VP.

Owen called Josh. A woman answered sounding a lot like "Tracy?"

He remembered instantly what a bad idea it was to guess the owner of an unexpected woman's voice answering a man's phone.

She laughed. "Surprised?" playing with him. "This is Captain Logan's very personal assistant. The Captain is busy at the moment. How can I make your day more enjoyable?" and laughed again.

The genuine sound of her laughter made Owen smile despite his mood. She was a treasure, no question about that. "If Captain Logan can break away for a moment there is something I need to speak to him about."

Owen could hear the sounds of a light hearted struggle as they fought for the phone, heard Josh's claim "with one hand tied behind my back," then his voice; "Owen, sorry, my assistant is a bit feisty this morning. What do you need?"

"The SFO trip tonight...they want to use 412."

"Did the PCU get changed?"

"No, the parts won't be available until tomorrow morning,"

"What are you worried about?" Josh asked, "You've got that tone in your voice. Was flying ok yesterday and I would guess she's flying ok now, if that's what your worrying about? Why don't you quit worrying and come have lunch with us?"

"It's the old guy's job to worry since you young guys seem incapable of it. Tracy going with you tonight?"

"Of course."

Owen didn't know what else to say. "I have too much going on to go to lunch, but if you are around Friday I'll meet you for cocktails," and ended the call before it went any further.

Sat and thought about things for awhile. Both of them on 412. Wouldn't get back until 7:00 tomorrow morning. 20 hours. Long time to wait.

Owen drove to the Bentworth building 30 minutes early. Drove by, around the block, parked on a side street, out of sight. 2 minutes away. Didn't want to be late... or early. Walk in the door on the dot. His notes were handwritten on a yellow pad and he had placed them in his blond leather briefcase. A relic from his aborted attempts at sales when there were no flying jobs available, it held the assorted paperwork the Chief Pilot position required. He thought it would look more VP like to walk in with the case instead of just the yellow pad.

Owen had stopped at home to change clothes, then been unsure how to dress. Wear the tie and his black sport coat? His only-non uniform tie, painted looking and colorful, a gift from a long ago girl-friend that Owen wore for the annual Christmas party and that was about it. He wondered about the dress code for a VP. Andrew didn't often come into work with a tie and jacket, more likely to be in khakis with an open neck dress shirt, like everyone else who worked in the Alpha offices. Casual everyday, jeans on Friday. Maybe he should see about the pay raise first, then worry about new clothes. Buy a suit? Wear a tie and jacket everyday? Dressed for success? Not his favorite concept.

The security guard looked up as Owen approached his desk; "Captain Swift?" and when Owen nodded, came out from behind the desk and walked him to the left most of 3 elevators, then punched in a code on the key pad labeled "executive level". The door opened silently, then closed as Owen stepped inside. There were 2 buttons. Owen pressed "Up".

The elevator door opened on a small lobby where Christine Saunders sat waiting behind a polished oak desk. "Captain Swift," she stood while greeting him, "please follow me."

Plush grey carpet with splashes of crimson, off white walls with black and white framed newspaper headlines about "black Friday", "banker jumps to his death," and other disasters from the depression era. A morbid sense of humor, Owen wondered, or a reminder not to get too complacent.

Christine rapped softly on the door at the far end of the hall then opened it and ushered Owen inside, closing the door after him.

What could be bad about this?

Printed in Great Britain
by Amazon